The Global Governance of HIV/AIDS

ELGAR INTELLECTUAL PROPERTY AND GLOBAL DEVELOPMENT

Series Editor: Peter K. Yu, *Kern Family Chair in Intellectual Property Law and Director, Intellectual Property Law Center, Drake University, USA*

Rapid global economic integration and the increasing importance of technology and information goods have created the need for a broader, deeper and more critical understanding of intellectual property laws and policies. This uniquely-designed book series provides an interdisciplinary forum for advancing the debate on the global intellectual property system and related issues that intersect with transnational politics, international governance, and global economic, social, cultural and technological developments. The series features the works of established experts and emerging voices in the academy as well as those practising on the frontlines. The series' high-quality, informed and accessible volumes include a wide range of materials such as historical narratives, theoretical explanations, substantive discussions, critical evaluations, empirical analyses, comparative studies, and formulations of practical solutions and best practices. The series will appeal to academics, policy makers, judges, practitioners, transnational lawyers and civil society groups as well as students of law, politics, culture, political economy, international relations and development studies.

Titles in the series include:

Intellectual Property and Sustainable Development
Development Agendas in a Changing World
Edited by Ricardo Meléndez-Ortiz and Pedro Roffe

Internet Domain Names, Trademarks and Free Speech
Jacqueline Lipton

Shaping China's Innovation Future
University Technology Transfer in Transition
John L. Orcutt and Hong Shen

Copyright and the Public Interest in China
Guan Hong Tang

Genetic Resources and Traditional Knowledge
Case Studies and Conflicting Interests
Edited by Tania Bubela and E. Richard Gold

The Global Governance of HIV/AIDS
Intellectual Property and Access to Essential Medicines
Edited by Obijiofor Aginam, John Harrington and Peter K. Yu

The Global Governance of HIV/AIDS

Intellectual Property and Access to Essential Medicines

Edited by

Obijiofor Aginam

Senior Academic Officer, United Nations University Institute for Sustainability and Peace, Tokyo, Japan

John Harrington

Professor of Law, Cardiff University, Wales, UK

Peter K. Yu

Kern Family Chair in Intellectual Property Law, Drake University Law School, USA

ELGAR INTELLECTUAL PROPERTY AND GLOBAL DEVELOPMENT

Edward Elgar

Cheltenham, UK • Northampton, MA, USA

Published by
Edward Elgar Publishing Limited
The Lypiatts
15 Lansdown Road
Cheltenham
Glos GL50 2JA
UK

Edward Elgar Publishing, Inc.
William Pratt House
9 Dewey Court
Northampton
Massachusetts 01060
USA

A catalogue record for this book
is available from the British Library

Library of Congress Control Number: 2011942545

This book is available electronically in the ElgarOnline.com Law Subject Collection, E-ISBN 978 1 84980 492 9

MIX
Paper from
responsible sources
FSC® C018575
FSC
www.fsc.org

ISBN 978 1 84980 490 5

Typeset by Columns Design XML Ltd, Reading
Printed by MPG PRINTGROUP, UK

Contents

Contributors

Frederick M. Abbott is the Edward Ball Eminent Scholar at Florida State University College of Law. He is highly regarded for his scholarship and professional activities in international intellectual property rights and global economic issues. He is Rapporteur for the Committee on International Trade Law of the International Law Association, consultant to the UNCTAD/ICTSD Project on Intellectual Property and Sustainable Development, the World Health Organization (WHO) and the World Bank. He is on the Panel of Experts of UNCTAD's Program on the Settlement of Disputes in International Trade, Investment and Intellectual Property. Professor Abbott serves as a panellist for the World Intellectual Property Organization Arbitration and Mediation Center. He is on the editorial board of the *Journal of International Economic Law* (Oxford). He is former Chair of the American Society of Law Intellectual Property Interest Group and the International Law Section of the American Association of Law Schools, and former Director of the American Society of International Law Research Project on Human Rights and International Trade. He is Chair of the Intellectual Property Advisory Committee of the Foundation for Innovative New Diagnostics. Professor Abbott is the author of numerous books and articles in the fields of international economic law, international intellectual property law, and public international law. His books include *Global Pharmaceutical Policy: Ensuring Medicines for Tomorrow's World* (with Graham Dukes) (2009), *International Intellectual Property in an Integrated World Economy* (with Thomas Cottier and Francis Gurry) (2nd edn 2011), *UNCTAD-ICTSD Resource Book on TRIPS and Development* (principal consultant with Carlos Correa) (2005) and *The International Intellectual Property System: Commentary and Materials* (with Thomas Cottier and Francis Gurry) (1999).

Obijiofor Aginam Ph.D. (UBC) was Professor of Law at Carleton University, Ottawa, Canada from 2001 to 2007 where he taught and researched global policy issues that cut across international law, globalization, global health governance, South-North relations, and Third World Approaches to International Law. Since 2007, he has served as Academic Officer and Head of International Cooperation and Development in the

United Nations University's Institute for Sustainability and Peace in Tokyo, Japan where he oversees research on policy and institutional frameworks on pressing global issues within the mandate of the United Nations. He has worked as Legal Officer and Global Health Leadership Fellow at the WHO headquarters in Geneva, Switzerland. He has held numerous fellowships including Global Security and Cooperation Fellowship of the Social Science Research Council in New York. Dr. Aginam has been a visiting professor at the University for Peace in Costa Rica, International University of Peoples' Institutions for Peace in Rovereto, Italy, and the University of the Witwatersrand in Johannesburg, South Africa. He is the author of *Global Health Governance: International Law and Public Health in a Divided World* (University of Toronto Press, 2005) and numerous other peer-reviewed publications. He is also the editor of *HIV/AIDS and the Security Sector in Africa* (United Nations University Press, 2012, with Martin R. Rupiya). Dr. Aginam has been a legal consultant for the WHO on aspects of trade and health; and the UN Food and Agriculture Organization (FAO) on the regulatory framework for food safety and biotechnology in developing countries. In the latter capacity, he has recently worked as a member of the FAO Expert Legal Team on the review of biotechnology and food safety laws in Bangladesh. He has been a recipient of the Social Sciences and Humanities Research Council of Canada research grant.

Tahir Amin LL B, Dip LP is the Co-Founder and Director of Intellectual Property for the Initiative for Medicines, Access & Knowledge (I-MAK). He practised as a solicitor of the Supreme Court of England and Wales with two of the leading IP firms in the United Kingdom and also served as an in-house global IP manager for a multinational company. He has over 10 years of experience in prosecuting, licensing, opposing and litigating trade marks, patents, and designs. Prior to founding I-MAK, he spent two years in India with the Alternative Law Forum researching public interest IP issues and working on pharmaceutical patent oppositions. He has served as a legal consultant to many groups, including the WHO, the International Centre for Trade and Sustainable Development (ICTSD), Clinton Foundation HIV/AIDS Initiative and Oxfam. Amin has published in many prominent fora, including *Health Affairs*, *Nature Biotech* and the WHO. He has also recently co-authored and edited a report by the EPO, UNEP and ICTSD on 'Patents and Clean Energy' (2010). Amin is currently a Fellow at the Harvard Medical School in the Department of Global Health and Social Medicine, where he was also a 2008 Echoing Green Fellow and a 2009 TEDIndia Fellow.

Laura Biron MA (Cambridge) Ph.D. (Cambridge) is a Research Fellow in Philosophy at Queens' College, Cambridge, and currently a Greenwall Fellow in Bioethics and Health Policy at Johns Hopkins and Georgetown. Her research and publications to date have focused on the ontological and justificatory foundations of intellectual property, taxation and global justice. Through Cambridge University's Forum for Philosophy in Business, she has worked as a consultant for KPMG, Pfizer and, most recently, BT, exploring conceptions of trust and integrity within the communications industry. In 2007, Biron helped to found the non-profit organization Incentives for Global Health, which is led by Thomas Pogge at Yale University. She has also worked as an advisor to the UK Intellectual Property Office, contributing to their work on the Rationale for Patents.

Avram Denburg MD M.Sc. FRCP(C) is a paediatrician with the Department of Paediatrics at the University of Toronto and a Clinical Fellow in the Division of Haematology/Oncology at the Hospital for Sick Children in Toronto, Canada. He has a Master of Science in Health Policy, Planning and Financing from the London School of Economics and the London School of Hygiene and Tropical Medicine. His research explores the intersection of ethics and child health policy and has focused on issues of access to essential medicines for children, the social determinants of child health, global child health ethics, and the ethics of international research in paediatric oncology.

Gail E. Evans BA (Hons), Dip.Ed., LL B, SJD (USyd) is Reader in International Trade and Intellectual Property Law in the Centre for Commercial Law Studies at Queen Mary, University of London and the co-director of the Queen Mary Intellectual Property Research Institute (Business and Professional). Nominated in 2008 and 2010 for the Queen Mary, University of London Drapers' Award for Excellence in Teaching, she lectures in International Intellectual Property Law; Trade Mark Law; and Intellectual Property Transactions. Dr Evans' areas of research are the international regulation and commercialization of intellectual property. Recent publications include 'Substantive Trademark Law Harmonization: On the Emerging Coherence between the Jurisprudence of the WTO Appellate Body and the European Court of Justice', in Graeme Dinwoodie and Mark Janis (eds), Trademark Law and Theory (Edward Elgar, 2009); 'Online Technology Contracts', in Hossein Bidgoli (ed.), *Handbook of Technology Management*, vol. 3 (2010); and 'The Comparative Advantages of Geographical Indications and Community Trade Marks for the Marketing of Agricultural Products in the European

Union', (2010) 41 *International Review of Industrial Property and Copyright Law* 645–74.

John Harrington LLB (Dublin) BCL (Oxon) is Professor of Law at Cardiff University and Senior Research Fellow at the British Institute in Eastern Africa in Nairobi, Kenya. He was Director of Liverpool's Institute of Medicine, Law and Bioethics (2007–2010) and a Jean Monnet Fellow at the European University Institute, Florence (2001–2002). He has published extensively on the interaction between law and medicine, setting this relationship in its broader political and economic context. He has also written on global health law issues, including the effect of privatization on health care regulation in Tanzania and on the consequences of criminalization for AIDS prevention policy. He has edited special issues of *Social Science and Medicine* and *Law Social Justice and Global Development* on international health law themes. An edited collection, *Global Health and Human Rights: Legal and Philosophical Perspectives* (with Maria Stuttaford), was published in 2010.

James Harrison is Associate Professor in the Law Department at the University of Warwick. His core research interests focus on analysing the broader social and environmental impact of economic laws and regulations. In much of his work he has utilized a human rights methodology for analysis. He has published a number of articles in this area and a monograph entitled *The Human Rights Impact of the World Trade Organisation* (2007). He has worked as a consultant for a wide range of organizations including the Council of Europe, the Office of the High Commissioner of Human Rights, the Canadian Council for International Co-operation and the Scottish Human Rights Commission. He previously worked as a solicitor and at a number of non-governmental organizations and has directed research projects and training programmes in locations throughout Africa, Asia, Europe and the Middle East. For more details of publications and experience see http://www2.warwick.ac.uk/fac/soc/law/staff/academic/harrison.

Kelley Lee D.Phil., D.Litt., FFPH is Professor, Associate Dean, Research and Director of Global Health in the Faculty of Health Sciences at Simon Fraser University. She is also Professor of Global Health Policy at the London School of Hygiene and Tropical Medicine. She has chaired the WHO Resource Group on Globalisation, Trade and Health. Her research focuses on the impacts of globalization on communicable and non-communicable diseases, and the implications for emerging forms of global governance. She has authored more than 80 scholarly papers, 40 book chapters and seven books including *Globalization and Health: An Introduction* (2003), *Global Change and Health* (2005), *The World Health Organization* (2008), *Asia's Role in Governing Global Health* (2012), and *Global Health and International Relations* (2012). Her current research focuses on analysing internal documents of the tobacco industry; the role of discourses and normative frameworks in global health governance; Asian contributions to global health governance; and global health diplomacy.

Kenneth C. Shadlen Ph.D. (UC Berkeley, Political Science, 1997) is Reader in Development Studies at the London School of Economics. He works on the politics of intellectual property and the politics of trade and integration. Some of his recent work on these topics has been published in *Comparative Politics*, *Global Governance*, *International Studies Quarterly*, *Journal of Development Studies*, *Review of International Political Economy*, *and Studies in Comparative International Development*. He is co-editor of *Intellectual Property, Pharmaceuticals, and Public Health: Access to Drugs in Developing Countries* (with Samira Guennif, Alenka Guzman and N. Lalitha) (2012), *The Politics of Intellectual Property: Contestation over the Ownership, Use, and Control of Knowledge and Information* (with Sebastian Haunss) (2009) and *The Political Economy of Hemispheric Integration: Responding to Globalization in the Americas* (with Diego Sánchez-Ancochea) (2008).

Peter K. Yu holds the Kern Family Chair in Intellectual Property Law and is the founding director of the Intellectual Property Law Center at Drake University Law School. He has served as Wenlan Scholar Chair Professor at Zhongnan University of Economics and Law in Wuhan, China and a visiting professor in the Faculty of Law at Washington and Lee University, the University of Haifa, the University of Hong Kong and the University of Strasbourg. Born and raised in Hong Kong, Professor Yu is a leading expert in international intellectual property and communications law. He also writes and lectures extensively on international trade, international and comparative law, and the transition of the legal systems in China and Hong Kong. A prolific scholar and an award-winning teacher, he is the author or editor of five books and more than 100 law review articles and book chapters. He serves as the general editor of *The WIPO Journal* and the editor of two book series (Edward Elgar Publishing). Professor Yu has spoken at events organized by the World Intellectual Property Organization, the International Telecommunication Union, the UN Conference on Trade and Development (UNCTAD), the UN Educational, Scientific and Cultural Organization (UNESCO), the Chinese, US and EU governments and at leading research institutions from around the world. His lectures and presentations have spanned more than 25 countries on six continents, and his publications have appeared in Chinese and English and have been translated into Arabic, French, Japanese, Persian, Portuguese, Spanish and Vietnamese.

Acknowledgements

This volume draws primarily on papers delivered at the 'Global Governance of HIV/AIDS: Intellectual Property and Access to Essential Medicines' Conference held at the University of Liverpool on 8 October 2008. The conference was the product of a multi-continent research project initiated by the Peace and Governance Programme of the United Nations University (UNU) in Tokyo and jointly implemented by the UNU, the Institute for Medicine, Law and Bioethics (IMLAB) at the University of Liverpool, UK, and the Intellectual Property Law Center at Drake University Law School in Iowa, USA. The papers included in this volume have since been updated to reflect developments after the conference. We wish to thank all the conference participants, including those speakers who were unable to contribute to this volume.

We are grateful to IMLAB and UNU for providing the much-needed funding for this conference. Thanks are also due to Yoshie Sawada at UNU and Kayte Kelly at IMLAB, both of whom provided invaluable administrative support for the conference, their contributors and project coordinators. In addition, we acknowledge the crucial assistance of Kalle Huebner, an intern at UNU in 2009; Vishwas Devaiah, PhD (Liverpool); as well as Ben Booth, John-Paul McDonald, Laura Seward and David Fairclough at Edward Elgar Publishing. Finally, we thank our home institutions for providing generous institutional support and making this project possible.

Obijiofor Aginam
John Harrington
Peter K. Yu
September 2011

1. Introduction

Obijiofor Aginam and John Harrington

The enjoyment of the highest attainable standard of health is one of the fundamental rights of every human being without distinction of race, religion, political belief, economic or social condition.

– Constitution of the World Health Organization (WHO, 1946, Preamble)

[T]heir relations in the field of trade and economic endeavour should be conducted with a view to raising standards of living.

– Marrakesh Agreement Establishing the WTO (WTO, 1994, Preamble)

1. JUSTICE, GOVERNANCE AND ACCESS TO ESSENTIAL MEDICINES

The global AIDS pandemic remains the greatest health challenge of the twenty-first century. The cost of HIV/AIDS is immense, above all in terms of human suffering, but also through its impact on broader human welfare and development in the Global South. Our response to the pandemic is first and foremost a matter of justice. The chances of being affected by HIV/AIDS are crucially determined by established inequalities of class, 'race', gender, geographical location and national origin. The prospects of those already affected by HIV/AIDS are similarly determined. These inequalities are man-made and man-sustained. They benefit some; they harm others. In so far as we fail to meet the challenge presented by the pandemic, we collude in and perpetuate this structural violence; we turn our backs on the insistent and pre-eminent claims of global justice.[1]

The injustices of AIDS have called forth practical responses across the range of human activity: in the natural sciences, clinical medicine, public health, education, public administration and law. The availability of essential drugs has been a central focus for these responses. With the development of effective antiretrovirals (ARVs) in the mid-1990s, public health campaigns aimed at prevention were augmented by a drive to secure access to therapy. This has been largely successful in developed countries thanks to the internal redistribution of health resources through insurance and various forms of socialized medicine. Local injustice is tempered to varying degrees in Europe and North America. That has not been the case in developing countries. For one thing, internal inequalities are much wider, with access to health care depending to a far greater extent on the private resources of the individual. For another, the poorer nations are bound into a global political economy shaped by colonial domination and resource extraction and now structured by trading relations of inequality and dependency. The development, production, distribution and purchase of ARVs are crucially influenced by these broader structures. High prices ration access to life-saving drugs, and these prices are a function of the international intellectual property (IP) regime. The entitlements of patent holders – enabling them to extract monopoly rents – set the baseline for legal, political and economic interventions to extend access.

The patent system, as part of the world trade system, favours the rich over the poor, the centre over the periphery, developed over developing nations. As Thomas Pogge has shown, the contemporary political economy of drug access, including its legal underpinnings, demands *both* a profound justice-based critique *and* hard-headed strategies for overcoming man-made scarcity in meeting health needs.[2] The chapters in this book take up the challenge of global injustice in the context of HIV/AIDS by investigating critically the different legal, political and economic determinants of drug access. As such, this collection contributes to our understanding of the emerging field of global health governance.[3] All chapters go beyond the merely descriptive, however. All are concerned with the practical question of how elements of the governance regime can be adapted, reformed or removed in order to increase the availability of affordable ARVs.

At the heart of the different arguments in this book lies the central tension between IP and access to essential medicines. Legal scholars, policymakers, and civil society activists have been occupied with unravelling the strands of this difficult legal and political problem since the end of the Uruguay Round of Multilateral Trade Negotiations in 1994. The most remarkable feature of the Uruguay Round was the transformation of the international trading system from the flexible framework of the General Agreement on Tariffs and Trade (GATT) to the 'rule-based' international trade architecture that is now built on the pillars of the World Trade Organization (WTO) – a multilateral organization that is equipped with powers to enforce trade norms and agreements (Jackson, 1997; Malhotra, 2003; Matsushita, Schoenbaum and Mavroidis, 2006;

Trebilcock and Howse, 2005). The implementation of the 1994 WTO Agreement on Trade-Related Aspects of Intellectual Property Rights (TRIPs) raises critical questions for the right to health and the availability of ARVs. The TRIPs Agreement obliges WTO member states to establish minimum patent protection for drugs, whether produced locally or by multinational pharmaceutical corporations.[4]

TRIPs provides the decisive legal underpinning for the governance of access to essential medicines. It calls into being a worldwide network of patent granting and enforcing institutions, from national courts, legislatures and patent offices to the dispute settlement mechanisms and negotiating fora of the WTO itself.[5] The network extends beyond official state governance to include private pharmaceutical manufacturers, university research laboratories and philanthropic bodies (Santoro and Gorrie, 2005; Zacher and Keefe, 2008). The globalized patent regime mandated by TRIPs does not simply result in a cascade of legal norms from international to regional, national and local levels. It also sets the horizon for private and public investment in scientific research and drug production. An adequate practical response to global injustice in the context of HIV/AIDS will have to be sensitive to the multiple dimensions of the access problem and to the specific ways in which they are manifested at different points in the governance network.

Struggles over the relative weight to be given to IP rights and the protection of health have played out most prominently at the WTO (Joseph, 2003; Thomas, 2002). The tension between trade and health is reflected in the terms of TRIPs itself. The Agreement provides for certain flexibilities, allowing the patent regime to be suspended or derogated from in cases of emergency. In the years after 1995, activists and developing countries became aware of the dangers to public health of granting maximal IP rights over pharmaceuticals (Drahos and Braithwaite, 2002; Sell, 2004). This awareness was focussed by the spreading catastrophe of HIV/AIDS in the poorest regions of the world. Pressure from developing countries and civil society organizations from North and South forced the WTO to clarify and confirm TRIPs flexibilities in relation to essential medicines ('t Hoen, 2002; Orbinski, 2002). Thus, the Doha Declaration on the TRIPS Agreement and Public Health of November 2001 stated that developing countries could override patents in the interest of public health by issuing compulsory licenses for the import or production of affordable generic drugs (Abbott, 2002; Charnovitz, 2002; Gathii, 2002). The Declaration failed to address the vital question of exports to needy countries that lacked facilities for pharmaceutical production. Was India, for example, permitted to allow its drug manufacturers to sell generic versions of on-patent medicines in

African states affected by the pandemic? This issue was addressed by the 2003 Decision of the General Council on the Implementation of Paragraph 6 of the Doha Declaration on the TRIPS Agreement and Public Health (General Council Decision). The Decision provided that such sales would not amount to a violation of TRIPs. However, it set conditions of extreme complexity for the lawfulness of exports. Commentators agree that the gains for access embodied in Doha have been recouped by the General Council Decision (Abbott, 2005; Correa, 2004).

As has been mentioned, legal provisions interact with the commercial calculations of drug producers in determining the availability of affordable medicines. From this perspective it is important to note that the dynamic pharmaceutical industries of India, Brazil and South Africa are increasingly shifting their focus to research-led production. The consequent imperative on these states to reform their IP laws to comply with TRIPs means that the supply of generic drugs in both these countries and other less developed countries is seriously at risk. In addition, the leading industrialized countries are continuously seeking, and have increasingly achieved, TRIPs-plus protection for major multinational companies through bilateral and regional free trade agreements (FTAs) or economic partnership agreements (EPAs) (Blouin, Heymann and Drager, 2007; Malhotra, 2003). These developments in the global economic arena present complex challenges for global health governance, especially for the right to health as codified in a number of international human rights treaties.

The chapters in this book are grouped under three main themes. The first concerns the governance contexts which frame access to essential medicines – the legal and political landscape of neo-liberal globalization, the structure of the global pharmaceutical industry and the multiple stratification of patient groups. The second set of chapters focuses on the specifically legal aspects of the access problem, attending to both the impact of human rights norms and the evolving content of IP law rules. The essays in the third group all propose concrete strategies for improving the availability of ARVs. These range from the creative use of patent licensing contracts to the alignment of market incentives with real health needs to the creation of South-South alliances in international trade diplomacy.

2. GOVERNANCE CONTEXTS

In his chapter, Obijiofor Aginam highlights key features of global health governance and explores the shortcomings of this framework in the context of HIV/AIDS. Relying on Paul Farmer's postulation that international policy initiatives and governance responses to the global AIDS crisis have so far been a failure, the author posits his discourse on two levels of inquiry. The first level focuses on the tensions between human rights and IP rights. The second level focuses on the opportunities and impediments for South-South cooperation to increase access to ARVs in developing countries. The promise of these two levels, according to Aginam, is limited by the normative parameters of contemporary global governance. Scholars have long contended that whenever there is a need to rank IP rights and human rights, the latter should be given more weight. Aginam argues that although this position remains popular in the academy and in the activist domain of global civil society, it is yet to be fully tested pragmatically in IP-driven disputes at the WTO. On the opportunities for, and impediments to, post-TRIPs South-South cooperation, this chapter considers the limits of TRIPs flexibilities, especially the General Council Decision. Based on the difficulties encountered by Canada's Access to Medicines Regime (CAMR), the author proposes South-South cooperation to increase access to drugs in the less developed South. One example of such cooperation is the 2007 joint venture agreement between the Government of Uganda and Cipla, an Indian generic drug manufacturer, to produce cheaper generic ARVs in a local facility in Uganda.

Most political and ethical claims for increased access to ARVs assume a ready supply of generic medicines. All that is required are sufficient resources to purchase them. Kenneth Shadlen's chapter questions this assumption in the light of the changing patient needs and developments in the structure of global pharmaceutical production. Increasing drug resistance means that the precise composition of ARV treatment must be continually renewed. Expensive, on-patent drugs will have to be substituted for cheap, off-patent equivalents. However, there is a decreasing likelihood that supplies of new generics will become available to bring down the price of the necessary new therapies. Why? Over half of generic ARVs are currently produced in India. The prospects for adequate supply are therefore crucially influenced by the legal and business landscape in that country. In particular, the implementation of a TRIPs-compliant patent regime has pushed the Indian pharmaceutical industry away from cheap generics and towards more costly drugs for sale in the developed countries. If India, then, is no longer the 'pharmacy of the developing world', how can affordable ARVs be made available? Shadlen considers a number of different responses to this problem, from reforming TRIPs, or increasing production capacity in the poorest countries, to a programme of expanded ARV access in India itself with spill-over benefits for developing countries. All are, however, subject to political, legal and economic obstacles.

Avram Denburg and Kelley Lee analyse a significant specific gap in global health governance/policy literature – access to paediatric medicines in the global political economy of drug production and supply. Focusing on paediatric HIV/AIDS and ARVs, Denburg and Lee argue that 'while the challenges facing paediatric medicines are global, this neglect is felt more acutely in developing countries'. Children, they argue, face unique barriers to access to essential medicines due to factors such as price discrepancies vis-à-vis adult medicines, missing appropriate dosages and formulations, or a lack of data from pharmacokinetic studies for research and development (R&D). Additionally, as developed countries move towards universal patent protection under TRIPs, increased product segmentation within the generic market is limiting the financial viability of the production of ARVs for children in most developing countries. These developments have been exacerbated through the neglect of paediatric drugs by global health institutions. Only a few years ago, emerging policies such as the 2007 World Health Assembly's Resolution 60.20 entitled 'Better Medicines for Children' and the subsequent WHO campaign to 'Make Medicines Child Size' in 2008 have been developed, due, in part, to civil society influence. As to the way forward, Denburg and Lee highlight future challenges and propose sustainable strategies for increasing access to paediatric medicines. These strategies include improving the financing and development of generic fixed dose combinations for children through South-South cooperation, public-private partnerships, and legal/regulatory reforms, especially those related to TRIPs, that create incentives for voluntary licensing. According to the authors, 'efforts to address these challenges will require a coordinated response from multiple echelons of governance, in concert with industry and civil society, if they are to effect lasting change'.

3. LEGAL DEVELOPMENTS

Concern with global justice in access to ARVs is commonly articulated in the language of human rights (e.g., Hunt and Leader, 2010; O'Connell, 2010). However, as James Harrison argues, the full potential of human rights is not realized where they are used solely as a tool of political mobilization. Developments in international human rights law, particularly in the field of social and economic rights, mean that they can have a significant additional effect as legal norms. General Comments produced by the UN treaty-monitoring bodies have given precision and force to state obligations to protect and promote the right of all to the highest attainable standard of health. More than this, detailed authoritative guidance is now available concerning the relationship between the human right to health and the interests protected by IP. The objective of patents, to stimulate scientific progress by endowing inventors with limited monopoly rights, needs to be aligned with other important social concerns, such as public health. The strategic gain from taking the legal nature of human rights seriously is evident in the crucial context of international trade law. The legal instruments of the WTO, exemplified in the General Council Decision and in TRIPs itself, as well as the implementing provisions of national law, are highly technical and detailed. If the right to health is to do the work of justice on the terrain of law it will have to partake of the same form. Of course, the scope and meaning of the right to health depends on what is understood by 'health'. The norm has to be 'thickened out', with public health standards defining the content of the obligation and providing evidence of its violation. In this regard, Harrison argues that human right to health impact assessments (HRIAs) have a crucial role to play in evaluating the effect of IP law on access to ARVs. He accepts that the rallying potential of human rights must not be neglected – the access question can never be finally depoliticized. But the struggle for essential drugs is waged in many fora, each with different terms of engagement.

Legal engagement for access to medicines is not limited to human rights. As Tahir Amin argues, the terms of patent law are subject to interpretation and application in a more or less pro-patient fashion. He presents a comparative evaluation of how a select group of developing countries have timed and implemented patent protection under TRIPs to safeguard access to essential ARVs. Under the Agreement, developing countries had 10 years to create pharmaceutical product patent regimes, but not all countries have used the flexibilities provided by TRIPs during this period. Some complied with TRIPs sooner than was legally required, while others went further by agreeing to TRIPs-plus provisions in FTAs which were even more restrictive of access to essential medicines. Amin focuses specifically on three well-defined elements of national patent laws. Countries such as India and the Philippines define the 'scope of patentability' narrowly – small or merely incremental changes to a pharmaceutical product will not justify an extension of the patent and, thus, the continued exclusion of lower-priced generics from the market. In addition to this, India and Brazil have facilitated opposition and observation procedures whereby public health bodies and civil society groups are afforded procedural rights to challenge dubious applications, either before or after they are granted. According to Amin, these are significant steps toward democratizing the patent system. Finally, he considers the extent to which authorities have resorted to compulsory licensing and government-use provisions in order to increase supply and reduce prices. In the latter context, he too emphasizes the importance of public health science as a guide to when there is in fact a 'health emergency' such as would justify governments overriding the interests of drug patent holders.

The availability of ARVs is affected not only by the changing IP regime in producer countries of the South, but also by the posture of authorities in the North. In this regard, Frederick Abbott examines a number of recent cases where Dutch customs authorities have seized generic drugs in transit through Amsterdam's Schiphol Airport. Medicines lawfully produced in India and destined for lawful sale in Brazil or Nigeria simply happened to be passing through the Netherlands owing to the established pattern of global transportation routes. This allowed multinational patent holders to disrupt the vital trade at its 'weakest link'. As Abbott shows, the actions of the Dutch authorities, subsequently endorsed by local courts, run counter to the fundamental principle of the territorial nature of patents laid down in TRIPs and in the Paris Convention for the Protection of Industrial Property. These legal moves facilitate the business strategy of patent holders seeking to snuff out competition from generic producers by eliminating their foreign markets. The political consequences are stark. Abbott argues that the current world trade regime was crafted precisely to take account of the dependence of developing countries on India as a source of generic drugs. The 'long-arming' of European jurisdiction in the Dutch cases is a frontal assault on this compromise, one which risks undermining the legitimacy of the global patent regime as a whole.

4. STRATEGIES FOR IMPROVING ACCESS

Political strategies to overcome or modify TRIPs will play an important role in guaranteeing access to ARVs. However, incremental legal reform and the provision of economic incentives for drug production may be more effective in the medium term. In this spirit, Gail Evans analyses the content and scope of restriction clauses in patent licensing contracts to assist in building research capacity in developing countries and in ensuring wide availability of essential medicines. Evans reviews models of technology transfer from academia to private business in developing and least developed countries, the impact of restructuring the global pharmaceutical industry, and the entry of new manufacturing companies from emerging economies like India and China on public-private partnerships with research institutions. At first glance the growing commodification of academic knowledge seems to run counter to the core scholarly and humanitarian values of universities. However, it is through their very position as patent holders – i.e., through the exercise of property rights – that universities can control the development and distribution of those pharmaceutical products which their basic research has made possible. Evans carefully details the different types of license which could be used by patent holders, setting them in their broader legal context, particularly having regard to the limits set by competition law. She concludes that contract doctrine is sufficiently flexible to carve out a space for the development of much-needed health products.

Laura Biron discusses the proposal made by Aidan Hollis and Thomas Pogge in 2008 for the establishment of a Health Impact Fund (HIF), which aims at supplementing the IP system to ensure widespread access to essential medicines. She notes that a patent confers a time-limited monopoly on inventors, allowing them to recoup the huge costs of drug development. However, as has been seen throughout this collection, patents price many potential buyers out of the market for drugs. These buyers could pay somewhat more than the cost of production, but not the amount of the monopoly rent extracted by the patent holder. The HIF aims to address this market failure by rewarding pharmaceutical innovators directly on the basis of the health impact of their products. The greater the number of Quality Adjusted Life Years (QALYs) a registered drug produces, the larger the company's share of the Fund. In return producers agree to sell at cost price, effectively making the drugs available to those in greatest need. Like Evans, Biron argues for pragmatic innovation with tangible results, rather than radical change. Implementation of the HIF would leave the global patent system untouched, making the cooperation of pharmaceutical companies more likely. Of course it could not function without significant financial support from the developed countries. Biron notes that a contribution of 0.03 per cent of gross national income would generate a fund of US$6 billion. While this would be considerably greater than most current overseas aid budgets, it would be considerably less than the drug expenditure of the wealthier countries.

The need for cooperation between developing countries is a notable theme in many of the chapters in this volume. Commercial joint ventures for the production of generic drugs, policy learning as regards the creative use of flexibilities in IP law and scientific collaboration between researchers and producers are all instances of fruitful exchange between developing countries. In his chapter, Peter Yu explores the potential for

South-South alliances in trade negotiation. In doing so, he returns us to the broader governance context within which the legal and economic framework for drug access is established. The likelihood of millions of people living with HIV/AIDS gaining access to essential medicines is crucially determined through processes of multilateral bargaining at the WTO, the World Intellectual Property Organization (WIPO), and in regional and bilateral fora. The gains to the developed countries and their commercial interests codified in TRIPs and the General Council Decision, as well as in subsequent FTAs or EPAs, have been achieved as a result of the isolation and weakness of developing countries in these negotiations. Yu explores the potential of what he calls 'IPC4D' – IP coalitions for development – as a means of resisting this 'divide and conquer' tactic. He is cautiously optimistic about the benefits of IPC4D – legal expertise can be pooled, negotiation fatigue overcome and the costs of dispute settlement reduced. The latter is particularly salient given the importance of the WTO's adjudication machinery in determining the precise content of states' obligations under TRIPs. The potency of South-South coalitions is enhanced where civil society organizations and concerned academics in the North can be enrolled as allies. Yu is careful to point out the likely obstacles to successful IPC4D. The interests of the least developed countries, often those worst affected by the AIDS pandemic, do not fully coincide with those of middle-ranking states, whose own industries themselves seek the protection of IP rights. Historical antagonisms and varying economic structures as between states may also be impediments to cooperation.

In the epilogue, Yu continues to explore the 'rugged road ahead' for HIV/AIDS governance, due in part to the ongoing tensions between the protection and enforcement of IP rights and the need for access to essential medicines and in part to the growing complexity of the international regulatory environment. He identifies some promising changes that have taken place in this environment since the launch of the Doha Development Round of Trade Negotiations. He also outlines the many remaining challenges that continue to haunt the HIV/AIDS governance regime while reducing access to essential medicines in developing countries.

To provide handy references, we include in the appendices selected provisions of the TRIPs Agreement, the Doha Declaration, the General Council Decision and the accompanying chairperson's statement, the proposed amendment to the TRIPs Agreement (Article 31*bis*), as well as other key WTO documents that have been discussed in this volume. Due to the limited space in this volume, we have omitted all the footnotes in the documents.

Access to essential medicines is a highly complex problem, at both the global and domestic levels. While this book does not resolve once and for all the highly acrimonious South-North debate that often pitches developing countries and civil society groups against the global pharmaceutical giants and their supportive developed countries, each contributor in this volume offers pragmatic insights into addressing at least one or more aspects of the complex interactions between the protection and enforcement of IP rights and access to essential medicines, with a primary focus on access to drugs for the treatment of HIV/AIDS.

NOTES

1. For a reflection on the nature of global health justice, see Baxi (2010).
2. Pogge has addressed both demands in his scholarly and practical work: see Pogge (2002, 2006) and Chapter 9 in this volume.
3. For an elaboration of the idea of global health governance, see Dodgson, Lee and Drager (2002) and Chapter 2 in this volume.
4. For a detailed analysis, see Matthews (2002).
5. On network governance in global health, see Burris (2004).

BIBLIOGRAPHY

Abbott, Frederick M. (2002), 'The Doha Declaration on the TRIPs Agreement and public health: Lighting a dark corner of the WTO', *Journal of International Economic Law*, **5**, 469–505.

Abbott, Frederick M. (2005), 'The WTO medicines decision: The political economy of world pharmaceutical trade and the protection of public health', *American Journal of International Law*, **9**, 317–58.

Baxi, Upendra (2010), 'The place of the human right to health and contemporary approaches to global justice: Some impertinent interrogations', in John Harrington and Maria Stuttaford (eds), *Global Health and Human Rights: Legal and Philosophical Perspectives*, London: Routledge, pp. 12–27.

Blouin, Chantal, Jody Heymann and Nick Drager (2007), *Trade and Health: Seeking Common Ground*, Montreal and Kingston, Canada: McGill-Queen's University Press.

Burris, Scott (2004) 'Governance, microgovernance and health', *Temple Law Review* **77**, 335–58.

Charnovtiz, Steve (2002), 'The legal status of the Doha Declarations', *Journal of International Economic Law*, **5**, 207–11.

Correa, Carlos (2004), *Implementation of the WTO General Council Decision on Paragraph 6 of the Doha Declaration on the TRIPs Agreement and Public Health*, Geneva: World Health Organization.

Dodgson, Richard, Kelley Lee and Nick Drager (2002), *Global Health Governance. A Conceptual Review, Discussion Paper No. 1*, Geneva: WHO, available at http://whqlibdoc.who.int/publications/2002/a85727_eng.pdf (accessed 8 September 2010).

Drahos, Peter and John Braithwaite (2002), *Information Feudalism: Who Owns the Knowledge Economy?*, London: Earthscan.

Gathii, James Thuo (2002), 'The legal status of the Doha Declaration on TRIPs and public health under the Vienna Convention on the Law of Treaties', *Harvard Journal of Law and Technology*, **15**, 291–317.

Hunt, Paul and Sheldon Leader (2010), 'Developing and applying the right to the highest attainable standard of health: The role of the UN Special Rapporteur (2002–2008)', in John Harrington and Maria Stuttaford (eds), *Global Health and Human Rights: Legal and Philosophical Perspectives*, London: Routledge, pp. 28–61.

Jackson, John H. (1997), *The World Trading System: Law and Policy of International Economic Relations*, Cambridge: MIT Press.

Joseph, Sarah (2003), 'Pharmaceutical corporations and access to drugs: The "fourth wave" of corporate human rights scrutiny', *Human Rights Quarterly*, **25**, 425–52.

Malhotra, Kamal (2003), *Making Global Trade Work for People*, London: Earthscan.

Matsushita, Mitsuo, Thomas J. Schoenbaum and Petros C. Mavroidis (2006), *The World Trade Organization: Law, Practice, and Policy*, 2nd Edition, Oxford: Oxford University Press.

Matthews, Duncan (2002), *Globalising Intellectual Property Rights: The TRIPs Agreement*, London: Routledge.

O'Connell, Paul (2010), 'The human right to health in an age of market hegemony', in John Harrington and Maria Stuttaford (eds), *Global Health and Human Rights. Legal and Philosophical Perspectives*, London: Routledge, pp. 190–210.

Orbinski, James (2002), 'AIDS, Médecins Sans Frontières, and access to essential medicines', in Peter I. Hajnal (ed.), *Civil Society in the Information Age*, Aldershot: Ashgate, pp. 127–35.

Pogge, Thomas (2002), 'Responsibility for poverty-related ill health', *Ethics and International Affairs*, **16**, 72–9.

Pogge, Thomas (2006), 'Human rights and global health: A research program', in Christian Barry and Thomas W. Pogge (eds), *Global Institutions and Responsibilities: Achieving Global Justice*, Oxford: Blackwell Publishing, pp. 190–217.

Santoro, Michael A. and Thomas M. Gorrie (eds) (2005), *Ethics and the Pharmaceutical Industry*, New York: Cambridge University Press.

Sell, Susan K. (2004) 'The quest for global governance in intellectual property and public health: Structural, discursive, and institutional dimensions', *Temple Law Review*, **77**, 363–99.

't Hoen, Ellen (2002), 'TRIPs, pharmaceutical patents, and the access to essential medicines: A long way from Seattle to Doha', *Chicago Journal of International Law*, **3**, 27–46.

Thomas, Caroline (2002) 'Trade policy and the politics of access to drugs', *Third World Quarterly*, **23**, 251–64.

Trebilcock, Michael J. and Robert Howse (2005), *The Regulation of International Trade*, 3rd edn, Abingdon, Oxford/New York: Routledge.
World Health Organization [WHO] (1946), Constitution of the World Health Organization, signed on 22 July and entered into force on 7 April 1948.
World Trade Organization [WTO] (1994), Marrakesh Agreement Establishing the World Trade Organization, 15 April.
Zacher, Mark W. and Tania J. Keefe (2008), *The Politics of Global Health Governance: United by Contagion*, New York: Palgrave Macmillan.

2. Communitarian globalism and disease: A normative orientation for global health governance

Obijiofor Aginam

Our response to AIDS has so far been a failure. There has been scientific progress, but with few dividends for people living with poverty as well as HIV. In most of sub-Saharan Africa, they have access to neither prevention nor treatment. Three million deaths this year, and not yet counted millions of new infections, bespeak massive failure (Farmer, 2003, p. 699)

1. INTRODUCTION AND OVERVIEW OF THE ARGUMENT

It is now widely accepted that the global HIV/AIDS crisis is defying, in very complex ways, what international scholars refer to as the governance architecture of the international system (Aginam, 2005; Cooper, Kirton and Shrecker, 2007; Fidler, 2004; Zacher and Keefe, 2008). Despite realizing over a decade ago that AIDS was not just a health issue but a cross-cutting theme in the national, regional and global development agendas, it appears that, as Farmer (2003, p. 699) put it, global policy initiatives and governance responses to AIDS have 'so far been a failure'. Although AIDS, especially in most developing countries with high prevalence of the disease, raises complex governance challenges for the agricultural, education, security, health and other public sectors, the 'massive failure' foreseen by Farmer is reinforced by the paradox of misery in the midst of plenty – the few tangible dividends that poor people living with the virus have derived from the enormous progress so far made by the global scientific community on AIDS treatment. While the relevant epistemic communities have explored the global HIV/AIDS crisis from a variety of disciplines – human security, development, human rights, intellectual property (IP), public health and epidemiology – the unequal access to essential medicines for AIDS treatment between infected populations in developed and developing countries continues to challenge the orthodoxy of global health (including AIDS) governance. Although global governance of AIDS encompasses both preventive and treatment therapies, this chapter explores the effectiveness and limits of existing global mechanisms for containing the HIV/AIDS crisis with a focus on the norms, rules and practices that facilitate or impede access to essential medicines for treatment of HIV/AIDS and other opportunistic infections.

2. DEFINITION AND KEY FEATURES OF (GLOBAL) GOVERNANCE

The word 'governance', especially with respect to emerging global issues, is paradoxically both widely accepted and intensely contested in relevant literature. The acceptance of the term is driven by the phenomenon of globalization and the transnational character of emerging global issues that defy both the geo-political boundaries of individual nation-states and the transnational governance architecture constructed on nation-states as the sole or dominant actors in the international system. The contestation of 'governance' arises partly from the fact that, as Rosenau (2000, p. 223) pointed out, the word is a recent phenomenon that never even existed in some of the world's leading languages such as German. 'Governance' is also doubtful in the thinking of many who still think of 'government' as 'the entity through which order is sought and goals framed and implemented' (Rosenau, 2000, p. 223). Even within the school of thought wherein 'governance' is widely accepted, scholars tend to agree more on the key features and characteristics of the term, especially when used in conjunction with the adjective 'global', than on its definition as such. Seminal writings and the policy frameworks of most intergovernmental institutions suggest that one conspicuous feature of governance at the global level is the emergence and involvement of multiple actors in the international arena who, along with nation-states as the dominant actors, now influence policy and institutional outcomes on a range of global issues that transcend the geo-political boundaries of sovereign nation-states. Global governance actors now include nation-states, regional and international organizations, charitable foundations, civil society and non-governmental organizations, private/corporate sector interests, international business associations, and transnational corporations. Most accepted definitions of global governance underscore the relevance and the often dynamic roles that these multiple actors now play alongside states in the global policy arena. About a decade ago, Lee and Dodgson (2000, pp. 227–8) argued:

> [T]he emergence of global governance as a central concept in international relations responds to a perceived change in the nature of world politics. In contrast to international governance, the defining feature of global governance is its comprehensiveness. Global governance views the globe as a single place within which the boundaries of the interstate system and nation-state have been eroded. Although the nation-state remains an important actor, processes and mechanisms of global governance are growing to encompass the structures of international governance that manage the system of nation-states … . The processes and mechanisms of global governance are diverse, as are the actors and structures that participate in them.

A governance framework, no matter how efficient, is not synonymous with government (Keohane and Nye, 2000, p. 12; Rosenau, 2000, p. 225). Government and governance rule systems differ markedly. While sovereignty and constitutional democracy legitimize government rule systems, the effectiveness of governance rule systems derives from 'traditional norms and habits, informal agreements, shared premises, and a host of other practices' (Rosenau, 2000, p. 225). Thus, 'as the demand for governance increases with the proliferation of complex interdependencies, rule systems can be found in nongovernmental organizations, corporations, professional societies, business associations, advocacy groups, and many other types of collectivities that are not considered to be governments' (Rosenau, 2000, p. 225). Driven by these exigencies, especially in the post-Cold War global transformations of the 1990s, the Commission on Global Governance (1995, p. 2) defined governance as:

> the sum of the many ways individuals and institutions, public and private, manage their common affairs. It is a continuing process through which conflicting or diverse interests may be accommodated and co-operative action may be taken. It includes formal institutions and regimes empowered to enforce compliance, as well as informal arrangements that people and institutions either have agreed to or perceive to be in their interest.

According to Keohane and Nye (2000, p. 12), governance refers to:

> the processes and institutions, both formal and informal, that guide and restrain the collective activities of a group … . Governance need not necessarily be conducted exclusively by governments and the international organizations to which they delegate authority. Private firms, associations of firms, nongovernmental organizations (NGOs), and associations of NGOs all

> engage in it, often in association with governmental bodies, to create governance; sometimes without governmental authority.

Given the contemporary 'complex interdependencies' between nations and peoples, global governance is necessitated by the dynamics of the transnational character of global issues that defy the territorial boundaries of sovereign countries. The (global) governance architecture that has been exclusively 'designed and constructed' by nation-states over three centuries ago since the Peace of Westphalia 1648 is no longer capable of addressing all the emerging and re-emerging global issues of our time (Aginam, 2007; Fidler, 2004; Zacher, 2002). As observed by Zacher and Keefe (2008, p. 138), 'for much of this century the dominant institutions in international decision making were states and intergovernmental organizations or what has often been referred to as "the Westphalian international order"'. In the absence of a world government, Held and McGrew (2002, p. 8) argued, 'the concept of global governance provides a language for describing the nexus of systems of rule-making, political coordination and problem-solving which transcend states and societies'. In an age of globalism involving globalized networks of interdependence, global issues – climate change, forced migration, financial crisis, transcontinental spread of infectious diseases, and many others – can only be effectively regulated through what Rosenau (2000, p. 225) called 'a bifurcated system'; i.e., one composed of the state-centric system driven by governments, as well as the 'multi-centric system' driven by a collection of non-state actors. Although states and non-state actors could compete, cooperate, and interact, 'the proliferating centres of authority on the global stage are thus dense with actors, large and small, formal and informal, economic and social, political and cultural, liberal and authoritarian, who collectively form a highly complex system of global governance' (Rosenau, 2000, p. 225).

Examples of governance frameworks based on the state-centric system include multilateral conventions, treaties, regulations and soft law declarations negotiated and adopted by states either bilaterally, regionally or multilaterally among themselves as the dominant actors in international relations, or by states under the auspices of international organizations like the United Nations, World Trade Organization (WTO), World Health Organization (WHO), and the Food and Agriculture Organization (FAO). These intergovernmental organizations are Westphalian institutions in so far as they admit only nation-states as members, and whatever mandates and powers they have are conferred on them by member-states through their respective constitutions or charters.

A governance framework based on the multi-centric system covers regulatory approaches to global issues either driven by non-state actors or involving their active interactions with states. This could take the form of public-private partnerships that have now proliferated on a number of global health issues in the past decade. Examples of these partnerships include the Global Alliance for Vaccines and Immunization (GAVI), Roll-Back Malaria Campaign, the Stop TB Initiative, the Medicines for Malaria Venture, the Global Fund to Fight AIDS, Tuberculosis and Malaria, and many others (Buse and Walt, 2002; Pinet, 2003). As Zacher and Keefe (2008, p. 135) observed, 'contemporary global health governance is complicated and messy; it is comprised of numerous and varied actors with competing values, interests and motivations'.

HIV/AIDS has become one of the global issues that the proliferating complex interdependencies and collectivities between states and non-state actors seek to tackle through 'a bifurcated system' of (global) governance (Rosenau, 2000). The sheer density and volume of seminal works on 'global health governance' that explore vast global health issues including AIDS attest to this phenomenon (Aginam, 2005; Cooper, Kirton and Schrecker, 2007; Fidler, 2004; Hein, Bartsch and Kohlmorgen, 2007; Poku, Whiteside and Sandkjaer, 2007; Zacher and Keefe, 2008). These works analyze the global AIDS crisis through a bifurcated governance framework.

3. GLOBAL GOVERNANCE OF HIV/AIDS: TWO LEVELS OF INQUIRY

If AIDS, as most scholars, international organizations and global civil society groups postulate, has become a global emergency, then the disproportionate distribution of the mortality and morbidity burdens of the disease between the poorer and industrialized regions of the world reinforces the 'life versus profit' debate that has emerged in global health scholarship at least in the past decade (Aginam, 2006; Beigbeder, 2004; Sell, 2004). This discourse is important because it pitches corporate profits against access to essential medicines by vulnerable populations in underdeveloped and developing countries, and the right to health against IP rights (Joseph, 2003; Santoro and Gorrie, 2005; Sell, 2004; Thomas, 2002). While HIV/AIDS is incurable, it is nonetheless a treatable disease. The impediments to access to antiretroviral (ARV) drugs by HIV-positive populations in most of the developing world are compelling factors that demand an assessment of the governance orthodoxy of the international system in which AIDS now features conspicuously as a global crisis.

Although such an assessment demands a multi-level inquiry, this chapter focuses on two levels. The first level of inquiry, which is academic, deals with the 'life versus profit' tensions between human rights and IP norms in the international system. The second level of inquiry, which is pragmatic, explores the emerging opportunities for South-South co-operation by developing countries to increase access to ARV drugs using the flexibilities of global IP regimes, especially the WTO Agreement on Trade-Related Aspects of Intellectual Property Rights (TRIPs).

3.1 Human Rights Versus Intellectual Property Rights

> The enjoyment of the highest attainable standard of health is one of the fundamental rights of every human being without distinction of race, religion, political belief, economic or social condition (World Health Organization, 2001).

The intense 'life versus profit' debate that has dominated the TRIPs Agreement has placed public health (the right to health) firmly on the global governance agenda. The post-1945 World Order, catalyzed by the establishment of the United Nations, is replete with human rights instruments. Most of these instruments codify the right of everyone 'to the highest attainable standard of health' (Hunt and Khosla, 2008; United Nations General Assembly, 2006; United Nations General Assembly, 2008).

In the same vein, international trading relations are also part of the post-World War II multilateral developments pioneered by the 1947 General Agreement on Tariffs and Trade (GATT) framework. However, IP rights were never part of international trade agreements before the end of the Uruguay Round of Trade Negotiations in 1994 that transformed the GATT into the WTO. The birth of the TRIPs Agreement as one of the trade agreements to be enforced by the WTO has had a fair share of insightful analysis by leading scholars (Sell, 2004 citing Drahos and Braithwaite, 2002, and Matthews, 2002). Partly due to civil society activism, the first decade of TRIPs (1995–2005), was characterized by such initiatives as the Doha Declaration on the TRIPs Agreement and Public Health in 2001 and the Decision of the General Council on the Implementation of Paragraph 6 of the Doha Declaration on the TRIPS Agreement and Public Health (General Council Decision) in 2003 – all aimed at balancing the imperatives of IP rights with the need for access to life-saving drugs. However, difficult questions still remain on how and when to use TRIPs flexibilities, the impact of TRIPs-plus obligations on access to drugs, and how to reconcile 'conflicting' provisions of IP and human rights treaties (Abbott, 2005; Charnovtiz, 2002; Gathii, 2002). Striking a balance between the imperatives of the preservation or promotion of health and the entitlement of an inventor to the material benefits of a scientific work (which could be derived from patents in pharmaceutical drugs) poses a difficult challenge. For instance, in addition to providing for the rights to life and health, the Universal Declaration of Human Rights (UDHR) of 1948, generally regarded as the cornerstone of the international human rights architecture, also provides in Article 27 as follows:

> 1. Everyone has the right freely ... to share in scientific advancement and its benefits.
> 2. Everyone has the right to the protection of the moral and material interests resulting from any scientific ... production of which he is the author.

Consistent with these provisions, Article 15(1) of the International Covenant on Economic, Social and Cultural Rights (ICESCR) of 1966 provides that:

> The States parties to the present Covenant recognize the right of everyone:
>
> (a) To take part in cultural life;
> (b) To enjoy the benefits of scientific progress and its applications;
> (c) To benefit from the protection of the moral and material interests resulting from any scientific, literary or artistic production of which he is the author.

While these UDHR and ICESCR provisions were construed to relate mainly to issues of copyright, the adoption of TRIPs – a more forceful agreement that could be compulsorily enforced through the WTO dispute-settlement mechanism – re-kindled the fierce debate on the linkages between IP and human rights (Cullet, 2003). In the event of a conflict between basic human rights such as the right to health (and in extreme cases the right to life) guaranteed by international treaties on the one hand and an international trade agreement like the TRIPs Agreement on the other, which one should prevail over the other? Should human rights 'trump' trade or vice versa? At the global, regional and national levels, trade agreements that drive IP norms seem to impede health 'regimes' that promote universal access to 'essential medicines', and the right of everyone to the highest attainable standard of physical and mental health. The WHO (1999, p. 10) defines essential medicines as 'those medicines that satisfy the health needs of the majority of the population; they should therefore be available at all times in adequate amounts and in the appropriate dosage form'.

Resolving these human rights and IP dilemmas remains a complex problem in the (global) governance of AIDS. Internationally, it is an arduous task, for instance, to locate a perfect synergy in the policy frameworks and mandates of the WHO and the WTO. Nationally, in the policy arenas of most developing countries, there is a lack of coherence and coordination between the relevant sectors – health, trade, agriculture, foreign policy, and science and technology (Blouin, Heymann and Drager, 2007). This is complicated by the fact that most underdeveloped and developing countries with a high prevalence of HIV/AIDS have no clout in contemporary global economic diplomacy where IP issues have become part of international trading relations – one of the important engines that drive contemporary economic globalization. In situations where human rights norms and those of IP are totally or partially irreconcilable, there is a consensus in academic literature that the challenge would always be how to make life-saving drugs available at costs affordable to the vulnerable groups that need them. According to Cullet (2003, p. 155), 'the central concern that should guide the implementation of all international treaties concerning health directly or indirectly is the promotion of better health care'. From an international legal perspective, tensions exist between TRIPs and human rights instruments like the UDHR, the International Covenant on Civil and Political Rights (ICCPR), the ICESCR, and many others. Leading scholars and academic commentators argue that whenever 'prioritization' of IP and human rights obligations is necessary, human rights should be given more weight than intellectual property rights (Aginam, 2006; Cullet, 2003; Howse and Mutua, 2000). While this argument is popular in human rights scholarship, as well as in the activist domain of global civil society, including organizations like Médecins Sans Frontières (MSF), the Treatment Action Campaign, and many others, it has yet to be fully tested pragmatically in trade disputes that play out in the WTO dispute settlement mechanism.

3.2 Opportunities and Impediments for South-South Cooperation to Increase Access to ARV

Post-TRIPs debate on IP versus access to ARV drugs, albeit a long and tortuous battle, nonetheless served as the catalyst that expanded the opportunities for pragmatic uses of TRIPs flexibilities. The 2001 Doha Declaration affirmed that TRIPs can and should be interpreted and implemented in a manner 'supportive of WTO Members' right to protect public health, and in particular, to promote access to medicines for all'. It also affirmed that WTO member states (mostly the underdeveloped and some developing countries) with insufficient or no manufacturing capacities in the pharmaceutical sector could face difficulties in making effective use of compulsory licensing under the TRIPs Agreement. The Doha Declaration was supplemented by the General Council Decision. The decision provides the criteria aimed at facilitating access to essential medicines, including ARV drugs for HIV/AIDS, by vulnerable populations in the underdeveloped and developing countries.

Both the Doha Declaration and the General Council Decision were fraught with serious structural impediments. While the Doha Declaration offered an interpretive paradigm that raised the visibility of public health and universal access to medicines in the TRIPs regime, it offered no concrete road map and technical details on how to resolve the IP versus public health dilemmas in pragmatic ways. This is further complicated by two factors. First, past efforts by countries like South Africa and Brazil to deploy the time-hallowed and universally acclaimed TRIPs flexibilities, especially compulsory licensing and parallel importation to address public health (especially HIV/AIDS) 'emergencies', were challenged by both the United States and global pharmaceutical corporations in different forums ('t Hoen, 2002). There is no evidence that these challenges by either the 'Big Powers' or 'Big Pharma' have abated or will abate soon. While the challenges may no longer be overt, they remain covert.

Second, any progress made under the Doha Declaration and the General Council Decision towards expanding the TRIPs opportunities is now gradually being reversed globally by the proliferation of bilateral and regional 'free trade agreements'. These agreements impose what is now known as TRIPs-plus obligations on developing countries, which are always the weaker partners to such agreements. The objective of the General Council Decision was to facilitate access to essential medicines (including ARV drugs for HIV/AIDS), especially for underdeveloped and developing countries with insufficient or no manufacturing capacities in the pharmaceutical sector.[1] These countries cannot issue compulsory licenses for the production of generic ARV drugs simply because they lack the technological capacity to manufacture them domestically. The only viable option is to import generic versions of the drugs from an industrialized country that is willing to amend its patent legislation in order to produce those drugs exclusively for export to poor countries. The General Council Decision imposes key obligations on exporting and importing countries in relation to these medicines. There is an obligation on developing countries to notify the WTO of an intention to become an eligible importing member, and specifically to identify the products and quantities.

Canada was the first industrialized country that amended its patent laws – in what is now known as 'Canada's Access to Medicines Regime' (CAMR) – to allow domestic production of generic drugs exclusively for export to a poor country hit by HIV/AIDS that files a request at the WTO for importation of such drugs.[2] Following the CAMR as well as the requirements of the General Council Decision, Apotex, a leading Canadian generic pharmaceutical manufacturer – at the request of MSF – developed a new fixed-dose combination tablet that combines existing ARV drugs – zidovudine (AZT), lamivudine (3TC), and niverapine – into a single tablet for the first time for export under compulsory license to developing countries (Elliott, 2007). In July 2007, Rwanda became the first country to initiate the use of a procedure under WTO rules that allows developing countries to import low-cost, generic medicines produced in other countries under compulsory licenses. In a notification deposited at the WTO, Rwanda notified the organization of its intention to use the 2003 procedure to import 15.6 million of the fixed-dose combination produced by Apotex in Canada (Elliott, 2007).

In the long process that eventually led to the production of the three drugs into one fixed dose, Apotex held complex negotiations with three Canadian pharmaceutical companies that owned patent rights on the three drugs before it finally got a compulsory license issued on 19 September 2007. Canada subsequently notified the WTO of this development as required by the General Council Decision. At the time of export to Rwanda, this generic single fixed-dose combination cost about US$0.40 per tablet as opposed to US$20 per tablet in the United States using the patented brands (Elliott, 2007). Although the CAMR is commendable, it is fraught with serious administrative bottlenecks, especially the long, tortuous, and often frustrating procedure of negotiations between the patent holders and generic drug producers for compulsory licenses. Because these negotiations took years, there is little or no incentive for most generic drug companies to pursue such CAMR initiatives in the future in Canada. Even for Canada and other industrialized countries that might contemplate amending their patent legislation to take advantage of General Council Decision, the real question remains whether such industrialized countries could withstand the pressure and corporate lobbying by the powerful pharmaceutical industry. One lesson to learn from the TRIPs negotiations in the 1990s is the power of industry lobby in global economic diplomacy. As Sinclair (2000, p. 22) observed, 'corporate pressure is nothing new in WTO negotiations. Such pressure, largely exerted by U.S.-based firms, is widely acknowledged to have been a driving force in the negotiations'.

The limits of the CAMR and the unwillingness of other industrialized countries to expand TRIPs flexibilities along the lines provided in the General Council Decision will leave most developing countries with the option of pursuing South-South cooperation as a way to increase access to ARV drugs for their HIV-positive populations.[3] This could take the form of foreign direct investment (FDI)-driven joint ventures with countries like India and Brazil that have well-established pharmaceutical sectors for generic ARV drug production. In 2007, for instance, Uganda commissioned a facility to produce generic ARV drugs locally based on a joint venture with Cipla, Indian generic producer. Available data from the WHO and the Joint United Nations Programme on HIV/AIDS (UNAIDS) suggest that about 41% of Ugandans who need ARV drugs currently receive the treatment (World Health Organization/UNAIDS, 2005). The joint venture initiative between Uganda and Cipla will likely drive down costs and make ARV drugs more accessible to those who need them in Uganda. Many other African countries have started working towards local production of generic ARV drugs along the lines and structure of the Uganda-Cipla venture. Whether these South-South initiatives for increased access to ARV drugs in developing countries are sustainable is open to debate. Nonetheless, such initiatives have opened a new vista in the global governance of AIDS as countries like India and Brazil emerge as part of the 'Southern' engines of growth. However, one major challenge for future South-South cooperation is the rapidly changing orientation of the pharmaceutical industry in these so-called BRICS countries towards patent regimes driven by the obligation on these countries to amend their IP laws to become TRIPs compliant.[4]

4. THREE POLICY CONCLUSIONS

Global governance of AIDS is a complex phenomenon with no easy solutions in an asymmetrical international system with inequalities and disparities among underdeveloped, developing, and industrialized countries. These disparities are not peculiar to HIV/AIDS issues. They are embedded in the orthodoxy of global governance architecture as a whole. In the context of the issues raised in this chapter, it is worthwhile to conclude with three policy conclusions for the future of global AIDS governance, especially focusing on reconciling IP and human rights and exploiting the opportunities of TRIPs flexibilities in a sustained way.

First, although the TRIPs Agreement created flexibilities that are arguably supportive of the poorer countries' drive to strengthen their institutional capacity to generate and promote public goods given each country's specific social and economic conditions, these flexibilities, in practice, were impeded by the interests of the big powers and pharmaceutical corporations. In reconciling their different international trade (including TRIPs) and human rights obligations, developing countries must ingeniously deploy human rights arguments pragmatically, especially the right to life, to exploit whatever opportunities and flexibilities that exist in global trade agreements. Trade liberalization must take into account the asymmetries and differential levels of development between the industrialized and poor countries and how these asymmetries are complicating the global HIV/AIDS crises. It is arguable that this was precisely what TRIPs, from the onset, set out to achieve with flexibilities such as compulsory licensing and parallel importation.

Second, countries like Brazil and India have now developed their domestic pharmaceutical sectors for sustained production of generic ARV drugs. They have also emerged as global economic players. As they continue to be part of the 'Southern' engines of economic growth, most developing countries will find them attractive for some form of South-South cooperation to boost access to ARV drugs for HIV/AIDS and other opportunistic infections. The vision and policy framework for these joint ventures should be articulated in ways that are TRIPs compliant, in order to meet the basic human rights obligations that these countries owe their HIV-positive populations.

Third, the solution to the crisis of HIV/AIDS in most developing countries is not just access to drugs. The healthcare infrastructure and health systems in most developing countries are either dysfunctional or inefficient. The healthcare system in developing countries, where dysfunctional, cannot support and sustain life-long ARV therapies. Availability of drugs without a functioning healthcare system to administer them effectively does not offer a sustainable solution to the HIV/AIDS and other public health crises in most of the underdeveloped and developing countries (World Health Organization Commission on Macroeconomics and Health, 2001). While access to ARV treatment must be actively promoted and pursued as an indispensable component of the global governance of AIDS, it is also extremely important to address the critical issues of healthcare reform in a sustainable way.

NOTES

1. It is estimated that more than 80 per cent of developing and underdeveloped countries lack a functional pharmaceutical sector with a capacity for domestic production of generic ARVs for the treatment of HIV/AIDS and other opportunistic infections. This point is well illustrated in 't Hoen (2002); Abbott (2005); Callahan and Wasunna (2006); Joseph (2003); Santoro and Gorrie (2005) and Thomas (2002).
2. This section benefited from the concise but excellent review of CAMR and the request by Rwanda written by Richard Elliott (2007).
3. For a discussion of the prospects and challenges of such South-South cooperation, see Chapter 10 in this volume.
4. 'BRICS' refers to Brazil, Russia, India, China and South Africa. For a discussion of the changing orientation of the pharmaceutical industry in some of the BRICS countries towards a more restrictive patent regime, see Chapter 3 in this volume.

BIBLIOGRAPHY

Abbott, Frederick M. (2005), 'The WTO medicines decision: Pharmaceutical trade and the protection of public health', *American Journal of International Law*, **9**, 317–58.

Aginam, Obijiofor (2005), *Global Health Governance: International Law and Public Health in a Divided World*, Toronto: University of Toronto Press.

Aginam, Obijiofor (2006), 'Between life and profit: Global governance and the trilogy of human rights, public health and pharmaceutical patents', *North Carolina Journal of International Law & Commercial Regulation*, **31**, 901–21.

Aginam, Obijiofor (2007), 'Global governance', in Sandro Galea (ed.), *Macrosocial Determinants of Population Health*, New York: Springer, pp. 159–68.

Beigbeder, Yves (2004), *International Public Health: Patients' Rights vs. the Protection of Patents*, Aldershot, UK: Ashgate.

Blouin, Chantal, Jody Heymann and Nick Drager (eds) (2007), *Trade and Health: Seeking Common Ground*, Montreal: McGill-Queen's Press.

Buse, Kent and Gill Walt (2002), 'Globalisation and multilateral public-private partnerships: Issues for health policy', in Kelley Lee, Kent Buse and Suzanne Fustukian (eds), *Health Policy in a Globalising World*, Cambridge: Cambridge University Press, pp. 41–62.

Callahan, Daniel and Angela A. Wasunna (2006), *Medicine and the Market: Equity v. Choice*, Baltimore: Johns Hopkins University Press.

Charnovtiz, Steve (2002), 'The legal status of the Doha Declarations', *Journal of International Economic Law*, **5**(1), 207–11.

Commission on Global Governance (1995), *Our Global Neighborhood: The Report of the Commission on Global Governance*, New York: Oxford University Press.

Cooper, Andrew F., John J. Kirton and Ted Schrecker (2007), *Governing Global Health: Challenges, Response, Innovation*, Aldershot, UK: Ashgate.

Cullet, Philippe (2003), 'Patents and medicines: The relationship between TRIPs and the human right to health', *International Affairs*, **79**(1), 139–60.

Drahos, Peter and John Braithwaite (2002), *Information Feudalism: Who Owns the Knowledge Economy?*, London: Earthscan.

Elliott, Richard (2007), 'First test of WTO mechanism for procuring generic medicines under compulsory license, via Canada's access to medicines regime', *HIV/AIDS Policy & Law Review (Canadian HIV/AIDS Legal Network)*, **12**(2–3), 23–5.

Farmer, Paul (2003), 'AIDS as a global emergency', *Bulletin of the World Health Organization*, **81**(10), 699.

Fidler, David P. (2004), *SARS, Governance and the Globalization of Disease*, London: Palgrave Macmillan.

Gathii, James T. (2002), 'The legal status of the Doha declaration on TRIPs and public health under the Vienna Convention on the Law of Treaties', *Harvard Journal of Law and Technology*, **15**(2), 291–317.

Hein, Wolfgang, Sonja Bartsch and Lars Kohlmorgen (eds) (2007), *Global Health Governance and the Fight Against HIVIAIDS*, New York: Palgrave Macmillan.

Held, David and Anthony McGrew (2002), 'Introduction', in David Held and Anthony McGrew (eds), *Governing Globalization: Power, Authority and Global Governance*, Cambridge: Polity, pp. 1–21.

Howse, Robert and Makau Mutua (2000), *Protecting Human Rights in a Global Economy: Challenges for the World Trade Organization*, Montreal: International Centre for Human Rights and Democratic Development.

Hunt, Paul and Rajat Khosla (2008), 'The human right to medicines', *International Journal on Human Rights*, **5**(8), 99–114.

Joseph, Sarah (2003), 'Pharmaceutical corporations and access to drugs: The 'Fourth Wave' of corporate human rights scrutiny', *Human Rights Quarterly*, **25**(2), 425–52.

Keohane, Robert O. and Joseph S. Nye Jr. (2000), 'Introduction', in Joseph S. Nye and John D. Donahue (eds), *Governance in a Globalizing World*, Washington, D.C: Brookings.

Lee, Kelley and Richard Dodgson (2000), 'Globalization and cholera: Implications for global governance', *Global Governance*, **6**, 213–36.

Matthews, Duncan (2002), *Globalising Intellectual Property Rights: The TRIPs Agreement*, London: Routledge.

Pinet, Geneviève (2003), 'Global partnerships: A key challenge and opportunity for implementation of international health law', *Medicine and Law*, **22**(4), 561–77.

Poku, Nana K., Alan Whiteside and Bjorg Sandkjaer (eds) (2007), *AIDS and Governance*, Aldershot, UK: Ashgate.

Rosenau, James N. (2000), 'Governance in a new world order', in David Held and Anthony McGrew (eds), *The Global Transformations Reader*, Cambridge: Polity, pp. 223–4.

Santoro, Michael A. and Thomas M. Gorrie (eds) (2005), *Ethics and the Pharmaceutical Industry*, New York: Cambridge University Press.

Sell, Susan K. (2004), 'The quest for global governance in intellectual property and public health: Structural, discursive, and institutional dimensions', *Temple Law Review*, **77**, 363–99.

Sinclair, Scott (2000), *GATS: How the World Trade Organizations New Services Negotiations Threaten Democracy*, Ottawa: Canadian Centre for Policy Alternatives.

't Hoen, Ellen (2002), 'TRIPs, pharmaceutical patents, and the access to essential medicines: A long way from Seattle to Doha' *Chicago Journal of International Law*, **3**: pp. 27–46.

Thomas, Caroline (2002), 'Trade policy and the politics of access to drugs', *Third World Quarterly*, **23**(2): pp. 251–64.

United Nations General Assembly (2006), *Report of the Special Rapporteur on the Right of Everyone to the Enjoyment of the Highest Standard of Physical and Mental Health*, 13 September, UN Doc A/61/338.

United Nations General Assembly (2008), *Report of the Special Rapporteur on the Right of Everyone to the Enjoyment of the Highest Standard of Physical and Mental Health*, 11 August, UN Doc A/63/263.

World Health Organization (1999), *Action Programme on Essential Drugs, Globalization, and Access to Drugs: Perspectives on the WTO/TRIPs Agreement*, Geneva: WHO.

World Health Organization (2001), *World Health Organization: Basic Documents*, Geneva: WHO, pp. 1–21.

World Health Organization Commission on Macroeconomics and Health (2001), *Macroeconomics and Health: Investing in Health for Economic Development*, Report of the Commission on Macroeconomics and Health, Geneva: WHO.

World Health Organization/UNAIDS (2005), *Progress on Global Access to HIV Antiretroviral Therapy: An Update on '3 by 5'*, Geneva: WHO/UNAIDS.

Zacher, Mark W. (2002), 'The decaying pillars of the Westphalian Temple: implications for international order and governance', in James Rosenau (ed.), *Governance Without Government*, Cambridge: Cambridge University Press, pp. 58–101.

Zacher, Mark W. and Tania J. Keefe (2008), *The Politics of Global Health Governance: United By Contagion*, New York: Palgrave Macmillan.

3. Is AIDS treatment sustainable?

Kenneth C. Shadlen

1. INTRODUCTION

The first decade of the twenty-first century witnessed a remarkable extension of antiretroviral (ARV) treatment to people living with HIV/AIDS in the developing world. Whereas ARVs reached less than five per cent of people in need of treatment as of 2002, by the end of the decade nearly half of those needing treatment were receiving these life-saving drugs. But to what extent can AIDS treatment continue to be increased? Can increased treatment be sustained?

In this chapter I present a cautionary view, focusing on fundamental changes that are transpiring in treatment regimens and the generic pharmaceutical industry. These changes could create a mismatch between the demand for and the supply of high-quality and affordable ARVs. To be sure, financial commitments for scaling-up treatment, the sense of urgency with which the international donor community has come to view the HIV/AIDS epidemic, and alleviation of some significant legal obstacles to accessing affordable medicines can all provide bases for optimism. Yet what has worked so far may not continue to work; more of the same may not be enough.[1] As the demand for treatment throughout the developing world increases and evolves, the world's ability to respond effectively may be limited. The reason why has to do with the effects that changes in the global political economy of intellectual property (IP) are likely to have on the availability of affordable ARVs.

The key issue regards the changing relationship between the demand and supply of particular sets of ARVs. The increase in ARV treatment has been possible because the drugs demanded for use in standard regimens throughout the developing world were also ARVs that generic producers (particularly in India) were able and willing to supply – legally and financially. As countries' treatment regimens change, however, both as first-line protocols become updated and as patients move from first-line to second-line regimens, the overlap between what drugs are needed and what are available may dissipate. The new global political economy of IP and subsequent transformation of the generic pharmaceutical industry are likely to complicate generic firms' ability to adjust their supply to the changed demand – or, importantly, their interest in adjusting their supply to the changed demand.

To advance this argument I build on the extensive literature on IP, pharmaceuticals, and health by problematizing what most analyses of AIDS treatment take as a constant – the existence of generic versions of essential drugs. If generic drugs exist, then analysts, activists, and policymakers can focus on the steps needed to increase consumers' ability to access them, such as how to overcome legal, IP-related barriers and how to increase purchasing power via the development of funding and pooled-procurement mechanisms; this is about increasing effective demand. But assuring adequate production and supply of essential drugs is also indispensable for increasing and extending treatment; and the constellations of political actors and strategies that facilitate the strengthening of demand may be less effective with regard to supply.

To highlight the distinct – and more complicated – political economy of production and supply, I show how the Agreement on Trade-Related Aspects of Intellectual Property Rights (TRIPs) sets new incentives for drug producers. Because these new incentives inspire new patterns of investment and specialization, they can have significant effects on the structure of generic pharmaceutical sectors in those countries that are capable of supplying essential medicines. The ensuing changes in market structure affect actors' economic and political interests and capacities, and new sets of interests and capacities have profound implications for the creation and maintenance of political coalitions in support of ongoing drug supply. The result, then, is that the global AIDS treatment campaign becomes marked by mismatches of interests and capacities: those actors capable of taking the steps necessary to increase the supply and availability of high-quality, affordable drugs have diminished interest in doing so, and those actors with an interest in expanding treatment may lack the capacities to address the problem of undersupply.[2]

The chapter consists of four sections. In the next section I highlight the remarkable increase in AIDS treatment. I provide background on the strategy led by the World Health Organization (WHO) for scaling-up treatment, and I discuss the critical and indispensable role that generic drugs play in extending and increasing treatment. In the third section I introduce the new IP environment, and I explain why in examining the relationship between patents and treatment it is imperative to focus on patents in supplier countries. To that end I show how the emergence of 'quasi-universal pharmaceutical patenting', where new drugs are likely to be patented in all countries with the ability to produce them, creates new and more complex challenges for the global treatment campaign. In the fourth section I examine these challenges in more detail by examining the incentives to generic suppliers. To do so I disaggregate the generic pharmaceutical sector, distinguishing among three basic segments according to price:cost ratios. I explain how new IP regulations transform market structure by turning the incentives dramatically against investing in production of generic versions of new drugs for AIDS treatment, and I consider the effects that the emerging market structure has on political coalitions for expanding treatment to meet the goals established by the international community. The analysis in this section is done with an eye on India, the country that is the most important supplier of generic AIDS drugs. In the conclusion I summarize the main findings and assess a range of mechanisms and strategies for restoring stability to the supply of essential medicines for AIDS treatment.

2. HIV/AIDS, ANTIRETROVIRALS AND TREATMENT

HIV/AIDS treatment entails combining various types of ARVs in order to slow down reproduction of the virus. ARVs do not cure HIV/AIDS, but they can prevent the virus from destroying the immune system and thus allow people who are infected to live normal lives. Indeed, the introduction of combination therapy in the 1990s converted HIV/AIDS into a chronic condition in much of the OECD (Organization for Economic Co-operation and Development). Notwithstanding the advances in science and the effective control of HIV/AIDS in developed countries, however, the global extension of ARV treatment progressed slowly. As of the early 2000s HIV/AIDS remained a death sentence in most of the developing world.

The daunting challenges to extending HIV/AIDS treatment in poorer countries and settings are widely acknowledged (Tayler, 2004; WHO, 2003; World Bank, 2004). Drugs are expensive, as is diagnostic equipment. Trained healthcare professionals are needed for diagnosing patients, delivering ARVs, monitoring patients, responding to medical emergencies and dealing with the emergence of opportunistic infections. Some medicines have refrigeration requirements, which add further complexities to supply management and to the already-immense challenges of procurement and patient care. The list goes on.

Despite the very real challenges, an increasing number of people living with HIV/AIDS in the developing world have begun to receive ARV treatment since the early 2000s. Figure 3.1 illustrates a remarkable trajectory of treatment. The solid line (corresponding to the left-hand vertical axis) shows the sharp increase in the number of people in developing countries receiving ARV treatment, from approximately 230,000 in 2002 to more than four million by the end of 2008. The dashed line (corresponding to the right-hand vertical axis) charts the associated growth in coverage, i.e., the number of people receiving treatment as a share of the total number of people in need of treatment, from less than five per cent to over 42 per cent by the end of 2008. The WHO measures coverage as the estimated number of people receiving ARV therapy as a share of the estimated number of people aged 0–49 in need of ARV therapy. Given the wide range of uncertainty regarding the number of people in a given country that have HIV/AIDS, and the further uncertainty in estimating how many of the people with HIV/AIDS at any given time are in need of ARV therapy, the figures for coverage are extremely rough.[3] But even with these caveats and the uncertainties regarding the specific figures, the rate of increase is unmistakable.

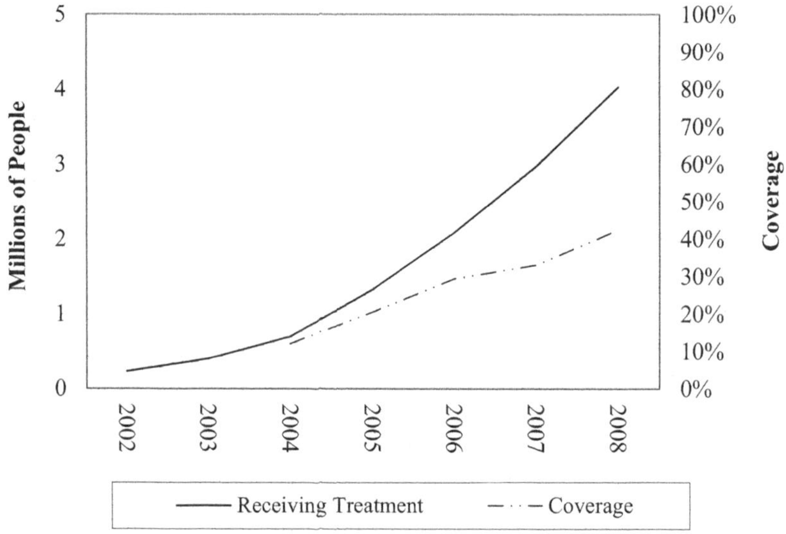

Sources: WHO, HIV/AIDS Progress Reports (Various Years), http://www.who.int/hiv/pub/progressreports/en/

Figure 3.1 AIDS treatment in the developing world

The dramatic increases in both treatment and coverage are the result of many factors, including a coherent international strategy spearheaded by the WHO, increased international financing, greater prioritization of

HIV/AIDS policies within developing countries (including investments in treatment infrastructure), and the relatively simple and ample availability of affordable versions of the ARVs in demand (Kapstein and Busby, 2009; Peiffer and Boussalis, 2010; Waning, Kyle, Diedrichsen, Soucy, Hochstadt, Barnighausen, and Moon, 2010). This final factor is the key point of the chapter, for it was the match between the profile of drugs available from multiple suppliers and the profile of ARVs demanded for initiation and expansion of AIDS treatment that facilitated the trajectory illustrated in Figure 3.1 – and it is the concern about the development of a mismatch between supply and demand that is the source of the concern about the future of ARV treatment.

Before turning to the analysis of the relationship between those ARVs in supply and those in demand, it is worth making a few observations about AIDS treatment in the developing world and the interaction between drug prices and national practices. The WHO strategy for scaling up ARV treatment in the developing world is a protocol-driven public health approach based on a formulary of recommended drugs, rather than individual treatment regimens. With testing and diagnostic technologies less available, and with severely constrained budgets for procuring medicines, the WHO strategy essentially strips treatment to the bare bones, providing a simple target for treatment eligibility and reliance on a reduced set of drug combinations. The idea is that a protocol-driven approach, whereby people whose CD4 count falls to a certain level are considered for receiving treatment that is drawn from a formulary of a small number of drugs, is simpler to implement (administratively, financially and medically) and thus more appropriate for resource-poor settings.

Specifically, the 2003 protocol called for treatment to begin when patients began showing advanced clinical disease symptoms and/or their CD4 count fell below 200 cells per cubic millimetre of blood. The recommended first-line treatment regimen consisted of combining two nucleoside reverse transcriptase inhibitors (NRTIs) with one non-nucleoside reverse transcriptase inhibitor (NNRTI). The five-drug formulary consisted of three NRTIs (lamivudine (3TC), zidovudine (AZT), and stavudine (d4T)) and two NNRTIs (efavirenz (EFZ) and nevirapine (NVP)).[4] In 2009 the WHO announced two significant revisions to the standard protocol.[5] First, the WHO called for treatment to begin earlier, at CD4 counts below 350 (rather than 200) and indicating that treatment should then commence regardless of symptoms.[6] Second, the WHO promoted tenofovir (TDF) as a recommended first-line NRTI in place of the highly toxic d4T.[7] Throughout this period, where first-line regimens are not having the intended effect of slowing down reproduction of the virus, the WHO has continued to emphasize the importance of moving patients to second-line treatment based on two NRTIs and a boosted protease inhibitor (PI).[8] Later in this chapter I will discuss the implications of these changes for the sustainability of treatment in the developing world, but for now it is worth simply making the obvious observation that by altering the threshold for eligibility the WHO significantly increased the number of people classified as 'in need of treatment'.[9] All else being equal, the treatment 'coverage' figure will decline on account of the larger denominator.

Though increasing and sustaining AIDS treatment depends on many factors, of course, the availability of the essential ARVs is absolutely indispensable. The cornerstone to an effective treatment program is that affordable medicines be available. Drugs are the key input because they are irreplaceable. Functional – if not optimal – substitutes can be found to address inadequacies in other components of treatment: different sorts of infrastructure can be made suitable, alternative healthcare providers can be deployed, and so on. But no amount of managerial creativity can substitute for ARVs. If drugs are not available, treatment is impossible, full stop.

Drug prices, of course, are not the only relevant issue, as the previous discussion of the challenges to treatment indicates; even if drugs were free, many countries may lack the infrastructure to extend treatment. Yet a key point regards the interaction between prices and infrastructure: for public health ministries operating with scarce resources, the incentives to invest in the development of the healthcare infrastructure that is essential for AIDS treatment is logically related to the price of drugs. Low prices can encourage resource mobilization, while high prices can discourage such mobilization; why bother investing in infrastructure that will go unused on account of the essential drugs being too expensive?[10] In short, because the availability of affordable drugs can make improving healthcare infrastructure a more useful investment, lower drug prices cannot just free resources but also create incentives to invest in the necessary infrastructure (Berwick, 2002, pp. 214; Nattrass and Geffen, 2005; Schwartländer, Stover, Walker, Bollinger, Gutierrez, McGreevey, Opuni, Forsythe, Kumaranayake, Watts, and Bertozzi, 2001).

A critical factor in lowering drug prices has been the existence of a vibrant market for high-quality 'generic' ARVs. Not only are generic drugs themselves ordinarily less expensive than their brand-name equivalents, but competition introduced by generics yields price reductions across the board. Indeed, the introduction and extension on the part of brand-name firms of tiered-pricing for ARVs has largely followed competition induced by generic suppliers (Lucchini, Cisse, Duran, de

Cenival, Comiti, Gaudry, and Moatti, 2003; Kovsted, 2005; MSF, various years; Wainberg, 2005; Waning, Kaplan, Fox, Boyd-Boffa, King, Lawrence, Soucy, Mahajan, Leufkens, and Gokhale, 2010). Absent generic competition, the supply of ARVs at affordable prices is overly reliant on the benevolence of the brand-name industry (Shadlen, 2004b).

In considering the role of generic suppliers, it is crucial to emphasize the dynamic and temporal dimensions. Because treatment must not be terminated, the need for drugs to be available is never-ending. But while the demand for drugs, in general, is constant, the demand for specific sets of drugs is not. Patients develop immunity to particular medications, resistant strands of the virus emerge, and treatment regimens need adjustment. The drugs that work today will be ineffective tomorrow; affordable and high-quality versions of *new* ARVs must be available as well. This means that the political, economic, and legal conditions that facilitate the availability of today's drugs must be continuously reproduced. The remainder of the chapter examines the challenges of such continuous reproduction and thus to the durability of generic competition, and, subsequently, the stability of supply of affordable ARVs.

3. TRIPS, QUASI-UNIVERSAL PHARMACEUTICAL PATENTING AND GENERIC ARVS

The TRIPs Agreement sets new and universal standards to which IP regimes in all countries that are WTO members must conform. Prior to the introduction of TRIPs many countries did not issue patents on pharmaceutical products, meaning that multiple suppliers could and often did exist for many drugs. That situation changes with TRIPs, which requires countries to grant patents in all technological fields (Article 27). As regards the ongoing extension of AIDS treatment, the essential issue is the effect of TRIPs and pharmaceutical patents on the *suppliers* of ARVs.

It is worthwhile to note that many ARVs are not patented in many developing countries. The reasons for this are multiple. First, the poorest (least developed) countries are not required to issue pharmaceutical patents until 2016. Second, those countries that did not grant patents to pharmaceuticals prior to 1995 did not have to begin doing so until 2005.[11] Third, even where countries begin to grant patents to pharmaceuticals, products that were already on the market prior to a country changing its patent laws typically cannot be patented (i.e., only new drugs are patentable). Fourth, notwithstanding the formal availability of patents, originator firms often choose not to patent each of their drugs in all countries, especially smaller markets.[12] Thus, many drugs that are patented in the OECD are still not patented in many developing countries.

The limited extent of pharmaceutical patents in the developing world has led some observers to conclude that patents are unimportant and that the concerns about the relationship between patents and access to ARVs are unwarranted (e.g., Attaran, 2004; Attaran and Gillespie-White, 2001). But such analyses, based on unweighted cross-country tallying of patents, are profoundly misleading. After all, few developing countries have the economic and technological capacity to produce their own ARVs, regardless of the patent situation. Most countries import their ARVs; where ARVs are produced locally, the active pharmaceutical ingredients (APIs) are generally imported (this is so for the most part even in big developing countries, such as Brazil, and in many developed countries too). From a treatment perspective, for example, the fact that ARV patenting is low in Malawi and Zambia is irrelevant, since neither country has the capacity to produce ARVs. Instead, they, like everyone else, are likely to depend on Indian (or Chinese) production.[13]

Thus, rather than examining patents across the board, our attention must be directed toward the more advanced developing (and also developed) countries with sophisticated pharmaceutical sectors, i.e., the potential suppliers. All larger countries – developed and developing – with the capacity to produce and export ARVs are WTO members (or wish to join, e.g., Iran) and are therefore bound by TRIPs to grant pharmaceutical patents. What this means, quite simply, is that eventually all new drugs are likely to be patented in all countries with the capacity to produce them. I call this situation 'quasi-universal pharmaceutical patenting'.

The most important supplier country for the sake of this analysis is India. With the most technologically sophisticated pharmaceutical sector in the developing world, India delayed the availability of product patents on pharmaceuticals until 2005, taking full advantage of the transition period allowed under TRIPs. Indeed, prior to 2005 India was the last country with significant production capabilities not to offer drug patents. The high level of scientific and technological capabilities combined with the absence of pharmaceutical patents allowed India's pharmaceutical sector to emerge as the principal supplier of generic drugs to the developing world: it is estimated that more than half of those receiving AIDS treatment in the developing world are treated with generic ARVs produced in India.[14] The active presence of Indian pharmaceutical firms in the global ARV market greatly increased the feasibility of extending

AIDS treatment in poor countries – directly, through the supply of affordable ARVs and, indirectly, by placing pressure on brand-name firms.

Extending ARV treatment in a world where all new drugs can – and almost certainly will – be patented in all countries with advanced production capabilities is the critical challenge facing the global ARV treatment campaign. That is not the same challenge that the treatment campaign has had to face thus far, as the success to this point (illustrated in Figure 3.1) has occurred in a world where the most important ARVs are not patented in many supplier countries. In fact, all of the drugs on the WHO's list of recommended ARVs for first-line or second-line treatment are available from generic producers in India.[15]

That ARVs have been available from India does not by any stretch of the imagination mean that securing access and expanding ARV treatment has been a simple task. The global treatment campaign has had to confront and overcome an array of significant obstacles. One obstacle regards the ability of importing countries to use compulsory licenses (CLs) and other policy tools in their national patent regimes to facilitate access to medicines. This has been, and remains, a matter of considerable conflict. While countries have ample rights under TRIPs to issue CLs, for example, a degree of uncertainty regarding these measures and considerable external pressures for countries to exceed their TRIPs obligations appear to have inhibited many developing countries from taking the necessary steps to improve access. In this regard the Doha Declaration on the TRIPS Agreement and Public Health of November 2001 (Doha Declaration), the outcome of a protracted campaign by developing countries and treatment activists, stands out as a landmark political event. Although the Doha Declaration does not reform TRIPs, by clarifying and clearly re-affirming countries' rights under TRIPs, it constitutes an important step in providing the political space for more countries to design and use their patent systems to secure stable access to affordable ARVs (Beall and Kuhn, 2012; Shadlen, 2004a). Of course, even when legal and political barriers are relaxed, drugs are still too expensive to make treatment feasible in many countries. Thus, a second obstacle has regarded funding and procurement. To that end, the global treatment campaign has relied on the creation of new mechanisms to increase importing countries' purchasing power through pooling procurement, jointly negotiating prices through bulk purchases, and of course the release of unprecedented amounts of money for AIDS treatment.

But what happens to the global treatment campaign if – and when – the ARVs *are* patented in India (and other export-capable countries)? That is the key question. After all, as explained above, and pending a major (and highly unlikely) revision of TRIPs, the world is moving toward a situation of quasi-universal pharmaceutical patenting, where all new ARVs will be patented in all countries with the ability to produce them. To understand the challenges posed by quasi-universal pharmaceutical patenting, it is essential to keep in mind that importing a good presupposes some other actor exporting that good. But TRIPs requires that goods produced in one country under a CL be 'predominantly' for domestic use (Article 31(f)). To the extent that new ARVs become patented in India and other export-capable countries, this requirement could hamper provision of generic versions of such drugs to developing countries. Most developing countries lack the capacity to produce drugs locally, which makes threats to issue CLs for local production empty threats – and so too are threats to issue CLs for import if potential exporters in more industrialized, production-capable countries are hamstrung by this provision of TRIPs.

The claim is not that patents in importing countries no longer present barriers to access, that the problems on the importing side were resolved by Doha. Patents in importing countries clearly can, have, and do present barriers, and overcoming these barriers continues to be a source of intense political conflict. Yet patents in exporting countries pose even greater and even more significant problems, for if patents in exporting countries curtail the supply of drugs then whatever steps are taken to overcome the obstacles posed by patents in the importing countries are inconsequential. Again, importation requires and presupposes exportation.

Addressing the issue of how the supply of generic ARVs may be affected by the restrictions that TRIPs places on producers in exporting countries has proved to be extremely difficult. In October 2001, on the eve of the Doha Ministerial Meeting, developing countries proposed a reading of TRIPs that would have simplified the export of generic drugs to poor countries.[16] The proposal was based on an interpretation of Article 30 of the TRIPs Agreement, which addresses the conditions under which actors can use patented knowledge without obtaining permission from the patent-granting state or the owner of the exclusive rights (i.e., automatic exceptions to patent-holders' rights). The developing countries sought to make a foreign public health emergency (such as an HIV/AIDS epidemic) one such condition. According to their proposal, firms in countries where a given drug is patented would be able to produce generic versions of the drug to supply countries that are experiencing public health crises but unable to produce the drug locally. For example, pharmaceutical firms in Canada or India (post-2005) would be allowed to produce generic versions of patented drugs to export to Malawi or

Zambia, even if these firms were not the patent holders in Canada or India – and they would be able to do so without requesting permission from the patent-holder or needing any steps to be taken by the Canadian or Indian governments. Under strong pressure from the transnational pharmaceutical industry, developed country governments, led by the United States, the European Union, and Switzerland, rejected this proposal (Abbott, 2005; Matthews, 2004).

The issue was unresolved at the WTO's 2001 Ministerial meeting. Paragraph 6 of the Doha Declaration simply recognized the special problems that TRIPs poses for developing countries that lack sufficient local manufacturing capabilities and called on the TRIPs Council to address the problem. In August 2003, after nearly two years of debate and on the eve of the WTO's Fifth Ministerial Meeting in Cancún, Mexico, a temporary resolution was finally agreed. The settlement, which constitutes a partial waiver to Article 31(f), includes increased regulations for issuing CLs for export to poor countries (and extensive safeguards against generic drugs being redirected back into wealthier markets). The August 2003 agreement, along with a supplementary statement from the Chair of the WTO's General Council (WTO, 2003a, 2003b), also included a list of developing and developed countries that pledged not to use the system as importers.[17]

Since 2003, a number of export-capable countries have revised their patent laws to incorporate the waiver of Article 31(f) (Matthews, 2006). Canada was the first to do so, and numerous other countries with advanced pharmaceutical sectors have followed. In India, the final version of the amended Patent Act, passed in March 2005, also permits CLs for export in conformity with the TRIPs waiver.

Are these changes (international and national) sufficient? It is too early to tell, for most countries have been able to continue importing the ARVs they need without recourse to these rules. After all, the ARVs in demand continue to be those that are not patented in India and thus available from Indian suppliers.[18] Yet while the world of quasi-universal pharmaceutical patenting is not here yet, the fact that it lies just over the horizon means that the adequacy of the existing arrangements for CL-for-export is of paramount importance for the sustainability of AIDS treatment.

To summarize, the global treatment campaign has depended, and continues to depend, on the supply of generic ARVs. When the ARVs in demand are unpatented in key supplier countries, such as India, improving access is a matter of addressing two sets of challenges: (1) assuring that patents do not create obstacles to importation in the country where the drugs will be used; and (2) negotiating prices with the generic suppliers and obtaining the resources to purchase the drugs at affordable prices. The international community has directed most of its efforts toward addressing these two challenges since the early 2000s, and tremendous advances have been made on account of the Doha Declaration and actors such as the WHO, UNAIDS, UNITAID, the Global Fund against Aids, Tuberculosis, and Malaria, the World Bank, the Clinton Foundation, the Gates Foundation, and the United States' Presidents' Emergency Plan for AIDS Relief (PEPFAR). However, when the ARVs *are* patented in supplier countries, e.g., India (as they will be, now that India grants pharmaceutical patents), expanding treatment in developing countries (low-income and middle-income)[19] requires addressing an additional – and arguably more difficult – set of challenges presented by such patents in *exporting* countries. The following section examines these challenges in more detail, focusing not just on the law but also the politics of supply.

4. INCENTIVES, INTERESTS AND CAPACITIES IN THE GENERIC PHARMACEUTICAL SECTOR

To understand the challenges to extending ARV treatment in a world of quasi-universal pharmaceutical patenting, it is essential to shift our analytic attention from law to politics. After all, the new international regulations and the subsequent changes to national IP laws create new *political* challenges. In Canada, for example, the requirement that drugs eligible for export under CLs be included on an official list of authorized drugs means that some actor – in industry or civil society – must petition relevant public officials for inclusion on this list. Similarly, under the Indian regulations, firms must request approval from the Controller General of Patents to export drugs produced under CL. Do the actors that might seek to elicit necessary measures by public officials have the interests and capacities to do so?

The central contention advanced here is that the global treatment campaign is threatened by a mismatch between interests and capacities. On the one hand, firms capable of taking advantage of legal opportunities to produce and export generic ARVs may lose interest in doing so, and if they are less vested in such operations they may also be less prepared to devote resources to get public officials to invoke the legal provisions that permit generic production for export. On the other hand, firms interested in taking advantage of legal opportunities to produce and export generic ARVs may lack capacity to do so, and the coalition of actors seeking to expand generic ARV supply may lack the resources to secure necessary public action.

To make sense of these mismatches and to understand the implications for ARV supply, it is useful to consider generic pharmaceutical exports according to three segments: commodity generics (CGs), specialty generics (SGs), and hybrid generics (HGs).[20] CGs are drugs whose patents have expired (or perhaps never existed) in both exporting and importing countries. Ibuprofen is a version of a CG: the molecule is in the public domain, and any pharmaceutical firm in any country can produce ibuprofen (marketing and sales, however, depend on approval from national health authorities). Hundreds of pharmaceutical firms in the world produce CGs, and low barriers to entry make this an intensely competitive segment of the market. SGs refer to new drug delivery systems, novel combinations of existing drugs, and non-infringing forms of patented drugs. Included as SGs are drugs whose patents in the United States and the European Union have recently expired or are about to expire, the most lucrative end of the generic market. In the United States, for example, the first generic producer to obtain authorization from the Food and Drug Administration (FDA) can receive six months of market exclusivity, in which its product competes only against the brand-name product.[21] HGs refer to drugs that are under patent in at least one country involved in trade (either importer or exporter), and thus made available through use of legally-derived limits or exceptions to patent rights. Drugs that are under patent in countries with greater manufacturing capacities, but produced under CL-for-export, fit this HG description.

Table 3.1 presents a simple overview of the variable price:cost ratios facing producers in the three segments of the industry. CGs have low prices (because minimal barriers to entry and intense competition drive prices down) and low costs (for production processes are well-known and there are few legal obstacles). Firms that specialize in CGs require high volumes to compensate for tight margins. SGs have relatively high prices (as the drugs are sold in wealthier and more regulated markets) and high costs (for more research and investment are required, and obtaining regulatory approval is more demanding). When a drug is no longer patented – i.e., when the knowledge is in the public domain – everyone with sufficient scientific and technical capacity can engage in production and sales, but for SGs considerable resources must be spent to become the first to reverse engineer the drug. Indeed, in the case of firms seeking to exploit the opportunities presented by US legislation, if the firm is not the first to receive FDA authorization the most significant advantages of entering the market dissipate. Moreover, administrative and legal factors create fairly high barriers to entry, as considerable resources must be dedicated to obtaining the approval of health authorities in more regulated markets, and becoming 'first to file' also exposes the firm to being sued for patent infringement. Thus, while only an option for those firms with sufficient technical capacity and financial and legal resources, the SG segment is the most profitable segment of the generics industry.

As regards HGs, and with specific reference to ARVs produced under CL-for-export mechanisms, these are likely to have the least favourable price:cost ratios. Prices will be low, for they will be sold for the most part in poorer countries with minimal purchasing power. Theoretically this need not be the case, but the fact that a number of middle-income developing and transition economies that do have greater purchasing power pledged *not* to import generic drugs under the TRIPS waiver to Article 31(f) greatly increases the probability that HGs of this sort will go exclusively to poor countries at exceptionally low prices. The costs of HGs can vary, depending on the age and complexity of the drug in question, but generally the costs of learning to produce and market generic versions of new, still-patented drugs are relatively high. Obviously, the costs involved in the production of HGs (and also SGs) are less than the costs of developing new patentable products, but they are significantly more than those presented by commodities. The reason for this is that learning how to replicate newer drugs is more difficult and expensive than replicating older drugs. Firms need to dedicate resources toward researching the compound and learning how to produce particular pharmaceutical formulations that are useful and satisfy demand. Furthermore, firms engaging in the production of HGs face transaction costs that derive from the political and legal environment, such as the necessity of making sure the drugs they seek to produce conform to national legislation on CL-for-export, requesting CLs from the government, and, potentially, defending themselves against complaints of patent infringement.

Table 3.1 Disaggregating the generic drug sector

Market segment	**Prices**	**Costs**	**Principal export markets**
Commodity Generics (CGs)	Low	Low	Developing and Least Developed ('less regulated')
Specialty Generics (SGs)	High	High	Developed ('regulated')
Hybrid Generics (HGs)	Low	High	Developing and Least Developed ('less regulated')

Source: Author's elaboration.

The generic ARVs currently used in HIV/AIDS treatment throughout the developing world can be regarded as CGs, as they are not protected by patents in India, the most important producer-exporting country. Indian firms, thus, face no legal, patent-related barriers to supplying these drugs to countries where they are not patented.[22] As discussed, mobilizing this source of supply has been a key to expanding treatment. Because of the tight margins involved, a crucial instrument for mobilizing supply has been the aggregation of demand through coordinated, bulk purchasing processes, largely facilitated by the Clinton Foundation and UNITAID (Waning, Kyle, Diedrichsen, Soucy, Hochstadt, Barnighausen and Moon, 2010). Yet the onset of quasi-universal pharmaceutical patenting changes this: newer ARVs are not CGs but rather HGs, as they are patentable – and will be patented – in India. The takeaway from this simple analysis, then, is that the future expansion and maintenance of the treatment campaign becomes increasingly dependent on HGs.

The higher costs of HGs of this sort is worth underscoring: the costs of learning how to reverse-engineer and replicate new molecules and drugs that are not yet in the public domain have not yet been borne, and ARVs for export often must meet the higher standards of good manufacturing practices that are conditions for participating in most international donor-funded access programs. What this means for production and supply is worrying, for the actors that are being counted on to supply these essential drugs that have low prices but high costs are for-profit enterprises operating under increasingly competitive conditions. But because firms that are capable of bearing the scientific, administrative and legal costs of HGs are also capable of bearing the costs of SGs, they are less likely to be attracted to the low-price, high-cost HG segment of the market. At the same time, smaller firms that seek to fill the niche may not be repelled by the low prices, but they are unlikely to be able to bear the costs of the HG segment.

A cursory examination of the case of India appears to bear out these concerns. The leading suppliers of ARVs are the more sophisticated and capable firms (Gehl Sampath, 2005; Grace, 2005). In fact, the bulk purchasing that contributed so critically to the initial expansion of treatment also had the effect of greatly concentrating supply among a consolidated set of firms (Waning, Kyle, Diedrichsen, Soucy, Hochstadt, Barnighausen and Moon, 2010). Yet in the context of TRIPs the prevailing strategy among India's leading firms has been to upgrade into SGs: they are developing new drug delivery systems and non-infringing processes for export to regulated markets (Chaudhuri, 2005; Gehl Sampath, 2005). Much of these firms' research and development effort is directed toward reverse engineering drugs nearing the end of their patent terms, with an eye toward receiving market exclusivity as 'first to file' in the United States (Bhandari, 2005).[23] Not only have exports to regulated markets been the fastest-growing component of Indian firms' portfolios (Chaudhuri, 2005),[24] but the government's Pharmaceutical Export Promotion Council reports that since 1998 Indian firms have filed more applications with the FDA than firms from any other country.[25] A detailed survey of emerging business strategies in the Indian pharmaceutical sector (Gehl Sampath, 2005) shows unambiguously that the highest priority for India's largest firms is to increase their share of generic exports to regulated markets. More than three-quarters of the firms indicated that they did not regard India's CL-for-export provisions (Article 92A) as a useful option.[26] And of the minority that regard Article 92A more positively, 60 per cent were small firms that lack the technical capacity and political resources necessary to take advantage of the legal opportunities in any case.

These firm-level observations are not surprising. After all, India's generic exports mean much more to the world than they do to Indian pharmaceutical firms. As reported, a conservative estimate is that Indian generics account for roughly 50 per cent of ARVs used in developing countries, but that figure is roughly four to 10 times the importance of these exports to the firms themselves, in terms of their total sales.[27] A recent study of the Indian pharmaceutical sector's exports to Africa (Chaudhuri, Mackintosh and Mujinja, 2010) reports similar figures: 'Among the major Indian companies which dominate both the domestic and the export market, Africa is a substantial foreign market only for Cipla'. The article then goes on to note that in 2006, 58 per cent of Ranbaxy's sales went to the United States and Europe with only 6.9 per cent to Africa, and that 'for other major Indian companies such as Dr Reddy's, Wockhardt, Kupin, Glenmark, and Torrent, Africa is in the residual category'.

To put it simply, Indian firms do lots of things besides producing generic ARVs for the developing world, and the asymmetry in this relationship is bound to intensify over time as the firms diversify in response to the new IP environment. ARVs already constitute a small part of the portfolio for the firms engaged in this activity, and these are the ones that are most integrated internationally and best prepared to take advantage of new opportunities in more-regulated SG markets. Moreover, they are now competing for market shares in an intensely competitive global environment, against some of the largest and best-resourced firms in the world (many of which are also focusing more on higher-end speciality generics). In such an environment, the strategies of the very same firms the world is counting on to export ARVs (the firms that MSF famously refers to as the 'Pharmacy of the Developing World') are likely to 'be dictated by survival needs and not by issues related to access to medicines of the general public, whether in India *or other least developed countries*' (Gehl Sampath, 2005, p. 67, emphasis added). Translated, to have a strategy 'dictated by survival needs' means they will have acute concern with price:cost ratios – they are likely to avoid sectors where prices are decreasing and costs increasing. Again, the fact that aggregating demand, which was critical to lowering prices, has also consolidated supply makes the situation that much more alarming since the set of firms on which the world is depending is quite small.[28]

The analysis becomes yet more worrying when we move from market structure to politics. The emerging industrial structure poses critical challenges for the global campaign to increase ARV treatment, because it means that the movement to secure public action for scaling up global treatment may not be able to count on an important and potentially powerful actor: to the extent that larger firms lose interest in producing and exporting generic ARVs, they are also likely to lose interest in lobbying to secure necessary actions on the part of public officials. But at the same time, those firms with an interest in doing so, in addition to lacking scientific and legal capacity, are also likely to lack the political resources to secure public action. As a result, the principal advocates of such government action in export-capable countries are poor people in need of treatment in faraway lands, and more generally the transnational network of treatment access activists. Hence the mismatch: actors capable of securing public action for scaling up global treatment (i.e., the ability to demand CLs for export to poor people in poor countries) may have few incentives to act, while actors needing action (i.e., people with HIV/AIDS in developing countries) may lack the necessary political resources.

This is not to suggest that poor people with HIV/AIDS who depend on the existence of high-quality, generic ARVs lack representation altogether, but they face significant hurdles in securing necessary public action. Quite simply, poor people with HIV/AIDS in sub-Saharan Africa are not powerful or important constituents in India. Instead, they are represented indirectly, through the transnational network of treatment activists. And while this activist network has been enormously successful in expanding access to generic ARVs by pressing for the relaxation of legal impediments and for increases in global funding ('t Hoen, 2002; d'Adesky, 2004; Friedman and Mottiar, 2005; Kapstein and Busby, 2009; Sell, 2002; Smith and Siplon, 2006), the new challenges in the realm of production and supply may stretch the capacities of the global treatment movement.

Indeed, it is important to emphasize how the emerging global political economy of ARV supply presents the transnational treatment activist network with new, formidable challenges. In addition to working to relax legal barriers and increase funding, treatment activists will now also need to get foreign governments – and, importantly, private firms in export-capable countries that already participate in intensely competitive market segments – to take politically risky and economically costly measures for poor people in other countries. Yet the capacity of activist movements to affect outcomes when private investors are involved depends on the structure of the relevant industries (Schurman, 2004). Producing generic versions of new ARVs for export to poor countries is an activity with exceptionally thin margins, a characteristic that becomes exacerbated as the costs – not just legal, but economic and political – of reverse engineering, producing, and exporting generic drugs increase. But at the same time that the new IP rules make this segment less attractive to larger, capable firms, the treatment activists need to get *more* firms involved and politically vested in this activity.

5. CONCLUSION

A key factor facilitating the expansion of treatment in the developing world has been that the main drugs in the WHO-recommended formulary are CGs that are easily provided by a number of large pharmaceutical firms in India. As the WHO's recommended protocol becomes updated and as patients move from first line to second (and third, and nth) line treatments, however, the drugs that will be demanded will increasingly be HGs – patented in India and available only through rather complex CL-for-export schemes. Not only do HGs present producers with less favourable incentives in terms of price:cost ratios, but this change in demand is occurring at the same time as the principal suppliers who have fuelled the global treatment campaign are directing their production and export strategies toward SGs.

Unless this mismatch is addressed, it is difficult to see how the current measures for increasing and extending treatment – measures which have focused on increasing importing countries' abilities to procure drugs by relaxing patent-derived barriers in importing countries, by aggregating demand to reduce prices and by providing resources to finance the acquisition of ARVs – can continue to achieve the desired results.

Thus, the emerging international regulations on IP engender changes that threaten the supply of high-quality, generic ARVs needed for AIDS treatment. Remember that the ARV treatment campaign depends, in large part, on the decisions made by private firms. We have to ask, then, to what extent we should expect private, for-profit enterprises to find it rational to include ARV provision for poor people in poor countries in their business models. To that end I have examined how IP institutions alter the interests of private firms, and how these transformed interests affect political coalitions needed to facilitate expanded ARV supply. One need not be apocalyptic to appreciate the concern and recognize the danger that looms over the horizon: at a time of projected increase in global demand for generic ARVs, supply may struggle to keep apace. Poorer developing countries, international organizations, and non-governmental healthcare providers may demand these drugs, but the critical sources of supply – upon which the world currently depends – may have been fundamentally transformed.

To fully appreciate the emerging mismatch between demand and supply, it is necessary to return briefly to the WHO's revised treatment guidelines. As indicated, the WHO recommends first-line treatment consisting of two NRTIs (3TC and either AZT or TDF) and one NNRTI (EFZ or NVP). To repeat, the inclusion of TDF came late, as part of the 2009 revisions to the WHO guidelines. Until recently TDF had minimal suppliers other than Gilead, which held patents on a number of polymorph versions of the molecule. While the Indian patent application was being examined, Gilead licensed TDF to a number of local firms under restrictive terms that prohibited firms from selling TDF outside of low-income countries in Gilead's 'global access program'. Only one firm, Cipla, was producing TDF unrestrained by Gilead's license.[29] This arrangement made TDF too expensive to include in the WHO's formulary, despite the drug's therapeutic benefits. In 2008, however, Gilead's patent was overturned in the United States, and the application was later rejected in India (it was also invalidated in Brazil). These events change the status of TDF from a drug controlled by one supplier (plus one renegade, and ultimately vindicated, Indian firm) to a drug that is open to generic competition, which in turn will lower the price of TDF. Thus, the potential crunch created by a new WHO recommendation leading to increased demand for a scarce drug with a single supplier was averted by legal decisions: d4T was replaced by TDF just as legal rulings transformed the latter from an HG (high legal barriers to exporting) to a CG (no CLs needed or other legal barriers to be overcome). But this timing is not a coincidence: the WHO did not recommend TDF previously because of price, and the eventual revisions to include TDF in the recommended first-line formulary *followed* these developments.[30]

Yet legal events (in this case favourable to extending treatment) only push the crunch and mismatch into the future. Just as d4T has been phased out and replaced by TDF, TDF or AZT or 3TC will eventually need to be phased out and replaced by other NRTIs (and EFZ and NVP will be replaced by other NNRTIs). There is no reason to expect the cycle by which the treatment regime is altered to coincide with the cycle by which HGs become CGs. Some drugs needed for treatment will be patented. Will it be worth firms' efforts to expend considerable resources to learn how to reverse engineer them and meet the legal requirements for CL-for-export in order to sell them at low cost?[31]

The bottom line is that first-line regimens for people just beginning treatment need to be continually updated, as resistant strands of the virus emerge. There is no reason to expect the combinations of ARVs that will be used for those starting treatment in 2015 or 2020 to be the same as those that are used for those starting treatment in 2010. This is not simply because there may be better drugs available, but because the drugs that serve as effective first-line treatments now will no longer be effective down the line. Likewise, patients receiving treatment need to move from first-line to second-line and third-line treatments and so on, and these regimens need to be updated too. When these updates are necessary and what drugs should be included in the revised treatment regimens are questions of science. Yet whereas cycles of drug demand are driven by science, cycles of what drugs are patented or not patented in key exporting countries (i.e., what drugs are SGs or CGs) are driven by entirely different factors, including patent filing strategies, opposition strategies, and legal decisions. There is no reason to expect these two types of cycles to match, as they so fortuitously have since the early 2000s.

How might the pending problem of undersupply be overcome? One strategy might be to shift attention away from larger, export-capable countries and focus instead on pharmaceutical manufacturing in poorer countries themselves. That is, since the least developed countries are not obligated to offer pharmaceutical patents until 2016, there should be no legal barriers to local production and export of generic ARVs – the constraints of Article 31(f) and the subsequent waiver do not yet apply.[32] Yet the challenges to creating sufficient generic pharmaceutical production capabilities in such countries are extensive. Putting IP laws in place that are appropriate for such purposes is more difficult than one might imagine. Many of the poorest WTO members have already fully implemented their TRIPs obligations – transition periods notwithstanding – and offer product patents on pharmaceuticals. They are not obliged to have done so, but re-revising their laws to, for example, make pharmaceuticals unpatentable would expose them to intense international pressures. Furthermore, even if such legal changes were made, the technical and economic obstacles to developing pharmaceutical sectors are immense (Chaudhuri, Mackintosh and Mujinja, 2010; Kaplan and Laing, 2005; WHO, 2004). In India, for example, the growth of the pharmaceutical sector was driven not just by the 1970 Patent Act, which made pharmaceutical products unpatentable, but also by an active state role in sponsoring research and transferring technology, knowledge, and skills from government labs to private firms (Chaudhuri, 2005, pp. 30–60; Kumar, 2003). The advanced chemistry skills that proved so effective in the emergence of India's indigenous pharmaceutical sector were developed only with the assistance of concerted government policies – policies that are largely absent in the poor countries that have a window of opportunity until 2016. Indeed, these countries would almost certainly need beyond 2016 to develop indigenous pharmaceutical sectors, but it may be difficult to inspire investment knowing that after a few years the IP regime will change. Or to put it differently, the pre-TRIPs legal environment that spurred high levels of domestic investment in India, for example, cannot be replicated because that legal environment did not have a known terminal point. Any firm responding to the incentives to scale up generic production in a least developed country would do so knowing that the end point of this strategy's feasibility is just around the corner.

A more sensible strategy is to reform global IP rules to facilitate continued supply of generic ARVs. That is essentially what the developing countries' 2001 proposed interpretation of TRIPs Article 30 would have accomplished, by removing the legal and political obstacles that stand in the way of pharmaceutical firms producing and exporting generic ARVs (see discussion above). This would make all ARVs for consumption in the developing world CGs, and it would do so in a way that firms with already-existing capabilities could participate as exporters. Of course, this proposal had little political viability in the past, so it may be logical to expect it to have no traction now either (Matthews, 2004; Shadlen, 2007). Yet this remains sensible from a public health perspective and perhaps it may be more politically feasible now, with TRIPs fully implemented in production-capable countries, than it was when first visited in the context of TRIPs implementation still being ongoing.

An alternative measure, one that does not require anything so magical as rapidly creating pharmaceutical capabilities in poor countries or obtaining agreement on a fundamental revision to TRIPs, is for India to embark on a universal treatment program. Were India to do so, even if new ARVs were patented in India the government could grant CLs to local producers under the term of TRIPs and the Doha Declaration. Local firms would have ample incentives to produce the drugs because of the size of local demand (India has roughly five million people who are HIV positive). And the firms producing the drugs under a CL would be free to export: so long as the drugs produced in India were 'predominantly' for local market, as they would be, then the residual can be exported without any legal obstacles imposed by TRIPs Article 31(f) or any need to invoke CL-for-export mechanisms. The virtues of this scenario are not just that universal treatment in India would make substantial contributions to WHO treatment targets, but that it would mobilize generic ARV production in the most important ARV provider and thus allow the supply of ARVs to respond flexibly to changing demand.

NOTES

1. In fact, "more of the same" may not be forthcoming either, as enthusiasm for increased funding appears to be waning in many donor countries, leading some to suggest that the "golden window" for treatment may be closing (McNeil, 2010).
2. In this chapter I focus explicitly on the relationship between changing patterns of demand for and supply of generic ARVs necessary to sustain AIDS treatment. In doing so I build on the analysis in Shadlen (2007).
3. Indeed, the denominator in the coverage ratio is an estimate made on the basis of a prior estimate.
4. The two NRTIs perform different functions, as they are different types of analogues. The WHO's recommendations were to combine 3TC (the 'pivotal' thiacytadine analogue) with either AZT or d4T, plus either EFZ or NVP. This yields the following four combinations: d4T/3TC/NVP, ZDV/3TC/NVP, d4T/3TC/EFV, ZDV/3TC/EFV. Other advanced NRTIs and NNRTIs along with later generation ARVs such as protease inhibitors, entry inhibitors, and integrase inhibitors are either reserved for second-line treatment or, in the most part, omitted from the WHO's recommendations.
5. These were not the first changes; a set of revisions were published in 2006 as well.
6. By way of comparison, note that the US and EU guidelines recommend treatment to begin at CD4 counts of 500. At the risk of stating the obvious, it is worth emphasizing that in developing countries, the point at which ARV treatment begins and the array and combination of drugs used in treatment (not to mention the availability of drugs for treating opportunistic infections) are substantially different from in wealthy countries.
7. According to the WHO (2009, p. 2), this change was made on account of d4T's 'long term, cumulative, and non-reversible toxicities'.
8. According to WHO (2007), as of 2006 roughly 98 per cent of the adults receiving ARV treatment were on first-line regimens, with the tiny fraction receiving second-line therapy concentrated in Brazil. An increasing number of people in Thailand must be receiving second-line treatment as well, given that Thailand is importing the key boosted PI (lop/r).

9. The WHO estimates that the new treatment guidelines increase the number of people classified as 'in need of treatment' by 3 to 5 million (Jack, 2009).
10. The existence of such an interactive effect rests on the fact that many expenditures for ARV treatment are HIV/AIDS-specific. After all, if the investments are for healthcare provision more generally, then governments might find these worth making regardless of the availability of ARVs per se. But many of the investments are ARV-treatment-specific, i.e., the creation of separate and parallel supply chains, storage facilities, and delivery systems.
11. Note that many developing countries with large and potentially important generic pharmaceutical sectors (e.g., Argentina, Brazil, Mexico, and Thailand) did not take full advantage of this transition period and began offering pharmaceutical patents prior to 2005.
12. Because patents are national, firms obtain and defend their patents in each country. Where markets are small, firms may decide that the costs of obtaining and maintaining a patent outweigh the benefits.
13. This point was made by a letter to the editor of the *Journal of American Medical Association* in response to Attaran and Gillespie-White (2001). See Boelaert, Lynen, Van Damme, Colebunders, Goemaere, Kaninda, Ciaffi, Mulemba, 't Hoen, Pécoul, Médecins Sans Frontières, Selgelid, Schuklenk, Attaran and Gillespie-White (2002) and also Grace (2005, pp. 18–9).
14. The estimate in the text was provided to me by a WHO official. Médecins Sans Frontières, which refers to India as the 'Pharmacy for the Developing World', provides even higher figures, reporting that roughly 80 per cent of the ARVs it uses in treatment locations are from India (MSF, 2007). Recent analysis of nearly 13,000 donor-funded, adult first-line ARV purchases also confirms the major role of Indian suppliers (Waning, Kyle, Diedrichsen, Soucy, Hochstadt, Barnighausen and Moon, 2010).
15. I discuss Tenofovir (TDF) below, in the conclusion.
16. See paragraph 9 of the developing country proposal to the TRIPs Council, IP/C/W/312, WT/GC/W/450, 4 October 2001.
17. Both the agreement and the supplementary statement were proposed as a permanent amendment to TRIPs in December 2005.
18. In 2008 a Canadian firm (Apotex) exported a standard first-line combination based on ARVs that are patented in Canada to Rwanda (Elliott, 2008). To date, this is the only instance of the CL-for-export rule being used. The fact that the 2003/2005 waiver to Article 31(f) has only been invoked once does not mean much in and of itself. After all, as noted, most ARVs in demand in developing countries are still unpatented in India, so there is little need to use the waiver. In fact, why it was invoked even this one time is not entirely clear. Multiple Indian firms produce the drugs that Apotex exported to Rwanda, so why Rwanda turned to a Canadian firm that had to jump through extensive hoops imposed by TRIPs and the Canadian legislation rather than simply import from India is an unanswered question that has produced a great deal of global head-scratching. I suspect that this was motivated in part by an effort to demonstrate the complexity (and thus user-unfriendliness) of the Canadian legislation.

19. The Doha Declaration (and much of the writing on this topic) makes a distinction between the challenges facing developing countries with sufficient local manufacturing capabilities and those without. Yet as significant as some developing countries' manufacturing capacity may appear to be, even the largest developing countries (e.g., Brazil) are heavily dependent on ARVs produced in India. Thus the more appropriate distinction is between ARV-exporters and ARV-importers (or to be blunt, India and not India).
20. This typology is drawn from Shadlen (2007), but the reader will notice that my definition of the categories and the application of these categories to ARV markets are different in the present text.
21. Specialty generics are also referred to as 'value-added generics'. Many analysts use the SG label to refer exclusively to new delivery systems (e.g., developing versions of drugs that can be injected directly into the blood). My usage is broader, including all generics that are technologically, legally, and administratively more complex, for these are the entry barriers that make SG more upmarket.
22. That is, provided they do not face difficulties in transhipment in European ports.
23. See also the comments of India's Minister of Commerce and Industry (Express Pharma Pulse, 2005) and Singh and Chatterjee (2004).
24. Indeed, the competitive pressures that Indian firms now face and the subsequent concern with upgrading export markets coincides with immense pressures in the OECD to reduce the costs of medicines, thus making India's high-quality yet inexpensive generic drug exports more welcome.
25. The data refer to drug master files (DMFs), the documents that producers must submit to register APIs and bulk drugs with US regulators. With 29.25 per cent of the DMFs from 1998 through September 2009, Indian firms accounted for nearly twice as many as US firms, which submitted 15.6 per cent of the total DMFs (Unnikrishnan, 2010).
26. 'The common reason was that it increased the procedural hassles associated with such exports enormously, and this was not considered worthwhile, especially since the economic returns from such exports were very low' (Gehl Sampath, 2005, p. 65).
27. These data were provided by a market analyst researching the Indian pharmaceutical sector.
28. This point, that an international public policy measure to achieve one goal can affect market structure in such a way as to make subsequent policy measures to achieve other goals more difficult is a valuable point made by Waning, Kyle, Diedrichsen, Soucy, Hochstadt, Barnighausen and Moon, 2010).
29. At the same time Cipla was collaborating with Indian NGOs to oppose Gilead's patent application. See Amin, Rajkumar, Radhakrishnan, and Kesselheim (2009).
30. Nevertheless, the WHO's revision was reported as a windfall for Gilead (Jack, 2009). For more discussion of TDF, including both conflicts over the patent and the relationship with the WHO recommendations, see Amin, Rajkumar, Radhakrishnan, and Kesselheim (2009).

31. According to the *Financial Times* (Jack, 2009), Cipla's CEO Yusuf Hamied 'said his concern was still more recent and expensive third- and fourth-generation medicines, which are subject in India to tougher patent restrictions. "Even if I received permission for those today, it would take three to five years to bring them to market," he said'.
32. Bangladesh, Kenya, and Tanzania are frequently cited as potential production sites.

BIBLIOGRAPHY

Abbott, Frederick M. (2005), 'The WTO medicines decision: World pharmaceutical trade and the protection of public health', *The American Journal of International Law*, **99**(2), 317–58.

Amin, Tahir, Rahul Rajkumar, Priti Radhakrishnan and Aaron S. Kesselheim (2009), 'Expert review of drug patent applications: Improving health in the developing world', *Health Affairs* **28**(5), 948–56.

Attaran, Amir (2004), 'How do patents and economic policies affect access to essential medicines in developing countries?', *Health Affairs*, **23**(3), 155–66.

Attaran, Amir and Lee Gillespie-White (2001), 'Do patents for antiretroviral drugs constrain access to AIDS treatment in Africa?', *Journal of the American Medical Association*, **286**(15), 1886–92.

Beall, Reed and Randall Kuhn (2012), 'Trends in compulsory licensing of pharmaceuticals since the Doha Declaration: A database analysis', *PLoS Med*, **9**(1), e1001154, available at http://www.plosmedicine.org/article/info%3Adoi%2F10.1371%2Fjournal.pmed.1001154 (accessed 22 February 2012).

Berwick, Donald (2002), 'We all have AIDS': Case for reducing the cost of HIV drugs to zero', *British Medical Journal*, **324**(7331), 214–6.

Bhandari, Bhupesh (2005), 'Patent regime? Not the end of the road', *Business Standard*, 2 February, available at http://www.rediff.com/money/2005/feb/02guest1.htm (accessed 8 September 2010).

Boelaert, Marleen, Lut Lynen, Wim Van Damme, Robert Colebunders, Eric Goemaere, Anne-Valerie Kaninda, Laura Ciaffi, Maryline Mulemba, Ellen 't Hoen, Bernard Pécoul, Médecins Sans Frontières, Michael J. Selgelid, Udo Schuklenk, Amir Attaran and Lee Gillespie-White (2002), 'Do patents prevent access to drugs for HIV in developing countries?', *Journal of American Medical Association*, **287**(7), 840–3.

Chaudhuri, Sudip (2005), *The WTO and India's Pharmaceuticals Industry: Patent Protection, TRIPs, and Developing Countries*. New Delhi: Oxford University Press (India).

Chaudhuri, Sudip, Maureen Mackintosh and Phares G. M. Mujinja (2010), 'Indian generics producers, access to essential medicines and local production in Africa: An argument with reference to Tanzania', *European Journal of Development Research*, **22**(4): 451–68.

d'Adesky, Anne-Christine (2004), *Moving Mountains: The Race to Treat Global AIDS*, New York: Verso.

Elliott, Richard (2008), 'Delivery past due: Global precedent set under Canada's access to medicines regime', *HIV/AIDS Policy & Law Review* **13**(1), available at http://www.aidslaw.ca/publications/interfaces/downloadFile.php?ref=1345 (accessed 8 September 2010).

Express Pharma Pulse (2005), 'Patent Act will not affect drugs export: Kamal Nath', 31 January, available at http://www.expresspharmaonline.com/20050210/happenings05.shtml (accessed 8 September 2010).

Friedman, Steven and Shauna Mottiar (2005), 'A rewarding engagement? The Treatment Action Campaign and the politics of HIV/AIDS', *Politics & Society*, **33**(4), 511–65.

Gehl Sampath, Padmashree (2005), 'Economic aspects of access to medicines after 2005: Product patent protection and emerging firm strategies in the Indian pharmaceutical industry', United Nations University-INTECH, available at http://www.who.int/intellectualproperty/studies/PadmashreeGehlSampathFinal.pdf (accessed 8 September 2010).

Grace, Cheri (2004), *The Effect of Changing Intellectual Property on Pharmaceutical Industry Prospects in India and China: Considerations for Access to Medicines*, London: DFID Health Systems Resource Centre.

Grace, Cheri (2005), *A Briefing Paper for DFID: Update on China and India and Access to Medicines*, London: DFID Health Systems Resource Centre.

Jack, Andrew (2009), 'Gilead set to benefit from HIV guidelines', *FT.Com*, 9 December, available at http://www.ft.com/cms/s/0/f8be7820-dea0-11de-adff-00144feab49a.html (accessed 8 September 2010).

Kaplan, Warren and Richard Laing (2005), *Local Production of Pharmaceuticals: Industrial Policy and Access to Medicines*, Washington DC: The World Bank.

Kapstein, Ethan B. and Joshua W. Busby (2009), 'Making markets for merit goods: The political economy of antiretrovirals', *Global Policy* **1**(1), 75–90.

Kovsted, Jens (2005), 'Scaling up AIDS treatment in developing countries: A review of current and future arguments', *Development Policy Review*, **23**(4), 465–82.

Kumar, Nagesh (2003), 'Intellectual property rights, technology and economic development: Experiences of Asian countries', *Economic and Political Weekly*, **38**(3), 209–25.

Lucchini, Stéphane, Boubou Cisse, Ségolène Duran, Marie de Cenival, Caroline Comiti, Marion Gaudry and Jean-Paul Moatti (2003), 'Decrease in prices of antiretroviral drugs for developing countries: From political 'philanthropy' to regulated markets', in Jean-Paul Moatti, Tony Barnett, Benjamin Coriat, Yves Souteyrand, Jérome Dumoulin and Yves-Antoine Flori (eds) (2003), *Economics of AIDS and Access to HIV/AIDS Care in Developing Countries: Issues and Challenges*, Paris: ANRS, pp. 169–211.

Matthews, Duncan (2004), 'WTO decision on implementation of Paragraph 6 of the Doha Declaration on the TRIPs Agreement and public health: A solution to the access to essential medicines problem?', *Journal of International Economic Law*, **7**(1), 73–107.

Matthews, Duncan (2006), 'From the August 30, 2003 WTO decision to the December 6, 2005 agreement on an amendment to TRIPs: Improving access to medicines in developing countries?', *Intellectual Property Quarterly* **10**(1), 91–130.

MSF (2007), 'Examples of the importance of India as the "pharmacy of the developing world"', available at http://www.msfaccess.org/fileadmin/user_upload/medinnov_accesspatents/Overview%20Jan%202007%20FINAL.pdf (accessed 8 September 2010).

MSF (various years), 'Untangling the web of price reductions: A pricing guide for the purchase of ARVs for developing countries', available at http://utw.msfaccess.org (accessed 8 September 2010).

Nattrass, Nicoli and Nathan Geffen (2005), 'The impact of reduced drug prices on the cost-effectiveness of HAART in South Africa', *African Journal of AIDS Research*, **4**(1), 65–7.

Peiffer, Caryn Anne and Constantine Boussalis (2010), 'Foreign assistance and the struggle against HIV/AIDS in the developing world', *Journal of Development Studies*, **46**(3), 556–73.

Schurman, Rachel (2004), 'Fighting "Frankenfoods": Industry opportunity structures and the efficacy of the anti-biotech movement in Western Europe', *Social Problems*, **51**(2), 243–68.

Schwartländer, Bernhard, John Stover, Neff Walker, Lori Bollinger, Juan Pablo Gutierrez, William McGreevey, Marjorie Opuni, Steven Forsythe, Lilani Kumaranayake, Charlotte Watts and Steffano Bertozzi (2001), 'Resource needs for HIV/AIDS', *Science*, **292**(5526), 2434–6.

Sell, Susan K. (2002), 'TRIPs and the access to medicines campaign', *Wisconsin International Law Journal*, **20**(3), 481–522.

Shadlen, Kenneth C. (2004a), 'Patents and pills, power and procedure: The North-South politics of public health in the WTO', *Studies in Comparative International Development*, **39**(3), 76–108.

Shadlen, Kenneth C. (2004b), 'Challenges to treatment: The price-infrastructure trap and access to medicines', *Journal of International Development*, **16**(8), 1169–80.

Shadlen, Kenneth C. (2007), 'The political economy of AIDS treatment: Intellectual property and the transformation of generic supply', *International Studies Quarterly*, **51**(3), 559–81.

Singh, Pragya and Dev Chatterjee (2004), 'Pharma's in the Den', *The Sunday Express*, 19 December, available at http://www.indianexpress.com/oldStory/61096/ (accessed 8 September 2010).

Siplon, Patricia and Raymond Smith (2006), *Drugs into Bodies: Global AIDS Treatment Activism*, Westport: Praeger.

Tayler, Yolanda (ed) (2004), *Battling HIV/AIDS: A Decision Maker's Guide to the Procurement of Medicines and Related Supplies*, Washington: The World Bank.

't Hoen, Ellen (2002), 'TRIPs, pharmaceutical patents, and access to essential medicines: A long way from Seattle to Doha, *Chicago Journal of International Law*, **3**(1), 27–46.

Unnikrishnan, Chnadrasekaran H. (2010), 'Indian firms overtake US in FDA drug filings', *livemint.com*, 17 March, available at http://www.livemint.com/2010/03/17220209/Indian-firms-overtake-US-in-FD.html (accessed 8 September 2010).

Wainberg, Mark A. (2005), 'Generic HIV drugs: Enlightened policy for global health', *New England Journal of Medicine*, **352**(8), 747–50.

Waning, Brenda, Warren Kaplan, Matthew P. Fox, Mariah Boyd-Boffa, Alexis C. King, Danielle A. Lawrence, Lyne Soucy, Sapna Mahajan, Hubert G. Leufkens and Manjusha Gokhale (2010), 'Temporal trends in generic and brand prices of antiretroviral medicines procured with donor funds in developing countries', *Journal of Generic Medicines* **7**(2), 159–75.

Waning, Brenda, Margaret Kyle, Ellen Diedrichsen, Lyne Soucy, Jenny Hochstadt, Till Barnighausen and Suerie Moon (2010), 'Intervening in global markets to improve access to HIV/AIDS treatment: An analysis of international policies and the dynamics of global antiretroviral medicines markets', *Globalization and Health*, **6**(9), available at http://www.globalizationandhealth.com/content/6/1/9 (accessed 8 September 2010).

World Bank. (2004), *HIV/AIDS Medicines and Related Supplies: Contemporary Context and Procurement*, Washington: The World Bank.

World Health Organization [WHO] (2003), *Scaling up Antiretroviral Therapy in Resource-Limited Settings: Treatment Guidelines for a Public Health Approach*, Geneva: World Health Organization.

WHO (2004), 'Manufacture of antiretrovirals in developing countries and challenges for the future, EB114/15, available at http://www.who.int/gb/ebwha/pdf_files/EB114/B114_15-en.pdf (accessed 8 September 2010).

WHO (2007), *Prioritizing Second-Line Antiretroviral Drugs for Adults and Adolescents: A Public Health Approach*, Geneva: World Health Organization.

WHO (2009), 'Key Messages: New WHO recommendations: Antiretroviral therapy for adults and adolescents', available at http://www.who.int/hiv/pub/arv/art_key_mess.pdf (accessed 8 September 2010).

World Trade Organization [WTO] (2003a), 'Implementation of Paragraph 6 of the Doha Declaration on the TRIPs Agreement and Public Health: Decision of the General Council of 30 August 2003', WT/L/540.

WTO (2003b), 'The general council chairperson's statement', 30 August, WT/GC/M/82, 13 November, para. 29.

4. Access to paediatric medicines: The global political economy of drug production and supply for children in the developing world

Avram Denburg and Kelley Lee

1. INTRODUCTION

Amid ongoing tensions between economic globalization and access to medicines, centred on the World Trade Organization (WTO) and its Agreement on Trade-Related Aspects of Intellectual Property Rights (TRIPs) ('t Hoen, 2003; CIPIH, 2006; Correa, 2002; Matthews, 2006; Westerhaus and Castro, 2006; WHO, 2002), limited attention to date has been given to access to medicines for children. Pharmaceutical research into, and development of, drugs for children lags markedly behind drugs for adults. Drug disposition and dynamics change as children grow, necessitating evidence and treatment tailored to age and developmental stage (Hoppu, 2008). Yet there is a relative paucity of pharmacokinetic studies, safety and efficacy data, and drug indications, dosages and formulations for paediatric medicines (Schaller, Lie and Hoppu, 2007). Most often, drugs licensed for use by children were developed for, and evaluated, in adults, with evidence of their clinical utility in children derived largely from data generated ex post (AAP, 1995). The implications of this inattention are significant. First, an inherent lag time exists in bringing paediatric drugs to market, as child indications necessarily follow adult ones. Second, fewer drugs are developed with paediatric physiology and pathology specifically in mind (IFPMA, 2008). As a corollary, many drugs prescribed to children are unlicensed for paediatric use: in Europe this figure approximates 50 per cent (Conroy, Choonara, Impicciatore, Mohn, Arnell, Rane, Knoeppel, Seyberth, Pandolfini, Raffaeli, Rocchi, Bonati, Jong, de Hoog and Anker, 2000).

While the challenges facing paediatric medicines are global, this neglect is felt most acutely in developing countries. Conceptual and practical similarities exist between paediatric medicines and the issue of drugs for neglected diseases. Neglected diseases are those that predominantly affect the developing world, where purchasing power is weak. There are thus inadequate market incentives for research and development (R&D) investment by the pharmaceutical industry. Classic examples of neglected diseases include: African sleeping sickness (trypanosomiasis), Chagas disease (American trypanosomiasis), leishmaniasis and schistosomiasis. Efforts to develop and license drugs to treat these diseases are either nonexistent or grossly inadequate. Notwithstanding recent swells in international attention, tuberculosis (TB), malaria and HIV/AIDS arguably remain neglected, by dint of their disproportionate burden in the developing world and the incommensurate political and fiscal responses to date. Certainly, they remain so in respect of health outcomes, which remain vastly discrepant between populations in the developed and developing worlds.

This chapter analyses access to paediatric medicines in the developing world, focusing on paediatric HIV/AIDS and antiretrovirals (ARVs). It begins by laying the theoretical and empirical foundations for a global political economy (GPE) analysis of drug production and supply for children in the developing world. It then examines the entwined economic and regulatory dimensions of paediatric access to medicines, by situating the realities of generic drug production within an existing model of generic market segments. Thirdly, the role of key institutions of global health governance in paediatric drug access is described. The chapter concludes with policy recommendations to improve paediatric drug access.

2. THEORY AND METHODOLOGY

2.1 Methods

This chapter reviews policy debates on access to paediatric medicines in the peer reviewed and grey literature, including government, civil society and industry documents. Electronic searches of major science and social sciences databases (ISI Web of Knowledge, WorldCat, Social Sciences Abstracts, Medline and PubMed) were supplemented by hand searches of relevant journals and ongoing 'snowball' searches from reference lists, as well as by review of technical and policy documents from relevant institutional websites. The search terms used included: 'p*ediatric medicines', 'p*ediatric HIV/AIDS', 'p*ediatric antiretrovirals', 'access to medicines', 'TRIPs Agreement', 'intellectual property rights', 'drug patents', 'political economy', 'pharmaceutical research and development', 'p*ediatric pharmacology', and 'global health governance'. Documentary analysis was informed by scholarship on international political economy and by a theoretical market paradigm for generic pharmaceuticals. With respect to the concept of 'access', this chapter restricts its lens to the development, regulation and purchase of paediatric drugs, in an attempt to sketch the political economy of drug production and supply for children in the developing world.

2.2 Conceptual Framework for Understanding Access to Medicines

Access to medicines subsumes a number of distinct, if interrelated, concepts. The World Health Organization (WHO) divides 'access' into four constituent parts: affordable prices; sustainable finance; rational selection and use; and reliable systems of supply and health care (WHO, 2000). Other paradigms focus principally on availability and accessibility: the former is often gauged in relation to drug research, development and production, the latter judged against a gamut of economic, sociocultural and health-system factors (Widdus, 2001). Most critical is the need to recognize the multifaceted nature of drug access, from 'bench' to 'bedside'. This chapter uses a four-pronged model which relates access to affordability, availability, appropriateness and accessibility. This framework extracts affordability from accessibility, to give it primacy as a structural determinant. It also lends specific weight to the appropriate type and composition of medicines, as a crucial component of access for children. The purpose of this chapter is not to identify and deconstruct all the component parts of access. Instead, it restricts its lens to the development, regulation and purchase of paediatric drugs, in an attempt to sketch the GPE of drug production and supply for children in the developing world.

2.3 Global Access to Paediatric HIV/AIDS Medicines for Children

Despite the availability of an effective treatment, an estimated two million people died from HIV/AIDS in 2007, of which 270,000 were children. Approximately 370,000 children were newly infected with HIV in 2007, primarily via mother-to-child transmission during pregnancy, delivery or breastfeeding. Of the two million children living with HIV infection globally, almost 90 per cent live in sub-Saharan Africa (UNAIDS, 2008). Moreover, the virus disproportionately affects children. While representative of just 6 per cent of those infected, they accounted for almost 15 per cent of AIDS deaths in 2007. At present, there are an estimated 780,000 children in immediate need of ARV treatment (WHO/UNAIDS, 2007).

Access to paediatric HIV/AIDS is indicative of wider drug access problems. As with sleeping sickness, market calculus has denied affordable and appropriate treatment to the majority of those suffering from the disease. In addition to the access barriers faced by adults, unique impediments compromise effective ARV treatment for children in resource poor settings. The issue of cost is paramount: paediatric drugs, including ARVs, are routinely more expensive than their adult equivalents – in some instances up to four times the price (MSF, 2007). The nature of paediatric formulations is as important as their cost. Until recently, few ARVs had been approved for use in children, and even fewer paediatric formulations existed. As of 2005, 13 out of 21 of the ARVs approved by the US Food and Drug Administration (FDA) were licensed for use in children, and only 11 of these had paediatric formulations (AAP, 2007). Increasing recognition of this problem has spurred efforts to expand the existing catalogue of affordable paediatric labelled ARVs. By December 2008, the number of FDA-approved generic ARVs had increased fivefold, from 15 to 78, with 16 constituted primarily for use in children (PEPFAR, 2009).

Among the gaps that persist, the lack of varied and appropriate fixed dose combination (FDC) therapies for children remains an impediment to expanded treatment access. FDCs are widely acknowledged as a key facet of enhanced treatment access for a number of diseases in resource poor settings, due to their simplified dosing and administration, ease of procurement and supply, and amenity to regimen standardization (Dionisio, Gass, McDermott, Racalbuto, Madeo, Braghieri, Crowley, Dos Santos, Graaff, Vasan, Eksaengsri, Moller, Khanna, Kraisintu, Juneja, Nicolaou, Sengupta, Esperti and Messeri, 2007). WHO has identified FDCs for HIV/AIDS, malaria and TB as priority developments in paediatric pharmacotherapy (WHO, 2008a). Generic FDCs, long a staple of adult-treatment regimens, are only a recent addition to the paediatric armamentarium (WHO-PAWG, 2008). In a positive step forward, the US FDA and WHO's prequalification programme granted approval for the use of the Indian generic manufacturer Cipla's Pedimmune Baby/Junior (d4T/3TC/NVP) in August 2007 (FDA, 2007). On the force of mounting attention to this problem, a number of generic paediatric FDC ARVs are now in production, and a first-line dispersible FDC tablet is available in over 30 countries through a partnership between the Clinton HIV/AIDS Initiative (CHAI) and UNITAID[1] (UNITAID, 2008). The bulk of these, however, contain the same active ingredients (d4T/3TC/NVP) in varying ratios.

There are consequent constraints to second-line treatment. Both side-effect profiles and resistance patterns demand effective and appropriate alternatives to first-line FDCs. Reliance on the exclusive use of stavudine (d4T) containing FDCs is particularly problematic, given the drug's significant side-effect profile. WHO has counselled against the use of d4T in first-line treatment where affordable alternatives exist; for low income countries, it has recommended universal dose decreases, based on evidence of high rates peripheral neuropathy, lactic acidosis and lipo-atrophy (WHO, 2008b). Furthermore, the risk of non-nucleoside reverse transcriptase inhibitor (NNRTI) resistance is particularly marked, due to the long half lives (approximately 21 days) of common drugs in this class, such as nevirapine (NVP) and efavirenz (EFV). NVP resistance can therefore occur rapidly with treatment interruption, due to the functional monotreatment at subtherapeutic levels (NIH, 2008). Compounding these problems, only one FDC meets the ideal dosing specifications of the WHO Paediatric Antiretroviral Working Group (WHO-PAWG); the rest contain drug ratios deemed unsuitable for younger, smaller children (WHO-PAWG, 2008).

Existing paediatric formulations, moreover, are often inherently problematic for resource-constrained settings. Liquid forms predominate: these are expensive to transport and store, as they require refrigeration (e.g., stavudine and most second-line agents); difficult to administer, due to both the poor taste and the large volumes required (for example zidovudine (AZT)); and concocted with potentially harmful excipients, such as alcohol and propylene glycol (AAP, 2007; GAA, 2006). Compounding the problem, adult formulations are often poorly adaptable to childhood dosing needs. In the absence of paediatric formulations, providers and caregivers are forced to split pills to approximate childhood doses. However, adult pills are rarely scored to permit accurate division. In addition, the respective distribution of drugs in FDC pills is not well known, resulting in the potential for inconsistent dosing with pill splitting (Dionisio, Gass, McDermott, Racalbuto, Madeo, Braghieri, Crowley, Dos Santos, Graaff, Vasan, Eksaengsri, Moller, Khanna, Kraisintu, Juneja, Nicolaou, Sengupta, Esperti and Messeri, 2007). Moreover, developmental changes in drug metabolism complicate the use of adult FDCs in children: NVP is metabolized differently in neonates than in older children, necessitating a higher dose relative to nucleoside reverse transcriptase inhibitor (NRTI) components than in adult regimens (WHO-PAWG, 2008). Even determining appropriate doses presents problems, due to a dearth of pharmacokinetic studies of ARVs in children, particularly infants. For example, evidentiary issues hamper the use of EFV, a recommended first-line agent in resource-constrained settings:

limited data exist on the pharmacokinetics of EFV in children under three years; it is consequently not approved for use in neonates (NIH, 2008). Lastly, paediatric dosing is based on body surface area, complicating attempts to standardize treatment with growth (AAP, 2007).

As is evident, similar structural conditions apply to paediatric HIV/AIDS as for neglected tropical diseases, *despite* the existence of the former in the Global North. Paediatric HIV/AIDS in the developing world is, in these respects, a different disease than its developed world counterpart. This situation is not exclusive to HIV/AIDS: the bulk of paediatric pathology is common to resource-rich and resource-constrained settings, albeit with vastly different patterns of morbidity and mortality. Pneumonia and diarrhoea remain the leading killers of children in the developing world despite their prevalence, and amenity to treatment, in the developed world (UNICEF, 2007).

Overall, children in the developing world are vulnerable to a 'double hit': (a) lack of R&D for paediatric drugs; and (b) lack of R&D for neglected disease largely specific to the developing world. The result is a critical lack of access to existing paediatric drugs, in formulations appropriate for both the context and population (Figure 4.1). The human cost of this neglect is profound: there is an estimated five-million deaths annually among children under five from drug-preventable causes (MacLeod, 2008).

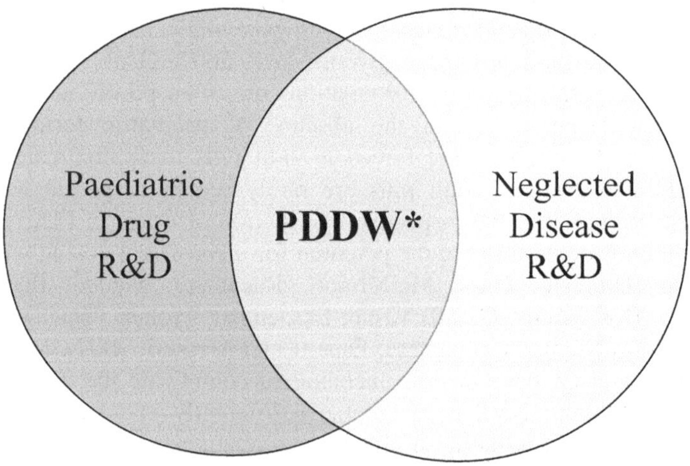

Note: *PDDW: paediatric drugs for the developing world.

Figure 4.1 The 'double hit' in paediatric drug development

3. ECONOMIC AND REGULATORY FACTORS

3.1 Intellectual Property and Generic Market Segments

The structural conditions imposed by TRIPs on pharmaceutical markets have considerably altered the GPE of drug development and supply (Abbott and Reichman, 2007). As of 2005, almost all WTO member states fall under the agreement's aegis (Kerry and Lee, 2007).[2] The extension of mandatory patent law to low- and middle-income countries has reconfigured the economic landscape for member states with vibrant generic drug industries. Companies in countries such as India and China, which have supplied the bulk of low-cost generics to the developing world, are now subject to global patent law (DFID, 2004; Tanner, 2006).

Compelling theory has been put forward to make sense of this new regulatory paradigm and its market effects. Shadlen's (2007; Chapter 3) model of generic market segments partitions the generic drug market into three broad compartments: commodity generics (CGs), specialty generics (SGs) and hybrid generics (HGs). Each conceptual family corresponds to a market segment indirectly created by TRIPs. CGs form the historical bedrock of trade in generics: drugs, like paracetamol (acetaminophen), whose patents have universally expired, and which are therefore open to unmitigated production and sale. There are thus low barriers to entry and intense competition in the CG market, effecting relatively low costs and prices (Grace, 2004). SGs, by contrast, represent generic industry innovation, and therefore display high barriers to competition. They include modified release formulations,[3] new modes of drug delivery (such as inhalable, injectable or transdermal products), scheduled drugs and biogenerics (Shankar, 2008). SGs often constitute the most lucrative segment of the generics market. They admit to substantial production costs, but generate correspondingly high returns, because they are sold in niche markets with greater regulation. Finally, HGs inhabit a middle ground: patents for these drugs exist in some countries, but have either lapsed, or never existed in others. They are thus produced in, and sold among the latter, but restricted from export to the former – unless the importing country issues a compulsory license[4] (CL) (Shadlen, 2007). ARVs for HIV/AIDS are a quintessential example of HGs.[5]

3.2 TRIPs and the Political Economy of Paediatric Drug Development and Supply

Market segmentation, as described above, has ramifications for the generic production and supply of paediatric ARVs. The likely profitability

– the relative difference between drug prices and production costs – of each segment is instrumental in this regard. The price:cost-risk profiles of CGs, SGs and HGs are inherently different. CGs are cheap to produce, but garner low market prices: they therefore achieve thin margins, necessitating large sale volumes to turn worthwhile profits (Shadlen, 2007). Conversely, SGs demand considerable production resources, but yield comparatively high returns. As a result, only firms of a certain size and stability are capable of entering the SG market; for those that can weather the costs and risks of production, this is a highly profitable arena (Grace, 2004).

HGs, by contrast, are neither cheap to produce nor highly priced, due largely to the existence of geographically select patents. ARVs – and particularly paediatric versions – fit this mould precisely. Unit prices cannot exceed purchasing power in developing world markets, the principal legal arena for their sale. The necessarily low prices, however, are not matched by low production costs. As with SGs, the knowledge and capacity for new drug development – such as the reverse engineering of new compounds and novel production techniques – generates considerable expense. These processes are more expensive still with respect to paediatric drugs, for which unique (and age-appropriate) formulations are required. Costs likewise accrue in attempts to meet the strict manufacturing and packaging standards of government-sponsored access programmes, as well as WHO prequalification requirements on bioequivalence, dissolution, shelf life and paediatric pharmacokinetics (WHO, 2004). All of this is relevant with reference to paediatric ARVs, given the gaps in pharmacokinetic data, the need for varied dosages and delivery methods, and the stated issue of excipients. In fact, more pharmacokinetic data exists on paediatric ARVs than for a number of other priority childhood diseases in the developing world, including TB. In some respects, therefore, the barriers to generic drug production for these diseases are higher still.

Substantial legal and regulatory costs are also involved in the production and sale of generic drugs for children. Given the relative lack of safety and efficacy data in children, and the limited knowledge of dosing requirements, the risk of drug side effects and adverse reactions is greater than in adults. Such risks are compounded by the limited generic formulations available for children. For instance, as discussed above, most existing paediatric FDC ARVs contain d4T, known to cause peripheral neuropathy, lipoatrophy and lactic acidosis (Murphy, Sunpath, Kuritzkes, Venter and Gandhi, 2007; van Griensven, Naeyer, Mushi, Ubarijoro, Gashumba, Gazille and Zachariah, 2007). These factors compound the legal costs associated with generic drugs more generally. The requirements for CLs introduced in various national fora have created political and economic obstacles to HG production and export. In Canada for instance, the issuance of a CL by the federal government is contingent upon prior inclusion of the drug in question on a priority list, which takes time and resources to amend (Elliott, 2006). Moreover, efforts to negotiate a voluntary license with the patent holder must precede CL requests. Finally, lengthy license approval/renewal processes, and a limited (two-year) license duration, hamper timely and sustained production (Faculty of Law, University of Toronto, 2007). As a result, Canada's Access to Medicines Regime (CAMR), adopted in 2004, has only issued one CL to date (Cohen-Kohler, Esmail and Perez, 2007). In addition to the time and expense associated with CL applications, there is the risk of patent infringement charges (Shadlen, 2007).

The spatial and temporal dimensions of paediatric markets further complicate the above conditions. Children a priori represent a narrower market than do adults. The paediatric ARV market, moreover, is expected to narrow further with improved prevention of mother-to-child transmission in the developing world (Dionisio, Gass, McDermott, Racalbuto, Madeo, Braghieri, Crowley, Dos Santos, Graaff, Vasan, Eksaengsri, Moller, Khanna, Kraisintu, Juneja, Nicolaou, Sengupta, Esperti and Messeri, 2007). In addition, paediatric markets are functionally partitioned according to age. Different forms of treatment pertain to different age brackets, based on available data on side-effect profiles, metabolic patterns and dosing requirements (AAP, 2007). In other words, temporal transitions in the treatment of HIV-positive children carry intrinsic costs. The 'segmented temporality' of paediatric markets also theoretically frustrates attempts at economies of scale, particularly for smaller generic firms. Lastly, the risk of drug resistance complicates sustained generic production of ARVs over time: the thin profit margins and high technical requirements for HG production are magnified by the eventual obsolescence of existing therapies.

3.3 The Impact of TRIPs on the Indian Pharmaceutical Industry

The above disincentives portend a shift in the economic and political landscape of paediatric drug development. The high cost and low yield of HGs, particularly paediatric versions, creates a significant challenge to the continued production of key generic drugs for children in the developing world. The example of India, a pivotal global player in generic drug manufacturing, is illuminating in this regard.[6] Historically, CGs represented the cornerstone of the Indian pharmaceutical sector: large-volume, low-cost sales to the developing world comprised a large share of revenues (Chaturvedi, Chataway and Wield, 2007). India signed onto TRIPs in 1995, with the cushion of a 10-year transitional period to achieve compliance with respect to the protection of pharmaceutical products. Even prior to full compliance, evidence from the domestic industry pointed to an increasing predilection for global markets, rather than those in the developing world. As of 1998, R&D for tropical or neglected diseases comprised only 16 per cent of industry expenditure; half of that, moreover, was directed towards diseases with global burden (Scherer and Watal, 2001).

Since 2005, Indian pharmaceutical firms have had to comply fully with TRIPs stipulations, as enshrined in the Indian Patent Ordinance of 2004 and the Patent (Amendment) Act of 2005 (Grace, 2005). The upshot has been a shift in focus from unregulated to highly regulated markets and, with it, a strategic emphasis on new chemical entities, branded products and niche, technology intensive drugs (Chaturvedi, Chataway and Wield, 2007). Some analysts predict that given their low cost structure and developing world expertise, Indian firms might retain a circumscribed CG focus to finance these more resource-intensive ventures (Grace, 2004). Even so, their propensity to undertake generic development of products patented post-2005 will likely remain low, given the associated CL requirements. For instance, the Patent Act stipulates a three-year moratorium on CL application from the date of patent approval (Grace, 2005). Evidence suggests this is deterring CLs issued for generic export among Indian firms, due to increased procedural costs and low expected returns on such products (Gehl Sampath, 2005).

Furthermore, the murky legal status of drugs in the Indian 'mailbox' – drugs patented between 1995 and 2005 – acts to deter generic production of this product pool. Though at times successful, the costs associated with pre-grant opposition efforts[7] are a distinct disincentive to investment by generic firms (Gehl Sampath, 2005). Thus, not only has patent law altered market incentives, it erects legal stumbling blocks to long-term generic production for the developing world. As resistance patterns give rise to the need for novel anti-infective drugs, these constraints will be even more keenly felt.

As is evident, in an era of universal TRIPs compliance, the thin margins reaped from the sale of generic ARVs – and, by the same token, paediatric FDCs for TB and malaria – might not outweigh the technical, legal and political costs involved in their production. Consequently, the few generic firms capable of meeting these costs – to date, the same ones that bear the brunt of HG production – face inducements to shift their focus to the more rewarding SG market. The resultant disincentives could drastically undercut the production and supply of drugs for children in the developing world.

In short, the extension of TRIPs and industry responses thereto has led to profound market failure in the production and supply of paediatric medicines to the developing world. The need for policy responses to address this resultant neglect is evident.

4. GLOBAL HEALTH GOVERNANCE AND ACCESS TO MEDICINES FOR CHILDREN

4.1 Persistent Neglect by Global Health Institutions

Problems with the development and licensing of paediatric drugs have been recognized since at least the 1950s concerning chloramphenicol-induced aplastic anaemia (MacLeod, 2008). Despite advances in paediatric pharmacology,[8] efforts to improve drug production and regulation for children remained slow and scattered (Hoppu, 2008). Domestic drug regulatory agencies in developed countries, including the FDA, enacted virtually no paediatric-specific legislation until the 1990s (Hirschfeld and Zajicek, 2007).

The global stage has been little different. Following the 1978 Declaration of Alma-Ata on Primary Health Care, global child health policy emphasized basic public health and primary care interventions – exemplified by United Nations Children's Fund's (UNICEF) focus on growth monitoring, oral rehydration, breastfeeding and immunization (GOBI) (Cueto, 2004). While access to medicines retained prominence in policy discussions, the debate by and large eschewed problems of paediatric drug dosing, formulations and licensing in favour of expanded access to existing medicines. The WHO/UNICEF co-sponsored Bamako Initiative of 1987, for example, privileged procurement of 40 existing generic medicines, and made little mention of gaps in paediatric pharmacotherapy (Ebrahim, 1993). WHO technical reports on the selection and use of essential drugs in the 1970s, the launch of its Action Program on Essential Drugs in 1979, and the bulk of its subsequent policy on access to medicines likewise paid little heed to the structural impediments to improved paediatric drug therapy (Bennett, 1989).

The precise reasons for this neglect are unclear. However, the role of agent and structural power in pharmaceutical policy-making is instructive in this regard. At the national level, asymmetries in lobbying power condition FDA policy priorities. The pharmaceutical industry is Washington's largest lobby, spending over US$1 billion over the last decade

(Ismail, 2008). Underlying this power is the structural importance of the industry to the US economy as one of its prime engines of growth in the latter half of the twentieth century. This power has afforded opportunities to influence FDA policy discussions, and even forestall or dilute legislation, on high cost regulatory issues like paediatric drug testing (Angell, 2004; Groopman, 2005). Moreover, the government has favoured policy 'carrots' rather than 'sticks'. Yet this has failed to stimulate voluntary paediatric studies throughout the 1990s (Boklan, 2006). The terms of current US paediatric drug legislation, while much improved, remain favourable to industry: rather than enforce paediatric drug testing through legislative fiat alone, the current regime also provides generous financial incentives to promote it (see below) (BPCA, 2002; PREA, 2007). What's more, it does not stipulate rigorous parameters or timetables for completion of paediatric studies. Consequently, 'a drug company can satisfy the law without generating meaningful data about how to prescribe its drug for children' (Coté, quoted in Groopman, 2005).

With respect to the developing world, neglect is likely to be conditioned both by economic disincentives and political partitions. During the latter decades of the century, GOBI and other public health programmes achieved far-reaching gains in child survival (Cueto, 2004). However, given the aforementioned market failure in paediatric medicines, without political steerage on paediatric drug issues, manufacturers continued to forego dedicated clinical testing in children, precluding the authorization of potentially valuable drugs for children (Hoppu, 2008).

Politically, the ascendance of the World Bank in global health abetted this trend (Bhatia and Mossialos, 2004). Its lead role in financing health development from the 1980s afforded unprecedented influence over health sector reforms (de Beyer, Preker and Feachem, 2000). Absent from the Bank's agenda, however, was recognition of the need for government intervention to enhance the production, testing and supply of paediatric medicines in a failing market because this ran counter to the neo-liberal doctrine of market non-interference. Such 'non-decision making' (Bachrach and Baratz, 1963; Lukes, 1974) limited feasible policy choices to a narrow set of cost-effective interventions. In short, Bank policy obscured market failure, making the problem of access to paediatric medicines an immutable reality of an increasingly global economy. Consequently, off-label and unlicensed prescribing to children has become familiar to medical practice, compromising the safety and efficacy of paediatric pharmacotherapy (Zucker and Rägo, 2007).

4.2 Making Medicines Child Size: Recent Policy Advances on Paediatric Medicines

A regulatory watershed came with the promulgation of American and, more recently, European Union (EU) legislation on paediatric medicines. Given limited industry initiative to design and test paediatric-specific drugs, the FDA introduced a clause on 'paediatric exclusivity' in the 1997 Food and Drug Modernization Act (Barton and Emanuel, 2005). This entitles a company to a six-month extension of exclusive patent rights for a given drug, to enable evaluation of its safety and efficacy in children (FDA, 2001). Paediatric drug development in the United States has been further buttressed by legislation to provide incentives for off-patent products and to mandate testing of specific drugs (BPCA, 2002; Hirschfeld and Zajicek, 2007; PREA, 2007). The European Medicines Agency (EMEA) has recently followed suit, equipping the EU with legislation that, in addition to FDA-informed principles, stipulates the development of age appropriate paediatric formulations (Permanand, Mossialos and McKee, 2007).

There are important opportunities from these national and regional initiatives. Mounting awareness of the global disregard for paediatric drug development spurred passage of World Health Assembly (WHA) Resolution 60.20 'Better Medicines for Children' in May 2007 (WHA, 2007). A WHO subcommittee has been created to better integrate paediatric needs into global medicines policy, beginning with the development of an essential medicines list for children (EMLc) in October 2007 (WHO, 2007). Close on its heels was the launch of a WHO campaign to 'Make Medicines Child Size' (WHO, 2008a). Where the realities of drug production and supply fall short of need, the campaign has identified priority research, development and access gaps, and set concomitant targets for improvement (Table 4.1).

Continued progress on paediatric medicines is conditional on the dialectic interaction of competing spheres of influence in global health policy. Recent attention has been partly attributable to civil society influence. Professional paediatric associations have used policy networks to voice calls for improved access. The International Pediatric Association (IPA) adopted 'essential medicines' as one of six core programme areas in 2000 (IPA, 1997; IPA, 2009). Collaboration between the IPA and the International Union of Basic and Clinical Pharmacology (IUPHAR) culminated in the creation of an International Alliance for Better Medicines for Children (IABMC) in 2006. Its founding Shanghai Declaration draws attention to impediments in research, clinical and regulatory spheres to improved paediatric pharmacotherapy – among them the lack

Table 4.1 WHO 'Make Medicines Child Size' targets

Priority research gaps: Medicines do not exist or safety and efficacy not known
Medicines for second-line treatment of TB (for TB resistant to existing medicines) Medicines for TB/HIV co-infection Medicines for neglected diseases including schistosomiasis, filariasis, and soil transmitted worms
Priority development gaps: Medicines, research or knowledge exist but medicines require development or adaptation
Four quality assured FDCs for malaria Four quality assured FDCs for HIV/AIDS Three quality assured FDCs for TB Antibiotics for neonatal infections
Priority access gaps: Medicines exist but are not reaching those who need them
Pain medication Oral rehydration salts with zinc in all areas with high incidence of diarrhoeal diseases Child-specific antibiotics for pneumonia Asthma medication

Source: Adapted from WHO (2008a).

of concerted global leadership (Gazarian, 2009). The IPA then held a symposium on 'Better Medicines for Children' at the 2007 International Congress of Paediatrics (Schaller, Lie and Hoppu, 2007). Because of these efforts, the issue of paediatric drug access has begun to permeate global health policy-making spheres. High-level contact between the IPA, IUPHAR and WHO have informed meetings and technical working groups on paediatric medicines, evincing the growth of policy networks around this issue (IPA, 2006).

However, the impact of these policies remains limited by entrenched power structures within global health governance. The WHO's policy influence, alongside other global health initiatives, reflects its constrained budget and membership structure. Resolutions are non-binding or, where binding, enact no punitive sanctions for non-compliance (Lee, 2008). Resolution 60.20 on paediatric medicines is illustrative: its language implies normative rather than legal force; it stipulates no benchmarks for evaluation; and it contains only weak mechanisms of accountability (WHA, 2007). Ultimately, implementation of its recommendations is subject to the decisions of individual member states. In this regard, market failure in paediatric medicines is not a politics-as-usual problem.

In recent years, the 'knowledge structure' underlying the GPE of access to medicines has faced concerted ideational challenges. A number of important WHA resolutions and WHO reports have addressed the impact of intellectual property rights (IPR) protections on access to medicines and, at least implicitly, to the power structures that underpin them. Established by a 2003 WHA resolution, the WHO Commission on Intellectual Property Rights, Innovation and Public Health (CIPIH) issued a landmark report (CIPIH, 2006). Its findings and recommendations inform the WHO 'global strategy on public health, innovation and intellectual property', adopted by the WHA in 2008 (WHA, 2008).

Unfortunately, challenges to the prevailing IPR regime have lagged with respect to policy on paediatric medicines. There is no explicit recognition in WHA Resolution 60.20, for instance, of market failures in paediatric medicines, or the legal and political conditions that perpetuate them. Rather than advocate legal reform of patent rules, it issues vague calls for states to 'encourage research and development' and 'collaborate ... to encourage fair trade' (WHA, 2007, paras 1(4), 2(5)). At its most politically aware, the resolution alludes to existing structural barriers in its call to 'use all necessary administrative and legislative means including ... the Agreement on Trade-Related Aspects of Intellectual Property Rights, in order to promote access to essential medicines for Children' (WHA, 2007, para 1(8)). Few, if any, of the child-specific barriers imposed by TRIPs have received concerted attention in WHA resolutions, strategies or WHO commission reports.

4.3 Political Ripple Effects: HIV/AIDS and Access to Medicines for Children

The political capital generated by HIV/AIDS has put paediatric medicines onto the global policy agenda, with a global network of intergovernmental and civil society organizations (CSOs) seeking to expand access to appropriate ARVs for children in the developing world. WHO/UNICEF collaboration has fostered the development of much needed dosing weight bands for existing ARV formulations, and a programming framework for the scale-up of treatment and care (WHO/UNICEF, 2008). The WHO-PAWG recently published recommendations on priority ARV formulations, including FDCs, to guide industry development and funding commitments (WHO-PAWG, 2008). The most high-profile evidence of global leadership has been the launch of UNICEF's 'Unite for Children, Unite Against AIDS' campaign, a multi-stakeholder collaboration to extend the reach of treatment, prevention and care activities for children with HIV/AIDS (UNICEF, 2005).

Instrumental advocacy work by organisations like the Global AIDS Alliance (GAA), Elizabeth Glaser Foundation and Médecins Sans Frontières (MSF) has also brought the issue to the policy table. MSF's 'access to essential medicines' campaign, in particular, has been pivotal for challenging the political and economic status quo (MSF, 2008a). Allied advocacy efforts, such as the Treatment Action Campaign, were instrumental in defeating an industry legal case against the South African government on the compulsory licensing of generic ARVs (MSF, 2001). This established a legitimate precedent for patent circumvention in public health emergencies, subsequently enshrined in the Declaration on the TRIPS Agreement and Public Health at the 2001 WTO Ministerial Meeting in Doha, Qatar (WHO/WTO, 2002). The political footing gained by CSOs has enabled a logical, if gradual, extension to policy on paediatric ARVs. MSF and GAA have both made paediatric drugs – particularly ARVs – a focus of recent advocacy efforts (GAA, 2006; MSF, 2008b). Philanthropic organizations, notably CHAI, have partnered with global health institutions to create predictable markets for paediatric ARVs, facilitating price cuts and creating incentives for the development of novel paediatric formulations (CHAI, 2009). Collaboration between CHAI and UNITAID, for instance, has generated average price reductions of 60 per cent on ARVs. It has also facilitated the bulk procurement and supply of Cipla's Pedimmune (d4T/3TC/NVP), a generic FDC tablet for children (UNITAID, 2008). Moreover, it has spurred the long-needed development of a paediatric FDC tablet without d4T: this AZT-containing pill, available since April 2008, is now available in seven developing countries (UNITAID, 2008).

These initiatives have been buttressed by financial support. UNITAID and the Global Fund to Fight HIV/AIDS, Tuberculosis and Malaria (GFATM) mobilized and disbursed funds for paediatric ARV treatment programmes (GFATM, 2008; UNITAID, 2008). Their drug procurement and management operations play an essential role in forecasting demand for paediatric ARVs, which in turn creates clear and viable market signals to guide industry production. UNITAID in particular has made paediatric ARVs a niche focus, allocating a significant proportion of its funds to paediatric treatment programmes and to the development of novel formulations, including FDCs (UNITAID, 2008).

Donor commitments to these endeavours reflect changes to the GPE wrought by HIV/AIDS and other global health concerns. The focus accorded to HIV/AIDS has begun to foster not only normative, but also pragmatic justifications for improving access to paediatric medicines. Politically, HIV/AIDS has absorbed the tropes of 'security' policy – a conceptual elision amplified by 9/11 (Barnett, 2006; Durodié, 2005; Feldbaum, Lee and Patel, 2006). The US National Intelligence Council (NIC) has emphasized the national security dimensions of the virus, arguing that AIDS 'will hurt prospects for transition to democratic regimes as they undermine civil society, hamper the evolution of sound political and economic institutions, and intensify the struggle for power and resources' (NIC, 2000). The perceived threats from bioterrorism (for example anthrax) and pandemic influenza have also influenced global policy on trade and medicines ('t Hoen, 2003, p. 55). Short- to medium-term political interests will continue to define global policy on trade and medicines and, by extension, access to paediatric medicines.

National economic considerations also figure prominently. Although forward-thinking, 2003 EU legislation on tiered pricing[9] for HIV, TB and malaria drugs evinces the power of the pharmaceutical industry over policy-making processes. Industry interests are reflected in the scheme's voluntary nature, and its emphasis on the prevention of parallel markets for re-importation (Council Regulation 953/2003, 2003). These provisions are pragmatic concessions to industry, and arguably necessary to entice involvement. Still, they undercut the force of the policy considerably. Without either mandatory measures or more forceful engagement of industry, the legislation has proved largely ineffectual. In its first year, no firms registered drugs for differential pricing. Five years on, only one company (GlaxoSmithKline) had done so – and it has offered tiered pricing on ARVs since 1997, well prior to the legislation (Wiechoczek, 2006). Moreover, all the registered products are components of ARV combination therapies whose companion drugs remain unregistered (European Commission, 2007). The structural power of the US pharmaceutical lobby is arguably stronger still, where deflections from global tiered-pricing proposals persist (Oxfam, 2007).

5. FUTURE CHALLENGES AND POLICY IMPLICATIONS

5.1 Financing Issues

Market failures in paediatric drug production and supply require creative fiscal solutions. These should exploit the potential of existing market models, and create conditions to transcend narrow market calculus. As the WHO 'Make Medicines Child Size' campaign highlights, deficits in R&D and production persist (WHO, 2008a). To fill priority development gaps, enhanced monopsony procurement of generic FDCs for AIDS, TB and malaria through bulk purchasing contracts – as for paediatric ARVs through GFATM, UNITAID and US President's Emergency Plan for AIDS Relief (PEPFAR) (PEPFAR, 2009) – will help lower prices and create assured markets. Where R&D gaps exist (as for second-line TB medications and paediatric TB/HIV drugs) the even stronger 'pull' of advanced market commitments (AMCs) could be used. The intent of AMCs is to mitigate tensions between the dual goals of innovation and affordability (Tremonti, 2005). Their core features include: legally binding donor commitments to drug procurement, based on *ex ante* price and volume commitments; two-stage pricing, comprised of a higher initial price to recoup R&D outlays and a lower tail price to ensure long-term market viability; and developing country guidance on disease and drug priorities (Grace, 2006). A relatively novel funding mechanism, AMCs were conceived, and presently exist primarily for vaccine development.[10] Their rationale and design, however, are applicable to paediatric neglected diseases more broadly.

Opportunities to improve the prevailing production and knowledge structures exist. A funding mechanism for not-for-profit drug development, channelled through existing public-private partnerships (PPPs), could augment R&D in priority areas (Chirac and Torreele, 2006; Trouiller, Olliaro, Torreele, Orbinski, Laing and Ford, 2002). Unlike the profit-driven use of patents by private industry, PPPs have used patents to forward public goals.[11] IPRs empower them to select optimal partners for development and distribution, contract out specific elements of development or distribution processes, and control price (Moran, Ropars, Guzman, Diaz and Garrison, 2005). In other words, such initiatives have tipped the conceptual balance in IPR, from the right of 'the legally constituted individual' (industry) towards a 'right of public domain' (society) (May, 2000, p. 167). A formal global funding channel for neglected disease drug development, drawing on the infrastructure of existing PPPs, could sustain emphasis on R&D for priority paediatric drugs, at prices geared for developing world markets (Orbinski, 2001).

Finally, in the medium- to long-term, support for South-South partnerships in active pharmaceutical ingredient (API) supply and generic production could be supported. Such partnerships are already proliferating in the developing world, enabling lower API prices, production tailored to domestic needs, and more robust competition with brand companies (Dionisio, Khanna, Nicolaou, Raghavan, Juneja, Sengupta and Messeri, 2008).[12] Donors could facilitate such partnerships through support for technology transfer agreements and funds earmarked for domestic production efforts (DFID, 2004). Improved technology and production capacity in the developing world would begin to shift structural power, perhaps enabling greater influence over agenda setting and decision making on access issues.

5.2 Data and Information Systems

Another clearly identified challenge is epistemic. Deep informational lacunae complicate efforts to catalogue treatment need, forecast drug demand and tailor product supply for children in the developing world. These gaps demonstrate the need for improved policies on data to prevent market failure. Most fundamentally, there is a need of more widely and routinely published paediatric treatment figures, from funding agencies and implementing partners alike (Dionisio, Gass, McDermott, Racalbuto, Madeo, Braghieri, Crowley, Dos Santos, Graaff, Vasan, Eksaengsri, Moller, Khanna, Kraisintu, Juneja, Nicolaou, Sengupta, Esperti and Messeri, 2007). Equally important are detailed procurement figures from global bodies, CSOs and national governments, following in the footsteps of the WHO Global Price Reporting Mechanism, CHAI and Brazil's Ministry of Health, respectively (WHO-AMDS, 2005). Both national and international data collection and monitoring will prove instrumental in entrenching reliable chains of production and supply. Disaggregated data on the procurement and consumption of paediatric drugs is the sine qua non of accurate attempts to forecast future need, and thereby stimulate sustained industry production in the long term – particularly given the vagaries of generic production described above.

The corollary of this is the need for consensus and clear articulation of paediatric drug priorities, including combinations, compositions and dosages. This implies access to reliable diagnostic methods, investigation of novel treatments, and information on drug kinetics and dynamics – especially for infants, in whom the knowledge gaps are often greatest (AAP, 2007; GAA, 2008; Hoppu, 2008). Evidence-informed policy on the need for different drug admixtures, second-line agents, and age-appropriate concoctions would help streamline industry efforts to develop the essential drug armamentarium for children. Through the laudable work of WHO-PAWG, this process is in its incipient stages with respect to ARVs. It will require broad and sustained leadership for coherent guidance on paediatric drug development more generally. The EMLc, a valuable template for paediatric drug needs, likewise demands continued update based on emerging pharmacokinetic studies, clinical trials and data from pharmacovigilance activities. The creation of a dedicated locus of governance for paediatric drug issues – ideally, under the auspices of the WHO – would prove invaluable in these efforts. This could serve to harness the considerable momentum of the 'Make Medicines Child Size' campaign for coordinated and sustainable policy-making on paediatric medicines at the global level.

5.3 Legal and Regulatory Issues

Focused legislative and regulatory reform would likewise facilitate paediatric drug production and supply. First, improved access will depend on robust national legislation to ensure the safe and ethical conduct of clinical trials in children; to mandate up-to-date licensing and labelling requirements for paediatric medicines; and to bring domestic regulatory authorities up to WHO technical standards, enabling greater cross-border harmonization of drug approval processes (WHO, 2008a). These reforms would benefit from analogues at the global level: the lack of detailed, formally adopted international guidelines on paediatric drug research, approval and labelling is particularly glaring (Gill, 2004; MacLeod, 2008).

Second, improved guidelines for the use of TRIPs flexibilities are required. Increased clarity, in both national and international regulations, on the legitimate use of CL provisions will prove crucial to their effective use. National governments should work to ensure expedited CL application and approval procedures vis-à-vis paediatric medications for developing world populations (Elliott, 2006). Incentives for generic production could be built into CL legislation, including extended CL tenability for longer-term market prospects and reduced procedural costs (Faculty of Law, University of Toronto, 2007). Eligibility of compounds for CLs should be based on the articulated needs of developing world governments, in concert with WHO stewardship (Cohen-Kohler, Esmail and Perez, 2007). More fundamentally, the potential for further TRIPs reform at the international level bears noting, including selective relaxation of stringent CL requirements for paediatric drugs of high priority.

In addition to CL considerations, enhanced voluntary licensing (VL)[13] mechanisms deserve mention. Given the aforementioned risks and marginal rewards associated with CLs, some see VLs as a more sustainable tactic for generic firms. Though a decided second-best to widespread CL adoption and competition, VLs are defended by proponents – including a number of influential generic manufacturers – as practicable improvements over a piecemeal and highly contested CL system. Purported benefits include: faster licensing time, due to minimal political wrangling; independence from national legislation; improved clarity over operational and legal boundaries; and better assurances of quality control, due to enhanced knowledge and technology transfer between brand and generic firms (Dionisio, Khanna, Nicolaou, Raghavan, Juneja, Sengupta and Messeri, 2008). However, serious potential drawbacks exist as well – principally cost and control issues. The cost of drugs under VLs depends largely on the terms negotiated with the patent holder, not least agreements on licensing fees and product royalties. IP controls continue to dictate the latitude afforded generic companies in the production and sale of the drug, and leave crucial public health decisions about access to medicines in industry hands (Abbott and Reichman, 2007; Westerhaus and Castro, 2006).

To mitigate these concerns, Dionisio et al. (2008) have developed an incentive-bound, WHO-brokered VL paradigm as a supplement to CL efforts. Their model proposes UNITAID-led bulk purchasing of generic drugs under VLs, fiscal relief from governments to generic firms (achieved through debt cancellation and tax revenues), and WHO oversight of VL negotiations. These provisions are seen as a means of effecting price reductions in essential drugs, whilst ensuring that the scope and terms of VL agreements cleave to global public health priorities. Such a strategy has its merits – particularly in the context of a system in which only 61 of the 157 WTO member states have ratified the public health waiver of TRIPs constraints on CLs for export (Paragraph 6 Decision) (WTO, 2011).[14] However, its pursuit in lieu of enhanced CL provisions would be myopic. Firstly, this model allows industry to undercut the capacity of global health governance institutions to steer drug policy by placing ultimate authority in the former's hands. Moreover, it relies upon the real and robust threat of CLs to both provoke and condition VL negotiation for the public good. Provided it is implemented in concert with policies to protect CL rights, a WHO-brokered VL system has the potential to improve access to affordable medicines for children in the developing world.

6. CONCLUSION

This chapter argues that the drivers of, and constraints on, paediatric drug development and supply stem from a confluence of economic and political factors. The role of regulation – specifically, national, regional and international agreements – is fundamental. Its mandated move towards universal patent protection induces product segmentation within the generic pharmaceutical market, limiting the financial viability of generic ARV production for children in the developing world.

The global health governance architecture has also conditioned the response to these gaps. Historical inertia has given way more recently to growing political momentum in attending to child-specific access barriers – particularly with respect to paediatric HIV/AIDS. However, crucial challenges remain: notably, data gaps, the need for larger and more predictable funding commitments, disparate national and regional responses to pharmaceutical trade regulation, and the lack of international standards for R&D, licensing and pharmacovigilance of paediatric medicines. Efforts to address these challenges will require a coordinated response from multiple echelons of governance, in concert with industry and civil society, if they are to effect lasting change.

NOTES

1. UNITAID is an international drug-purchase facility created in 2006 by France, Brazil, Chile, Norway and the United Kingdom, with the professed goal of scaling-up treatment access for people living with HIV, TB and malaria in developing countries, through 'sustained strategic market intervention to drive price reduction and increases in supply'. It now has 29 member countries, 19 of which are in Africa, and is funded in the main by taxes levied on airline tickets (UNITAID, 2008).
2. The sole exception is the group of least developed countries, which remain exempt from their WTO obligations on protecting pharmaceuticals until 2016.
3. Modified-release implies changes in the rate at which a drug is released from a resinate. Variations in this rate are used to create extended or sustained release forms of existing medicines.
4. A compulsory licence is 'the permission given by a government to a third party to use or produce an invention without the consent of the patent holder' (Lee and Drager, 2005, p. 83).
5. Save the earliest (mid-1980s) incarnations, which will soon become CGs, most existing ARVs are HGs; moreover, any newly developed ARVs will fall into this category.

6. A detailed case study is beyond the scope of this chapter. For a more comprehensive analysis, see Chaturvedi, Chataway and Wield (2007); Gehl Sampath (2005) and Grace (2004, 2005).
7. Indian patent law does not grant patents to new or improved versions of existing medicines, and affords interested parties the right to file an opposition to any patent under review by the patent office on these grounds. However, the legal interpretation of this principle remains highly disputed in practice.
8. These include, inter alia, sophisticated knowledge of developmental pharmacokinetics, the advent of technologies for non-invasive drug monitoring, and the delineation of ethical guidelines for paediatric clinical trials.
9. Tiered pricing is the practice of setting different prices for the same product, to reflect the characteristics of different markets or consumers.
10. A partnership between the Global Alliance for Vaccines and Immunisation (GAVI), the Bill & Melinda Gates Foundation and five G8 governments launched a pilot pneumococcal vaccine AMC in 2007 (Advanced Market Commitment for Vaccines, 2008).
11. The Drugs for Neglected Diseases Initiative (DNDi), for instance, is developing paramomycin for visceral leishmaniasis through a purely public model: research is being carried out by MSF and public labs in Kenya; distribution will be undertaken by a Dutch not-for-profit; and the drug sold at cost in development world markets (DNDi, 2007). On the force of a swell in PPP initiatives since 2000, there are approximately 63 drugs for neglected diseases (DNDs) somewhere in the development pipeline: 50 of these are part of PPPs, eight to nine of which are predicted to make the market by 2010 (Moran, Ropars, Guzman, Diaz and Garrison, 2005).
12. APIs account for the majority of ARV development costs, ranging anywhere from 55–99 per cent (Pinheiro, Vasan, Kim, Lee, Guimier and Perriens, 2006). The bulk of APIs for generic ARVs are produced in China and India. Discounts on APIs through South-South partnerships – as are occurring, for instance, between Indian Cipla and Ugandan Quality Chemicals – increase the viability of generic drug production for developing world markets (Pharmaceutical-Technology.com, 2008).
13. A voluntary licensing is a negotiated agreement with a patent holder for generic production and sale of a branded product (Dionisio, Khanna, Nicolaou, Raghavan, Juneja, Sengupta and Messeri, 2008).
14. As a result, the deadline for ratification, initially set for December 2007, has been postponed thrice until 31 December 2013; its formal acceptance is contingent on ratification by two-thirds of WTO member states.

BIBLIOGRAPHY

Abbott, Frederick M. and Jerome H. Reichman (2007), 'The Doha Round's public health legacy: Strategies for the production and diffusion of patented medicines under the amended TRIPs provisions', *Journal of International Economic Law*, **10**(4), 921–87.

Advanced Market Commitment for Vaccines (2008), 'Saving lives with new vaccines: Advanced market commitments', available at http://www.vaccineamc.org/files/AMC_FactSheet_v2.pdf (accessed 19 November 2009).

American Academy of Pediatrics [AAP] (1995), 'Guidelines for the ethical conduct of studies to evaluate drugs in paediatric populations', *Paediatrics*, **95**(2), 286–94.

AAP (2007), 'Increasing antiretroviral drug access for children with HIV infection', *Paediatrics*, **119**(4), 838–45.

Angell, Marcia (2004), *The Truth about Drug Companies: How They Deceive Us and What to Do about It*, New York: Random House.

Bachrach, Peter and Morton S. Baratz (1963), 'Decisions and non decisions: An analytical framework', *American Political Science Review*, **57**(3), 641–51.

Barnett, Tony (2006), 'A long-wave event: HIV/AIDS, politics, governance and "security": Sundering the intergenerational bond?', *International Affairs*, **82**(2), 297–313.

Barton, John H. and Ezekiel J. Emanuel (2005), 'The patents-based pharmaceutical development process: Rationale, problems and potential reforms', *Journal of American Medical Association*, **294**(16), 2075–82.

Bennett (1989), 'The dilemma of essential drugs in primary health care', *Social Science and Medicine*, **28**(10), 1085–90.

Best Pharmaceuticals for Children Act (BPCA), Public Law No. 107–109 (2002).

Bhatia, Mrigesh and Elias Mossialos (2004), 'Health systems in developing countries', in Anthony L. Hall and James Midgley (eds), *Social Policy for Development*, London: Sage, pp. 168–204.

Boklan, Jessica (2006), 'Little patients, losing patience: Pediatric cancer drug development', *Molecular Cancer Therapeutics*, **5**(8), 1905–8.

Clinton HIV/AIDS Initiative [CHAI] (2009), 'Treating HIV/AIDS and malaria: Clinton HIV/AIDS initiative', available at http://www.clintonfoundation.org/what-we-do/clinton-hiv-aids-initiative/what-we-ve-accomplished (accessed 18 November 2009).

Chaturvedi, Kalpana, Joanna Chataway and David Wield (2007), 'Policy, markets and knowledge: Strategic synergies in Indian pharmaceutical firms', *Technology Analysis and Strategic Management*, **19**(5), 565–88.

Chirac, Pierre and Els Torreele (2006), 'Global framework on essential health R&D', *Lancet*, **367**(9522), 156–61.

Cohen-Kohler, Jillian C, Laura C. Esmail and Andre Cosio Perez (2007), 'Canada's implementation of the paragraph 6 decision: Is it sustainable public policy?', *Globalization and Health*, **3**(12), 1–16.

Commission on Intellectual Property Rights, Innovation and Public Health, World Health Organization [CIPIH] (2006), 'Public health: Innovation and intellectual property rights', World Health Organization, available at http://www.who.int/intellectualproperty/documents/thereport/ENPublicHealthReport.pdf (accessed 19 November 2009).

Conroy, Sharon, Imti Choonara, Peiro Impicciatore, Angelika Mohn, Henrik Arnell, Anders Rane, Carmen Knoeppel, Hannsjoerg Seyberth, Chiara Pandolfini, Maria Pia Raffaeli, Francesca Rocchi, Maurizio Bonati, Geert 't Jong, Matthijs de Hoog and John van den Anker (2000), 'Survey of unlicensed and

off label drug use in paediatric wards in European countries', *British Medical Journal*, **320**(7227), 79–82.
Correa, Carlos M. (2002), *Implications of the Doha Declaration on the TRIPs Agreement and Public Health*, Health Economics and Drugs Series No. 12, Geneva: World Health Organization (WHO/EDM/PAR/2002.3).
Council Regulation 953/2003, *To avoid trade diversion into the European Union of certain key medicines*, 2003 OJ (L 135) 5.
Cueto, Marcos (2004), 'The origins of primary health care and selective primary health care', *American Journal of Public Health*, **94**(11), 1864–74.
de Beyer, Joy A., Alexander S. Preker and Richard Feachem (2000), 'The role of the World Bank in international health: Renewed commitment and partnership', *Social Science and Medicine*, **50**(2), 169–76.
DFID Health Resource Centre [DFID] (2004), 'Access to medicines in underserved markets: What are the implications of changes in intellectual property rights, trade and drug registration policy?', *DFID UK Health System Resource Centre*, available at http://www.dfidhealthrc.org/publications/atm/DFID_synthesis_aw.pdf (accessed 19 November 2009).
Dionisio, Daniele, Robert Gass, Peter McDermott, Vincenzo Racalbuto, Marina Madeo, Giuseppe Braghieri, Siobhan Crowley, Pinheiro Eloan Dos Santos, Peter Graaff, Ashwin Vasan, Achara Eksaengsri, Helene, Moller, Khanna, Arun Kumar Khanna, Krisana Kraisintu, Sandeep Juneja, Stavros Nicolaou, Aloka Sengupta, Francesco Esperti and Daniela Messeri (2007), 'What strategies to boost production of affordable fixed-dose anti-retroviral drug combinations for children in the developing world?', *Current HIV Research*, **5**, 155–87.
Dionisio, Daniele, Arun Kumar Khanna, Stavros Nicolaou, Vijay Raghavan, Sandeep Juneja, Alok Sengupta and Daniela Messeri (2008), 'For-profit policies and equitable access to antiretroviral drugs in resource-limited countries', *Future Medicine – Future HIV Therapy*, **2**(1), 25–36.
Drugs for Neglected Diseases Initiative [DNDi] (2007), 'DNDi portfolio map', available at http://www.research4development.info/SearchResearchDatabase.asp?OutputID=178797 (accessed 16 July 2008).
Durodié, Bill (2005), *Health, Foreign Policy and Security: The Concept of Risk*, UK: Nuffield Trust, UK Global Health Programme.
Ebrahim, G. (1993), 'The Bamako initiative', *Journal of Tropical Pediatrics*, **39**(2), 66–7.
Elliott, Richard (2006), 'Pledges and pitfalls: Canada's legislation on compulsory licensing of pharmaceuticals for export', *International Journal of Intellectual Property Management*, **1**(1–2), 94–112.
European Commission (2007), 'Annual report on application of Council Regulation (EC) No 953/2003 of 26 May 2003 to avoid trade diversion into the European Union of certain key medicines', available at http://trade.ec.europa.eu/cgi-bin/antitradediversion/annual_reports.pl?action=reports (accessed 10 August 2008).
Faculty of Law, University of Toronto (2007), 'Making Canada's access to medicines regime work for countries in need: A case study on Ghana', available at http://www.camr-rcam.gc.ca/review-reviser/camr_rcam_ut.stu_05-eng.pdf (accessed 19 November 2009).

FDA (2007), 'FDA grants tentative approval for 50th and 51st anti-retroviral drugs under President's emergency plan for AIDS relief', available at http://www.fda.gov/NewsEvents/Newsroom/PressAnnouncements/2007/ucm108964.htm (accessed 19 November 2009).

Feldbaum, Harley, Kelley Lee and Preeti Patel (2006), 'The national security implications of HIV/AIDS', *PLoS Medicine*, **3**(6), 171–5.

Food and Drug Administration [FDA] (2001), 'The paediatric exclusivity provision: January 2001 status report to Congress', available at http://www.fda.gov/downloads/Drugs/DevelopmentApprovalProcess/DevelopmentResources/UCM049915.pdf (accessed 19 November 2009).

GAA (2008), 'Scaling up access to early infant diagnostics: Accelerating progress through public-private partnerships', available at http://aidsalliance.3cdn.net/98430b280794df0a1d_ikm6bh00f.pdf (accessed on 18 November 2009).

Gazarian, Madlen (2009), 'Delivering better medicines to children: Need for better integration between the science, the policy, and the practice', *Pediatric Drugs* **11**(1), 41–4.

Gehl Sampath, Padmashree (2005), *Economic aspects of access to medicines after 2005: Product patent protection and emerging firm strategies in the Indian pharmaceutical industry*, Tokyo: United Nations University – Institute for New Technology.

GFATM (2008), 'Fighting AIDS', available at http://www.theglobalfund.org (accessed 23 June 2008).

Gill, Denis (2004), 'Ethical principles and operational guidelines for good clinical practice in paediatric research: Recommendations of the Ethics Working Group of the Confederation of European Specialists in Paediatrics (CESP)', *European Journal of Pediatrics*, **163**(2), 53–7.

Global AIDS Alliance [GAA] (2006), 'Children left behind: Stakeholders failing to adequately prevent or treat paediatrics HIV/AIDS', available at http://aidsalliance.3cdn.net/284bb9af0b1cb1b3eb_oam6ibfg3.pdf (accessed 19 November 2009).

Grace, Cheri (2004), 'The effect of changing intellectual property on pharmaceutical industry prospects in India and China: Considerations for access to medicines', available at http://www.dfidhealthrc.org/publications/atm/Grace2.pdf (accessed 19 November 2009).

Grace, Cheri (2005), 'A briefing paper for DFID: Update on China and India and access to medicines', available at http://www.dfidhealthrc.org/what_new/Final%20India%20China%20Report.pdf (accessed on 19 November 2009).

Grace, Cheri (2006), 'Developing new technologies to address neglected diseases: The role of Product Development Partnerships and Advanced Market Commitments', available at http://www.dfidhealthrc.org/publications/Issues_papers/push_pull_06.pdf (accessed 19 November 2009).

Groopman, Jerome (2005), 'The paediatric gap', available at http://www.jeromegroopman.com/articles/pediatric-gap.html (accessed 10 August 2008).

Hirschfeld, Steven and Anne Zajicek (2007), 'Brief selective history of pediatric initiatives in the United States of America', available at http://archives.who.int/eml/expcom/children/Items/USinitiatives.pdf (accessed 19 November 2009).

Hoppu, Kalle (2008), 'Paediatric clinical pharmacology: At the beginning of a new era', *European Journal of Clinical Pharmacology*, **64**, 201–5.
International Federation of Pharmaceutical Manufacturers and Associations [IFPMA] (2008), 'Principal focus and actions of the research-based pharmaceutical industry in contributing to global health', available at http://www.ifpma.org/Issues/GlobalHealth/fileadmin/templates/ifpmaissues/pdfs/2008_02_27_Contrib_2_Global_Health_Final_Industry_Focus_and_Actions_EN.pdf (accessed 18 November 2009).
International Paediatric Association [IPA] (1997), *Just say know to drugs*, Report of the IPA Workshop on Essential Drugs for Children, Halifax (NS), Geneva: International Paediatric Association.
IPA (2006), 'Archives: IPA year end newsletter 2006', available at http://www.ipa-world.org/News/Pages/Newsletter.aspx (accessed 25 November 2009).
IPA (2009), 'Program areas: Better medicines for children', available at http://www.ipa-world.org/Program_Areas/Pages/Better_Medicines_Children.aspx (accessed 18 November 2009).
Ismail, Mohammad Asif (2008), 'A record year for the pharmaceutical lobby in '07: Washington's largest lobby racks up another banner year on Capitol Hill', *Center for Public Integrity*, available at http://projects.publicintegrity.org/rx/report.aspx?aid=985 (accessed 10 August 2008).
Kerry, Vanessa Bradford and Kelley Lee (2007), 'TRIPs, the Doha declaration and paragraph 6 decision: What are the remaining steps for protecting access to medicines?', *Globalization and Health*, **3**(3), 1–12.
Lee, Kelley (2008), *The World Health Organization*, London: Routledge.
Lee, Kelley and Nick Drager (2005), 'The World Trade Organization and public health', in Kelley Lee and Jeff Collins (eds), *Global Change and Health*, London: Open University Press, pp. 83–94.
Lukes, Steven (1974), *Power: A Radical Approach*, London: MacMillan.
MacLeod, Stuart M. (2008), 'If not now … when? The opportune moment has arrived for major international impact in paediatric pharmacology and pharmacy', *Paediatric Drugs*, **10**(3), 141–2.
Matthews, Duncan (2006), 'From the August 30, 2003 WTO decision to the December 6, 2005 agreement on an amendment to TRIPs: Improving access to medicines in developing countries?', *Intellectual Property Quarterly*, **10**(1), 91–130.
May, Christopher (2000), *A Global Political Economy of Intellectual Property Rights: The New Enclosures?*, New York: Routledge.
Moran, Mary, Anne-Laure Ropars, Javier Guzman, Jose Diaz and Christopher Garrison (2005), *The New Landscape of Neglected Disease Drug Development*, Sydney: Pharmaceutical R&D Policy Project, The George Institute.
MSF (2001), 'Pharmaceutical industry must stop obstructing access to medicine in South Africa', available at http://www.msfaccess.org/media-room/press-releases/press-release-detail/?tx_ttnews%5Btt_news%5D=104&cHash=cf60d5c6e9 (accessed 18 November 2009).
MSF (2007), 'Untangling the web of price reductions: A pricing guide for the purchase of ARVs for developing countries', available at http://doctorswithoutborders.org/publications/article.cfm?id=3728&cat=special-report (accessed 18 November 2009).

MSF (2008a), 'Campaign for access to essential medicines', available at http://www.accessmed-msf.org/ (accessed 7 August 2008).

MSF (2008b), 'Children with HIV/AIDS deserve fair treatment', available at http://www.accessmed-msf.org/main/hiv-aids/introduction-to-hivaids/children-and-hivaids/ (accessed 11 August 2008).

Murphy, Richard A., Henry Sunpath, Daniel R. Kuritzkes, Francois Venter and Rajesh T. Gandhi (2007), 'Antiretroviral therapy-associated toxicities in the resource-poor world: The challenge of a limited formulary', *Journal of Infectious Diseases*, **1**(196, Suppl 3), S449–56.

National Institutes of Health [NIH] (2008), 'Guidelines for the use of antiretroviral agents in paediatric HIV infection', available at http://www.aidsinfo.nih.gov/ContentFiles/pediatricGuidelines.pdf (accessed 15 June 2008).

NIC (2000), 'Global trends 2015: A dialogue about the future with non-government experts', available at http://www.dni.gov/nic/NIC_globaltrend2015.html (accessed 10 August 2008).

Orbinski, James (2001), 'Health, equity and trade: A failure in global governance', in Sampson, Gary P. (ed), *The Role of the World Trade Organization in Global Governance*, pp. 223–41.

Oxfam (2007), 'Investing for life: Meeting poor people's needs for access to medicines through responsible business practices', available at http://www.oxfam.org/en/policy/bp109_investing_for_life_0711 (accessed 11 August 2008).

Pediatric Research Equity Act of 2007 (PREA) (2007), H.R. 3580, 110th Cong. §§ 401–4.

PEPFAR (2009), 'Celebrating life: Fifth annual report to Congress on PEPFAR', available at http://www.pepfar.gov/press/fifth_annual_report/ (accessed 19 November 2009).

Permanand Govin, Elias Mossialos and Martin McKee (2007), 'The EU's new paediatric medicines legislation: Serving children's needs?', *Archives of Diseases in Childhood*, **92**(9), 808–11.

Pharmaceutical-Technology.com (2008), 'Quality chemical industries, HIV drug plant, Uganda', available at http://www.pharmaceutical-technology.com/projects/qualitychem/ (accessed 14 July 2008).

Pinheiro, Eloan, Ashwin Vasan, Jim Yong Kim, E. Lee, Jean Marc Guimier and Joseph Perriens (2006), 'Examining the production costs of antiretroviral drugs', *AIDS*, **20**(13), 1745–52.

Schaller, Jane G., Sverre Lie and Kalle Hoppu (2007), 'Symposium on better medicines for children: Report from the 25th international congress of paediatrics, Athens, Greece', *Pediatric Drugs*, **9**(6), 357–60.

Scherer, Frederic M. and Jayashree Watal (2001), *Post-Trips Options for Access to Patented Medicines in Developing Countries*, Draft working paper for Working Group 4 of the Commission for Macroeconomics and Health, Geneva: World Health Organization.

Shadlen, Kenneth (2007), 'The political economy of AIDS treatment: Intellectual property and the transformation of generic supply', *International Studies Quarterly*, **51**(3), 559–81.

Shankar, B. (2008), 'Specialty generics – The next wave of generics growth', *Drug Delivery Technology*, **8**(2), 76–7.

Tanner, James A. (2006), 'WTO TRIPs and its effect on the supply and development of medicines in China', *Hong Kong Medical Journal*, **12**(1), 84–6.

't Hoen, Ellen (2003), 'TRIPs, pharmaceutical patents and access to essential medicines: Seattle, Doha and beyond', available at http://www.who.int/intellectualproperty/topics/ip/tHoen.pdf (accessed 11 August 2008).

Tremonti, Giulio (2005), 'Background papers to advanced market commitments to vaccines: A new tool in the fight against disease and poverty – Report to the G8 Finance Ministers/Tesoro, Ministero dell'Economia e delle Finanze', available athttp://www.dt.tesoro.it/Aree-Docum/Relazioni-/Working-Pa/Advanced-Market-Commitments-for-vacc.pdf (accessed 10 July 2008).

Trouiller, Patrice, Piero Olliaro, Els Torreele, James Orbinski, Richard Laing and Nathan Ford (2002), 'Drug development for neglected diseases: A deficient market and a public-health policy failure', *Lancet*, **359**(9324), 2188–94.

UNAIDS (2008), '2008 Report on the global AIDS epidemic', available at http://www.unaids.org/en/KnowledgeCentre/HIVData/GlobalReport/2008/2008_Global_report.asp (accessed 29 July 2008).

UNICEF (2005), 'A call to action: Children – The missing face of AIDS. The Global Campaign on Children and AIDS: Unite for Children, Unite Against AIDS', available at http://www.unicef.org/publications/index_29157.html (accessed 12 July 2008).

UNICEF (2007), 'Children and the millennium development goals: Progress towards a world fit for children', available at http://www.unicef.org/publications/files/Children_and_the_MDGs.pdf (accessed 12 April 2008).

UNITAID (2008), 'UNITAID annual report 2008', available at http://www.unitaid.eu/images/news/annual_report_2008_en.pdf (accessed 20 November 2009).

van Griensven, Johan, Ludwig De Naeyera, Thomas Mushib, Sowaf Ubarijorob, Diane Gashumbab, Claire Gazille, Rony Zachariah (2007), 'High prevalence of lipoatrophy among patients on stavudine-containing first-line antiretroviral therapy regimens in Rwanda', *Transcripts of the Royal Society of Tropical Medicine and Hygiene*, **101**(8), 793–8.

Westerhaus, M. and A. Castro (2006), 'How do intellectual property law and international trade agreements affect access to antiretroviral therapy?', *PLoS Medicine*, **8**(3), 1230–6.

Widdus, Roy (2001), 'Public-private partnerships for health: Their main targets, their diversity, and their future directions', *Bulletin of the World Health Organization*, **79**, 713–20.

Wiechoczek, Oliver (2006), 'The EU's contribution to global governance: The case of global infectious diseases', available at http://212.3.246.100/Objects/2/Files/EFPIAaward2006.pdf (accessed 25 November 2009).

World Health Assembly [WHA] (2007), 'Resolution WHA60.20: Better medicines for children', available at http://www.who.int/gb/ebwha/pdf_files/WHA60/A60_R20-en.pdf (accessed 2 July 2008).

WHA (2008), 'WHA61.21: Global strategy and plan of action on public health, innovation and intellectual property', available at http://www.who.int/gb/ebwha/pdf_files/A61/A61_R21-en.pdf (accessed 2 August 2008).

World Health Organization [WHO] (2000), *WHO Medicines Strategy: Framework for Action in Essential Drugs and Medicines Policy, 2000–2003*, Geneva: World Health Organization (WHO/EDM/2000.1).

WHO (2002), *Globalization, Patents and Drugs: An Annotated Bibliography*, Health Economics and Drugs series number 9, Geneva: World Health Organization (EDM/PAR/2001.1).

WHO (2004), 'Manufacture of antiretrovirals in developing countries and challenges for the future', available at http://www.who.int/gb/ebwha/pdf_files/EB114/B114_15-en.pdf (accessed 14 March 2008).

WHO (2007), 'WHO model list of essential medicines for children (First List, October 2007)', available at http://www.who.int/childmedicines/publications/EMLc%20(2).pdf (accessed 18 November 2009).

WHO (2008a), 'Make medicines child size', available at http://www.who.int/childmedicines/en/index.html (accessed 15 May 2008).

WHO (2008b), 'Addendum to 2006 WHO guidelines on antiretroviral therapy for HIV infection in adults and adolescents', available at http://www.who.int/hiv/pub/guidelines/adult/en/index.html (accessed 3 July 2008).

WHO AIDS Medicines and Diagnostics Service [WHO-AMDS] (2005), 'Relative market share of different antiretroviral compounds in low- and middle-income countries in 2004 and 2005: An analysis of two public domain data bases', available at http://www.who.int/hiv/amds/consumptionAMDS.pdf (accessed 18 November 2009).

WHO Paediatric ARV Working Group [WHO-PAWG] (2008), 'Preferred antiretroviral medications for treating and preventing HIV infection in younger children: Report of the WHO Paediatric Antiretroviral Working Group', available at http://www.who.int/hiv/pub/paediatric/ARV_WG_meeting_report_may2008.pdf (accessed 18 November 2009).

WHO/UNAIDS (2007), 'AIDS Epidemic Update. Joint United Nations Programme on HIV/AIDS', available at http://www.unaids.org/en/KnowledgeCentre/HIVData/EpiUpdate/EpiUpdArchive/2007/default.asp (accessed 18 November 2009).

WHO/UNICEF (2008), 'Scale up of HIV-related prevention, diagnosis, care and treatment for infants and children: A programming framework', available at http://www.unicef.org/aids/index_documents.html (accessed 10 July 2008).

WHO/WTO (2002), *WTO Agreements & Public Health*, Geneva: World Health Organization and World Trade Organization.

WTO (2011), 'TRIPs and public health: Members accepting amendment of the TRIPs Agreement', available at http://www.wto.org/english/tratop_e/trips_e/amendment_e.htm (accessed 1 June 2011).

Zucker, Howard and Lembit Rägo (2007), 'Access to essential medicines for children: The World Health Organization's global response', *Clinical Pharmacology and Therapeutics*, **82**(5), 503–5.

5. Trade agreements, intellectual property and access to essential medicines: What future role for the right to health?

James Harrison

1. INTRODUCTION

Pharmaceutical drugs are an essential component in the treatment of many of the world's most serious healthcare problems, including HIV/AIDS. But at the heart of the recent debate over pharmaceutical drugs have been their prices. The price of many drugs is greatly increased by the intellectual property (IP) protection that is granted to their inventors, allowing pharmaceutical companies a number of years in which they have exclusive rights to market and sell their products (Oxfam, 2006, p. 15f). This raises some fundamental questions about the legal and moral balances of our society. To what extent should inventors be allowed to profit from their inventions, and to what extent should countries limit the rewards they can obtain in order to take care of other important societal concerns such as public health? (Harrison, 2007, p. 115f)

In terms of international trade law, this argument has become particularly acute with regard to developing countries. While most developed countries have already instituted relatively strong systems of IP protection as a result of domestic policy choices, a number of developing countries have only recently established systems of IP protection as a result of international trade law obligations. These obligations arise from the World Trade Organization's Agreement on Trade-Related Aspects of Intellectual Property Rights (TRIPs Agreement) and bilateral and regional trade agreements, which often contain stronger forms of IP protection than that found in the TRIPs Agreement – the so-called TRIPs-plus provisions.

There is a great deal of debate about the developmental stage at which implementation of a system of IP protection is appropriate, which is beyond the scope of this chapter (e.g., Abbott, 2005a, p. 81f; Commission on Intellectual Property Rights, 2002). But there has also been much discussion of the narrower impact of TRIPs and TRIPs-plus provisions on the ability of many developing countries to successfully implement healthcare policies that maximize access to essential medicines for fighting diseases such as HIV/AIDS (e.g., Abbott, 2005b; Sun, 2004). Some organizations have criticized TRIPs and TRIPs-plus provisions from a developmental perspective, while others have done so from a health perspective. Some have critiqued its social iniquity, while others have attacked it from a purely economic perspective.[1] Amongst these broad-ranging critiques, a substantial number of actors have framed (some of) their arguments utilizing the discourse of human rights. Most of the actors who have utilized such a discourse focus upon the negative impact of the TRIPs Agreement on the right to health.

This chapter explores the rationale for this human rights discourse and investigates what it has added to the other types of critiques of TRIPs and TRIPs-plus provisions. It argues that the human rights discourse around the issues of the TRIPs Agreement and access to essential medicines has primarily focused on the strength of human rights as universal values that can be utilized as a rallying call to a range of actors coming together to campaign on the issue. The human rights discourse has also been used as a 'signal' of the importance of the issue in respect of those seeking to utilize TRIPs obligations to undermine the provision of essential medicines. But it is not greatly discussed or noted that the detailed *legal* obligations of human rights, which many see as one of their key strengths, have not been significantly engaged, for instance, to challenge the obligations of governments contained in the TRIPs Agreement. The chapter will relate the attempts, primarily by relevant UN organizations, to expand upon the legal content of the right to health in this context, and the limited attempts that have so far been made to apply that legal framework to the complex health and IP issues that arose after the adoption of the Doha Declaration on the TRIPS Agreement and Public Health (Doha Declaration). It will evaluate the ongoing case for the detailed *legal* obligations of human rights to be engaged in critiquing the impact of TRIPs and TRIPs-plus obligations on access to essential medicines, as well as the drawbacks of such an approach.

The next section of this chapter will therefore briefly introduce the TRIPs Agreement and comment on its regulatory philosophy, which is very different from traditional trade agreements, and explore what a human rights approach in this context might entail. Section 3 will then examine the impact of this human rights discourse on the TRIPs Agreement prior to the Doha Declaration. This will be followed by an assessment of the human rights discourse post-Doha Declaration. Section 5 then focuses on the increasing calls for human rights impact assessments (HRIAs) of the IP provisions in trade agreements and evaluates the potential of this policy mechanism. The chapter will end with some conclusions on the future role of the right to health in addressing some of the broader social justice issues raised by the TRIPs Agreement and TRIPs-plus bilateral and regional trade agreements.

2. KEY FEATURES OF THE TRIPS AGREEMENT AND THE RATIONALE FOR A HUMAN RIGHTS CRITIQUE

The TRIPs Agreement was introduced into the World Trade Organization (WTO) system during the Uruguay Round of Trade Negotiations largely as a result of lobbying by pharmaceutical companies (Abbott, 2002, p. 470). It establishes minimum levels of protection that each government has to give to the IP, including patents, of fellow WTO members. It sets out, *inter alia*, requirements for the grant of rights; powerful modes of enforcement (national enforcement and WTO dispute settlement); and time limitations on protection of intellectual property rights (IPRs) (a minimum of 20 years for patents). This is balanced by permitted exceptions which allow IPRs to be overridden in specified circumstances, through, for example, compulsory licenses and parallel importation. There are also transition periods for developing countries so that they have longer time periods to implement their obligations under the TRIPs Agreement.

This contribution will not explore the nature of these legal provisions in any detail and will assume some basic knowledge of how they function, as is done elsewhere in this volume.[2] But, taking a broader perspective, it should be recognized that the regulatory philosophy of the TRIPs Agreement is very different from 'traditional' trade agreements. Adherence to international trade rules is generally justified on the grounds that WTO Agreements promote trade liberalization, that such liberalization is welfare-enhancing, and that this, *inter alia*, has a positive impact on the protection and promotion of human rights (WTO, 2004, p. 10).[3] But the TRIPs Agreement places members under extensive positive regulatory duties to enforce patent rights. As such the 'welfare' balance required is far more difficult to ascertain than for agreements imposing only liberalization requirements. It is important to recognize this very different usage of global trading rules under agreements like

TRIPs – no longer centred around the unifying principle of trade liberalization – but taking on rules that aim at creating an increasingly 'uniform global regulatory infrastructure' (Heiskanen, 2004, pp. 13–4). This shift in regulatory philosophy leads to more fundamental questions about the purpose and justice of global regulation, which increases the need for an external critique of trade rules. The TRIPs Agreement is actually enforcing *rights*-based obligations – the rights of IP holders – combined with exceptions and limitations on the situations when those rights can be enforced, in order to allow for the protection of other key interests such as public health. This is essentially a rights-based approach to regulation, and so the norms and standards of human rights appear to be well-placed to provide an external critique of how the TRIPs Agreement functions.

The fact that human rights norms are the international and national legal obligations of States means that those States have international and national legal obligations to comply with human rights, alongside their international trade law obligations. This is often seen as a key strength of utilizing a human rights discourse and adds legitimacy to the demands for policy changes that are based on relevant, legally codified human rights (Hunt and MacNaughton, 2006, p. 13). From the legal perspective, it is the International Covenant on Economic, Social and Cultural Rights (ICESCR) that provides the most detailed international legal framework through which human rights norms and standards can be utilized to critique the balance of rights and exceptions created by the TRIPs Agreement. The ICESCR contains provisions relating to both the rights of inventors and the right to health of the general population. Article 15(1) of the ICESCR recognizes the right of everyone 'to benefit from the protection of the moral and material interests resulting from any scientific, literary or artistic production of which he [or she] is the author'. So, the rights of inventors of medicines are protected under the ICESCR. Article 12 of the ICESCR recognizes 'the right of everyone to the enjoyment of the highest attainable standard of physical and mental health'. The rights of the general population to the highest attainable standard of health are therefore protected by the ICESCR. The question remains, what balance the ICESCR should strike when these two sets of rights come into conflict. Such clashes of rights are not unusual (e.g., the clash between freedom of expression and the prohibition of racial discrimination). In the context of provision of essential medicines, if the TRIPs Agreement is enforcing its specific conception of rights – IPRs – in a way which is undermining the balance struck by the human rights approach, then serious questions need to be asked about the nature of the rights and obligations it is creating.

But, from a legal perspective, finding a definite violation of the right to health is not an entirely self-evident process. We need to apply relevant human rights frameworks (e.g., respect, protect and fulfil) in order to understand whether a violation has occurred and who is the violator (is it a domestic government, third country or international organization?). We need to be able to show a causal link between the harm created and the violation (e.g., has the TRIPs obligation in question actually led to decreased access to essential medicines?). We also need to understand the mechanisms by which human rights strike a balance between particular rights in particular situations where they come into conflict (e.g., is there a breach of a core obligation of either right?). Let us therefore consider some of the scenarios where it has been suggested that the TRIPs Agreement has undermined the protection and promotion of human rights with regard to provision of essential medicines to see what form of critique human rights actors have in fact provided and the extent to which the legal framework of human rights has been engaged.

3. THE IMPACT OF A HUMAN RIGHTS DISCOURSE ON THE TRIPS AND ACCESS TO MEDICINES DEBATE BEFORE AND DURING THE NEGOTIATION OF THE DOHA DECLARATION

In the early days of the TRIPs Agreement, there were well-documented attempts by the pharmaceutical companies, assisted by the United States and other Northern countries with strong pharmaceutical industries, to attempt to enforce a strong interpretation of patent rights in the context of medicines. Particularly infamous were the cases involving HIV/AIDS drugs.

Highest profile of all, in November 1997, at the height of the HIV/AIDS epidemic that was (and still is) ravaging the country, the South African government enacted legislation to increase the availability of affordable drugs treatment (The Medicines and Related Substances Control Amendment Act, 1997). This legislation authorized measures aimed at the provision of more affordable drugs for the treatment of HIV/AIDS including parallel importation of patented drugs and the production of generic medicines under compulsory licences, as apparently authorized by the TRIPs Agreement.

There was a swift response from the US government and international pharmaceutical producers. In early 1998, approximately 40 drug companies banded together and submitted a formal complaint to the Pretoria

High Court in South Africa, challenging the constitutionality of the Medicines and Related Substances Control Amendment Act and arguing its incompatibility with the TRIPs Agreement. Further, the US Trade Representative, at the request of the US pharmaceutical industry, placed South Africa on its 'Section 301 Watch List', and the US administration withheld several South African exports from preferential treatment (Sun, 2004, p. 131). Largely as a result of campaigning and publicity-raising by numerous NGOs, this legal action was brought to global attention and the companies dropped their case.

The South African case, although by far the most high profile, was by no means the only instance of such attempts to enforce a strict interpretation of TRIPs obligations. Another high-profile case saw the United States bring an action against Brazil through the WTO for abuse of IPRs in producing generic medicines to (very successfully – see OHCHR (2001)) fight HIV/AIDS (WTO, 2001). Looking more broadly at the situation in the 1990s, there were a great many other countries who suffered 'well-documented and intensive' pressure, particularly from the United States to strictly enforce provisions of the TRIPs Agreement, including Argentina, the Dominican Republic, Kenya and Thailand (Abbott, 2002, p. 472). What was becoming clear from these situations was that, even though TRIPs rules potentially had mechanisms to allow for the provision of more affordable essential medicines, there was a great deal of ambiguity about when they could be utilized. Such ambiguities could lead to legal action and political pressure against developing countries that attempted to utilize relevant provisions. Thus, it was at the instigation of the African Group that discussions commenced in the TRIPs Council in June 2001 with a view to clarifying the flexibilities in the TRIPs Agreement, and particularly how these flexibilities could be utilized to enhance access to essential medicines. This process eventually led to the adoption of the Doha Declaration on the TRIPS Agreement and Public Health on 14 November 2001 (Doha Declaration, 2001).

As a result of the developing countries' strength and unity on this issue, strong public feeling in favour of their positions, and the effects of the aftermath of the September 11 attacks, the Doha Declaration is one of the few occasions where the final text is much closer to that proposed by developing than developed countries (Abbott, 2002, p. 469). It is generally recognized that the Doha Declaration confirms that all of the key flexibilities of the TRIPs Agreement could be utilized by developing countries. So, '[e]ach member has the right to grant compulsory licences and the freedom to determine the grounds upon which such licences are granted'. Each member also has the right to determine what constitutes 'a national emergency or other circumstances of extreme urgency' for the purposes of the Agreement. The one outstanding issue that was not resolved at Doha was an issue where the existing TRIPs rules *did* need to be amended in order to promote access to essential medicines in many developing countries; it was recognized that WTO Member States with insufficient or no manufacturing capacities in the pharmaceutical sector could face difficulties in making effective use of compulsory licensing under the TRIPs Agreement. It took two years of further negotiations to find a solution to this issue in the form of the Decision on Implementation of Paragraph 6 of the Doha Declaration on the TRIPS Agreement and Public Health (Paragraph 6 Decision), which set up a mechanism allowing importation of generic medicines under compulsory licenses into countries with insufficient manufacturing capacity to produce such drugs themselves.

In a non-technical sense, this decision does seem like a 'victory' for human rights (although as we will see below a victory with many caveats). The Doha Declaration and the Paragraph 6 Decision were even hailed by trade insiders in evocative human rights-style language. The then Director-General of the WTO, Supachai Panitchpakdi, described the Decision as a 'historic agreement for the WTO … proving once and for all that the organization can handle humanitarian as well as trade concerns' (WTO, 2003). The then-EC Commissioner for Trade (now WTO Director-General), Pascal Lamy, described it as a deal that showed the WTO could 'put people before markets' (Lamy, 2003). But the more specific question we are seeking to answer here is: What role did an explicit human rights discourse play in these achievements? Certainly it did play some role.

Many of the disparate civil society groups campaigning against the TRIPs Agreement were united by the view that enforcing IPRs in a way that reduced access to essential medicines for fighting diseases like HIV/AIDS was a human rights issue (Sleap, 2004). More specifically, the fact that the South African Constitution explicitly recognizes the right to health could be seen as a factor in the decision of the pharmaceutical companies to drop their legal action against the South African government. It meant that any court case would have led to judges explicitly balancing right to health concerns against the IPRs of the pharmaceutical companies. It is impossible to know precisely how important this aspect was in the decision to discontinue the case (Scott and Wai, 2004, pp. 315–6). But certainly the very high profile campaign against the pharmaceutical companies was more important than detailed consideration of the way in which rights would have been weighed and balanced in the case itself. This is in contrast to a later challenge to the *domestic* policy of the South African government on the provision of antiretroviral drugs where the South African Constitutional Court did make a ruling on right to health grounds.[4]

It is also clear that the right to health was a factor in the negotiations over the Doha Declaration. Most obviously this can be seen in the draft declaration initially proposed by developing countries, the preamble to which explicitly invokes the obligations of countries to protect 'fundamental human rights', including the right to health as protected by the ICESCR (Proposal by the African Group, 2001). Due to strong opposition from many developed countries, the final Doha Declaration does not utilize the explicit human rights approach of the developing countries' draft, but the impact of that discourse can be seen. The Declaration states that 'the Agreement can and should be interpreted and implemented in a manner supportive of WTO members' right to protect public health and, in particular, to promote access to medicines for all'.

So, over this period there was significant campaigning on the basis of human rights, and 'right to health' language was even invoked in negotiations over the Doha Declaration itself. The discourse of human rights was primarily utilized to mobilize stakeholders working on particular issues to recognize their shared interests, as well as to heighten the sense of moral outrage at the nature of the obligations that the TRIPs Agreement appeared to be enforcing. It can perhaps even be seen as a bargaining chip in the process of negotiating the Doha Declaration itself. But human rights discourse generally appears to have been utilized as a mechanism for framing arguments, rather than to directly challenge TRIPs obligations utilizing detailed expositions of the *legal* obligations of the ICESCR and other relevant human rights instruments. There are a number of possible rationales for this.

First, the balance of rights and obligations created by the ICESCR was perhaps not well enough understood in the TRIPs context to be utilized in any other way. It was only in late 2000 that more detailed expositions of the nature of the relevant rights began to be produced by key UN actors. The Committee on Economic Social and Cultural Rights (CESCR) which monitors the implementation of the ICESCR in Member States produced a General Comment on the right to health in August 2000, which stated that provision of essential drugs was part of the core obligation of the right to health (CESCR, 2000, para. 43). The Office of the High Commissioner for Human Rights (OHCHR) produced a paper setting out a human rights framework for analysing the TRIPs Agreement very shortly before the Doha Declaration was negotiated (OHCHR, 2001). But there has been significantly more work done subsequently to 'flesh out' the nature of the relevant obligations as we will see below in discussions of post-Doha issues.

Second, the utility of using human rights discourse in any more technical, legal sense was limited. On the one hand, campaigners were united in perceiving clear violations of the TRIPs Agreement in situations such as South Africa. So, detailed exposition was unnecessary for internal unity on the issue, and no pressing external rationale was advanced. The South African case never came to court; the international human rights law system was not a strong institutional mechanism for resolving these issues; and negotiations and cases within the relatively 'self-contained' international trade law system were primarily concerned with international trade law obligations. So there was no need to interrogate the human rights dimensions of the issue in any detail. We might even speculate that activists and campaigners saw dangers in employing human rights arguments in a more technical and legalistic manner, and we will return to a consideration of these issues below. But we might conclude that since the 'right' results were generally perceived by campaigners and developing countries to have been achieved through the Doha Declaration, the level of engagement with the more detailed normative content of the human rights invoked was not particularly significant.

4. POST-DOHA DECLARATION: RIGHT TO HEALTH ISSUES

In spite of the triumphant pronouncements by trade diplomats, concerns about the impact of international trade law obligations on the ability of countries to provide essential medicines to their populations have not dissipated. There is considerable evidence that the solutions brokered through the Doha Declaration and the Paragraph 6 Decision have not been as successful as was first imagined for a number of reasons. First, there is evidence of ineffective utilization of flexibilities in the TRIPs Agreement by developing countries (Osewe, Nkrumah, and Sackey, 2008). Furthermore, the administrative complexity of the Paragraph 6 Decision and its implementation in legislation at the national level has led to a number of actors questioning whether it is in fact workable (Médecins Sans Frontières, 2006; Oxfam, 2006; WTO, 2010). Early experiences with importation of generic HIV/AIDS medicines from Canada to Rwanda, the first time the system had been tested, confirmed concerns of generic producers and campaigners over the problems of complexity (Elliott, 2007; Sekalala, 2010).

Outside the WTO system, another set of issues have grown in prominence. With the WTO system itself floundering, more and more bilateral and regional trade agreements are creating a 'spaghetti-bowl' of trade obligations across the globe (Bhagwati, 1995). These agreements often include provisions protecting IPRs that are far stronger than those contained in the TRIPs Agreement. The so-called TRIPs-plus provisions include the extension of the scope and term of patent protection, facilitation of 'ever-greening', increase in the term of data exclusivity and limitations on the ability of countries to utilize compulsory licensing and parallel imports (Krikorian and Szymkowiak, 2007). Many authors have argued that such provisions substantially reduce States' TRIPs flexibilities which allow for the production or importation of cheaper generic drugs (e.g., Bernieri, 2006; El-Said and El-Said, 2007; Krikorian and Szymkowiak, 2007).

What is clear is that the 'big bang' of the Doha Declaration and the Paragraph 6 Decision has not created the ultimate solution which deals with all the potential impediments to access to essential medicines created by the protection of IP through international trade law obligations. The impediments we now face are also considerably more complex, multifaceted and technical than those preceding the Doha Declaration. The fact that we are dealing with multiple bilateral and regional agreements, negotiated in national capitals, each with their own different IP provisions means that issues are more complex and global justice movements are harder to mobilize (Abbott, 2005b, p. 354). Because we are dealing with the minutiae of administrative legal arrangements (e.g., packaging requirements of generic drugs) rather than head-on legal battles over access to affordable drugs, raising public awareness and engagement with the underlying issues is far harder. So what use has been (and should be) made of the discourse of human rights in this post-Doha Declaration period?

Certainly a human rights framework continues to be utilized on this issue by UN human rights agencies, the World Health Organization and coalitions of NGO actors who are campaigning about various social justice dimensions of the international trading system, and IP provisions in particular (Canadian Council for International Co-operation, 2007; Sell, 2007, pp. 66–7). There has also been an increase in the number of human rights organizations campaigning on these issues.[5] Human rights therefore still appear to be effective as a rallying call to relevant international organizations and campaigning groups who are active on these issues. The question is whether the nature of the discourse has evolved and is capable of responding to the increasing complexity of the issues we now face? And does a more detailed appreciation of the legal obligations and their application assist in this endeavour?

Certainly, UN human rights bodies, in response to the pre-Doha Declaration TRIPs issues, began working to produce more guidance about the relevance of the legal obligations of international human rights instruments to the TRIPs debate. As stated above, in June 2001, the OHCHR produced a paper setting out a human rights framework for analysing the TRIPs Agreement. This was followed in December 2001 by the CESCR producing a statement on human rights and IP (CESCR, 2001). This statement has been further developed in 2006, when the CESCR produced a General Comment on Article 15(1)(c) of the Covenant which examines the balance to be struck between inventors' rights and other rights such as the right to health (CESCR, 2006). The General Comment emphasizes that IPRs are not human rights as such, but merely an instrumental mechanism through which States provide protection to individual authors and creators. Thus the protection afforded to inventors under Article 15(1) does not necessarily coincide with that under national and international IP systems. Rather, there is a need to ensure that such IP systems contribute to the progressive realization of all the Covenant rights, including the right to health. High prices caused by IP protection can affect the 'economic accessibility' of essential drugs, and therefore make it more difficult for States to comply with their right to health obligations. In particular, States have a duty to take action with regard to any IP regime that makes the costs of essential medicines 'unreasonably high' (CESCR, 2006, para. 35). But there is no exposition on the nature of the action, which should be taken from a human rights perspective, or what constitutes unreasonably high prices. This guidance is therefore difficult to apply to particular circumstances of potential violations.

CESCR, as well as the Committee on the Rights of the Child (CRC), has raised concerns about the impact of IP provisions in trade agreements on access to essential medicines in the context of particular trade agreements and their impact on particular countries. In the last few years, these committees have expressed concern in their Concluding Observations on a number of countries including Chile, Costa Rica, Ecuador, El Salvador, Kenya, Morocco, Nicaragua, Peru, the Philippines and Thailand.[6] Concerns include both the failure to utilize flexibilities permitted by the TRIPs Agreement and the impact of TRIPs-plus provisions in bilateral and regional trade agreements.

The approach of the Committees is generally to express concern about the possible or potential adverse consequences of such agreements, rather than to identify actual human rights violations.[7] This is to an extent symptomatic of the *modus operandi* of the UN Treaty Monitoring

Bodies. It is a weak system in terms of enforcement mechanisms, and so relies upon State co-operation combined with pressure from relevant actors (national and international NGOs etc.) for action to be taken. It is also symptomatic of the problems inherent in making a finding that a violation has occurred in a particular country (and who is responsible) due to the complexity of the issues involved. We need to understand the extent of the violation (how many people are without essential drugs and the extent of the impact upon them), what is causing the violation (e.g., obligations of bilateral trade agreements, failure to use TRIPs flexibilities, complexity of requirements of the Doha Declaration and national implementing legislation or reasons unrelated to trade agreements such as a lack of local distribution network for drugs etc.) and the actors who are to blame (e.g., third countries for enforcing obligations, home country for failure to use flexibilities, local administration for failures in distribution etc.). We then need to prove the causal link between the provisions of the trade agreement and the lack of access to drugs on the ground.

For all of these reasons, it is therefore unsurprising that both the CESCR and the CRC have called for States to conduct HRIAs of trade agreements to assess the impact of IP provisions of international trade agreements (as well as a range of other provisions of trade agreements).[8] It is hoped that HRIAs will allow the legal obligations of human rights to be utilized, in order to actually identify any negative impacts caused by trade agreements. The penultimate section of this chapter therefore examines the existing practice and future potential of HRIAs as a mechanism for engaging with post-Doha Declaration TRIPs and TRIPs-plus issues from a human rights perspective.

5. HUMAN RIGHTS IMPACT ASSESSMENTS

Calls for HRIAs have been made by the CRC, the CESCR and a range of other actors. The UN Special Rapporteur on the Right to Health also recommended that impact assessments of trade agreements be carried out in his report on the impact of the WTO on the right to health, and in his report on Peru (UN Special Rapporteur, 2004, para. 50; UN Special Rapporteur, 2005, para. 53). Such calls have also been taken up by civil society activists (3-D, 2006; Canadian Council for International Co-operation, 2007; FIDH, 2008). But as yet, only a very limited number of HRIAs have been undertaken. Only two of those HRIAs specifically deal with the human rights impact of IP provisions in a trade agreement – an impact assessment of the US-Thailand Free Trade Agreement (including its IP provisions) by the Thailand National Human Rights

Commission (TNHRC, 2006) and an impact assessment of the IP provisions of the Central American Free Trade Agreement on the right to health (Walker, 2009).

The calls for 'impact assessments' described above are not made in a vacuum. Social, economic, environmental and human rights impact assessments are increasingly widely used tools for measuring the impact of a wide range of activities.[9] While the number of HRIAs that have been undertaken with regard to trade agreements is very limited, economic, environmental and 'social' impact assessments of trade agreements have been far more widespread (Harrison and Goller, 2008, p. 9f). However, assessment of 'social' impact (most analogous to the human rights impact we are considering here) is often unsatisfactory. Where conclusions about social impacts are reached, they tend to be brief and not assessed according to any consistent methodology. There are a number of assessments, for instance, which specifically deal with the impact of trade agreements on essential medicines, particularly in the South American context (Health Ministry of Peru, 2005; Holguín Zamorano, 2004; Pan American Health Organization, 2004; Pan American Health Organization, 2005). These assessments include detailed economic assessment of projected price fluctuations of products as a result of liberalization, with, at best, passing references to social impacts on the population in question (e.g., Health Ministry of Peru, 2005, pp. 197, 222). They have been criticized for their weak methodological frameworks (Blanco, 2006). Human rights norms and obligations could therefore become the basis for a more rigorous form of analysis of the broader social impacts of such trade agreements.

But this will not necessarily be the case. Consideration of the Thailand National Human Rights Commission HRIA reveals that the methodology of the report is very disappointing from a human rights perspective. In general, the report makes only sporadic references to the provisions of relevant human rights instruments. Discussion of key human rights principles (e.g., non-discrimination) is absent. Conclusions about violations are generally not related back to the relevant standards or, when they are, only at a high level of generality, which adds little to the preceding analysis. With regard to the IP issues in particular, there is an economic analysis of the likely impact of the proposed provisions, particularly with regard to how it will impact upon access to essential medicines. It is concluded that the proposed provisions will lead to expensive drugs 'beyond the means of local consumers' and as a result 'the people in Thailand will be denied access to drugs, causing endless public health and social problems' (THNRC, 2006, p. 26). It is later stated that this would be in breach of the right to health (THNRC, 2006,

p. 59). But these conclusions are not reached on the basis of any kind of 'right to health' analysis; rather, it is simply presumed that a human rights violation will occur because of the preceding economic analysis of likely price increases. Thus human rights discourse is not doing any real work in the analysis of the issue and simply becomes an appendage, a label to be applied to an existing economic and social justice critique.

As I have argued elsewhere with regard to HRIAs of trade agreements more generally, conducting an HRIA of a trade agreement is a complex process (Harrison and Goller, 2008). Some work has already been done by the UN Special Rapporteur on the Right to Health to identify and concretize the relevant legal obligations and how they should be applied in this specific context (Hunt and MacNaughton, 2006, p. 13). More recently, the UN Special Rapporteur on Food has produced 'Guiding principles on human rights impact assessments of trade and investment agreements' (Human Rights Council, 2011). But much work is still to be done on constructing appropriate methodological frameworks if they are to provide a robust and useful mechanism for measuring the broader 'social' impacts of trade agreements. It is important that those bodies who are advocating HRIAs assist actors who are involved in the process of actually undertaking assessments on a range of issues including how to use human rights norms and standards to drive the assessment process; how to undertake case studies of affected populations; and how key causal issues which are likely to need exploration in the assessment should be tackled (Harrison and Goller, 2008, p. 24).

The HRIA of the IP provisions of Central America–Dominican Republic–United States Free Trade Agreement (CAFTA) and their impact on the right to health in Colombia by Simon Walker is a sophisticated model, which could be a sound basis on which future impact assessments could be built (Walker, 2009). It clearly sets out the relevant *legal* obligations of the right to health and uses them to underpin the subsequent analysis of the broader social impact of the IP provisions in CAFTA (Walker, 2009, p. 123f). But Walker's assessment is undertaken by an individual rather than an IGO or State organ. Institutional support and dissemination of such good practice is vital from key international actors (e.g., OHCHR) if lessons are to be learnt and methodologies are to be improved at the national level.

Properly constructed HRIAs have the potential to allow the legal obligations of human rights to play a more active and informative role in 'post-Doha' TRIPs and TRIPs-plus debates. It could also facilitate the identification of situations where governments are not in fact constrained by international trade law obligations to act in a way that conflicts with human rights norms and standards. Governments may be making domestic policy choices and regulatory decisions in ignorance of the real ambit of international trade rules, or for entirely different reasons (e.g., at the behest of domestic lobbying groups).

But the development of appropriate methodologies will be an ongoing learning process and will require responses to new issues raised by individual assessments as they take place. In the absence of increasing levels of consensus around robust methodological frameworks, there is a danger that poor HRIAs will fail to have any impacts upon debates and countries may claim that even the most superficial impact assessment process constitutes an HRIA.[10] Furthermore, there are legitimate questions over whether this process of engaging the legal obligations of human rights through conducting HRIAs will lead to substantively different and better outcomes from a social justice perspective.

6. CONCLUSIONS: WHAT FUTURE ROLE FOR THE RIGHT TO HEALTH?

The discourse of human rights will inevitably continue to play a role in trade debates more generally and in the debate around IP provisions and their impact on access to essential medicines specifically. Invoking human rights continues to be a way of forging coalitions of actors campaigning around the potential negative impacts of IP protections in international trade agreements on the provision of essential medicines for fighting pandemics like HIV/AIDS. Utilizing a human rights approach will also engage a wide range of human rights institutions (e.g., international human rights agencies, human rights NGOs, national human rights institutions etc.) which might not otherwise become involved in discussions about the impact of trade agreements.

The question remains of how much impact this discourse will have on those who are making technical decisions about the implementation of TRIPs and TRIPs-plus obligations – primarily national governments. It is an important critique of existing human rights approaches to international trade law that at the stage of actual policy formulation and evaluation 'human rights language recedes into the background' and that policy proposals often do not seem 'to be derived from human rights obligations in any direct way' (Lang, 2007, pp. 393–4). Faced with clear and potentially actionable legal obligations under the TRIPs Agreement and related bilateral and regional trade agreements, governments may take these obligations more seriously than vague and often poorly understood human rights obligations. This gives rise to the argument that, for the human rights discourse to maximize its effectiveness, it needs to engage audiences beyond the traditional human rights and development community, such as politicians and trade negotiators, many of whom are likely to strongly dispute the relevance of human rights to these debates (Howse, 2002, n. 7). By unpacking the legal obligations of key human rights instruments, a more substantial role is perhaps possible for human rights in future TRIPs and TRIPs-plus debates. In this context, HRIAs of specific IP provisions in specific trade agreements and their implementation at the national level could be seen as a positive step. The use of HRIAs is increasingly advocated by relevant UN bodies and campaigning groups. But there is a great deal of work to do on designing appropriate methodological frameworks. Poorly constructed technical and legal human rights arguments in the context of complex post-Doha TRIPs and TRIPs-plus debates will only reinforce views of sceptics that human rights have little or nothing to add to the debates about the social justice impact of international trade agreements and make engagement harder in the future.

A more nuanced and complex human rights discourse, based on the widely-recognized interpretations of relevant codified rights, has the potential to play an important role in the future debate about trade agreements, IP and access to essential medicines. But ongoing vigilance is required. This legalization of human rights can have negative consequences. Once it is argued that human rights should be taken into account in some legal decision-making process, the process of technical engagement can make activists, campaigners and human rights lawyers themselves lose touch with underlying values that make the human rights critique important (Koskenniemi, 2009, p. 14). Furthermore, decision-makers (who will often be trade specialists) can feel more comfortable in prioritizing their own values, safer in the knowledge that they have 'taken into account' legitimizing human rights values (Koskenniemi, 2002, p. 570). It must be remembered that human rights are far more than simply the technical legal provisions of international and national legal texts. They are moral values, driven by particular conceptions of justice. Viewing human rights as entirely constrained by what is set out in legal instruments and expounded upon by legal experts can be dangerous (Williams, 2007).

The human rights discourse will probably always be an important rallying call for campaigners on issues related to IP and access to essential medicines. It also has a future as a powerful slogan with which to discredit obvious and clear forms of injustice in international trade agreements. The question remains of the extent of the useful role the discourse can play in dealing with the legal and technical complexities of the post-Doha TRIPs and TRIPs-plus world. This chapter has presented attempts to flesh out the legal content of the right to health by relevant international bodies and the limited attempts that have been made so far in the application of precise legal obligations in the context of specific trade agreements through HRIAs. It has been suggested that conducting HRIAs appears to be the best way for human rights discourse to substantively engage in complex post-Doha TRIPs and TRIPs-plus debates. But it also recognizes the dangers inherent in this legalization of human rights. Impact assessments must be conducted with appropriate and sophisticated methodologies to avoid being, or at least appearing, simply reactionary. At the same time those utilizing the human rights discourse must retain a clear vision of the underlying ethos and value of human rights and be prepared to challenge those seeking to engage human rights language merely to justify the *status quo* rather than as a serious intellectual tool of enquiry into alternative social justice outcomes.

NOTES

1. For a development perspective, see, for example, Oxfam (2006). For a medical perspective, see the Médecins Sans Frontières Campaign for Essential Medicines at http://www.msfaccess.org/. For a selection of reports primarily cataloguing the economic impact, see the discussion in Section 4.
2. For further discussion, see Harrison (2007, Chapter 9).
3. For a critique of this position, see Harrison (2007, p. 33f).
4. *Treatment Action Campaign & Ors v. Minister of Health & Ors* (2002) 5 SA 721 CC.
5. A prominent example is the non-governmental organization '3-D' which campaigns exclusively on trade, human rights and an equitable economy, see http://www.3dthree.org. Organizations like International Federation of Human Rights and Amnesty International also increasingly campaign on a range of economic, social and cultural rights issues including the right to health and access to essential medicines.
6. See CESCR Concluding Observations on Chile (E/C.12/1/Add.105) 20 November 2004, para. 60; CESCR Concluding Observations on Costa Rica, E/C.12/CRI/CO/4, 4 January 2008, paras 27 and 48; CESCR Concluding Observations on Ecuador, E/C.12/1/Add.100, 7 June 2004, paras 55–6; CESCR Concluding Observations on El Salvador, E/C.12/SLV/CO/2, 27 June 2007, paras 19, 38; CESCR Concluding Observations on India, E/C.12/IND/CO/5, 8 August 2008, para. 46; CESCR Concluding Observations on Morocco, E/C.12/MAR/CO/3, 4 September 2006, paras 29, 56; CRC Concluding Observations on Ecuador, CRC/C/15/Add.262, 13 September 2005, para. 20; CRC Concluding Observations on El Salvador,

CRC/C/15/Add.232, 30 June 2004, paras 47–8; CRC Concluding Observations on Kenya, CRC/C/KEN/CO/2, 19 June 2007, para. 47f; CRC Concluding Observations on Nicaragua, CRC/C/15/Add.265, 21 September 2005, paras 16–7; CRC Concluding Observations on Peru, CRC/C/PER/CO/3, 14 March 2006, paras 48–9; CRC Concluding Observations on Philippines, CRC/C/15/Add.259, 21 September 2005, para. 58; CRC Concluding Observations on Thailand, CRC/C/THA/CO/2, 17 March 2006, para. 57.

7. One exception is the CESCR Concluding Observations on El Salvador, E/C.12/SLV/CO/2, 27 June 2007, where the Committee states at para. 19 that 'The Committee notes with concern the adverse effects of the implementation of the Free Trade Agreement, which entered into force in El Salvador on 1 March 2006, on the exercise of the rights established in the Covenant by the most vulnerable sectors of the population'. Even here, the Committee requests at paragraph 38 that an impact assessment be carried out, suggesting there is still a need to assess the evidence.
8. See, for example, CESCR Concluding Observations on Costa Rica, E/C.12/CRI/CO/4, 4 January 2008, para. 48; CESCR Concluding Observations on Ecuador, E/C.12/1/Add.100, 7 June 2004, para. 55; CESCR Concluding Observations on El Salvador, E/C.12/SLV/CO/2, 27 June 2007, para. 38; CRC Concluding Observations on El Salvador, CRC/C/15/Add.232, 30 June 2004, para. 48.
9. For access to the full text of a range of different HRIAs, see the Human Rights Impact Resource Centre at http://www.humanrightsimpact.org/ (accessed 20 November 2008). For information on a wider range of impact assessments, see International Association for Impact Assessment at http://www.iaia.org (accessed 20 November 2008).
10. For example, in its report to the CESCR, Costa Rica claimed that an HRIA had been carried out on the effects of a trade agreement involving that country, despite having little information at all about the impact of the agreement in question, see 3D (2007).

BIBLIOGRAPHY

3D (2006), *Trade-related Intellectual Property Rights, Access to Medicines and Human Rights – Morocco*, April 2006, available at http://www.3dthree.org/pdf_3D/3DCESCRMorocco_April06Eng.pdf (accessed 20 December 2009).

3D (2007), *UN Human Rights Body Gives Credence to Costa Rica's 'No' Coalition*, available at http://www.3dthree.org/pdf_3D/CostaRicaCAFTA.pdf (accessed 20 December 2009).

Abbott, Frederick M. (2002), 'The Doha Declaration on the TRIPs Agreement and public health: Lighting a dark corner of the WTO', *Journal of International Economic Law*, **5**(2), 469–505.

Abbott, Frederick M. (2005a), 'Towards a new era of objective assessment in the field of TRIPs and variable geometry for the preservation of multilateralism', *Journal of International Economic Law*, **8**(1), 77–100.

Abbott, Frederick M. (2005b), 'The WTO medicines decision: The political economy of world pharmaceutical trade and the protection of public health', *American Journal of International Law*, **99**(2), 317–58.

Bernieri, Rosa (2006), 'The intellectual property rights in bilateral investment treaties and access to medicines: The case of Latin America', *Journal of World Intellectual Property*, **9**(5), 548–72.

Bhagwati, Jagdish (1995), 'US trade policy: The infatuation with free trade agreements', in Jagadish Bhagwati and Anne O. Krueger, *The Dangerous Drift to Preferential Trade Agreements*, Washington: AEI Press, pp. 1–18.

Blanco, Hernan (2006), 'Sustainability impact assessment of trade policy and its application in the context of Latin America', *Impact Assessment and Project Appraisal*, **24**(4), 285–97.

Canadian Council for International Co-operation (2007), *Reconciling Trade and Human Rights: The New Development Agenda*, available at http://www.ichrdd.ca/site/_PDF/publications/globalization/TradeHRConfPDF.pdf (accessed 20 December 2009).

CESCR (2001), *Human Rights and Intellectual Property, Statement by the Committee on Economic Social and Cultural Rights*, 14 December (E/C.12/2001/1).

CESCR (2006), *The Right of Everyone to Benefit from the Protection of the Moral and Material Interests Resulting from any Scientific, Literary or Artistic Production of which He or She is the Author (Article 15, paragraph 1(c), of the Covenant) General Comment No. 17*, 12 January (E/C.12/GC/17).

Commission on Intellectual Property Rights (2002), *Integrating Intellectual Property Rights and Development Policy*, available at http://www.iprcommission.org/papers/pdfs/final_report/ciprfullfinal.pdf (accessed on 20 December 2009).

Committee on Economic Social and Cultural Rights [CESCR] (2000), *General Comment on the Right to the Highest Attainable Standard of Health*, 11 August (E/C.12/2000/4).

Doha Declaration (2001), *Declaration on the TRIPs Agreement and Public Health, Ministerial Declaration*, November 2001, WT/MIN(01)/DEC/2).

Elliott, Richard (2007), 'First test of WTO mechanism for procuring generic medicines under compulsory license, via Canada's Access to Medicines Regime', *HIV/AIDS Policy & Law Review*, **12**(2–3), 23–5.

El-Said, Hamed and El-Said Mohammed (2007), 'TRIPs-plus implications for access to medicines in developing countries: Lessons from Jordan–United States Free Trade Agreement', *Journal of World Intellectual Property*, **10**(6), 438–75.

Fédération Internationale des Ligues des Droits de l'Homme [FIDH] (2008), *Human Rights Impact Assessment of Trade and Investment Agreements concluded by the European Union*, available at http://www.fidh.org/IMG/pdf/positionpaperFIDH-HRIA_finalfevrier2008.pdf (accessed 20 December 2009).

FIDH (2008), *10th African Union Summit, Open letter to African Union Heads of State and Government Meeting in Addis-Ababa*, available at http://www.fidh.org/spip.php?article5137 (accessed 20 December 2009).

Harrison, James (2007), *The Human Rights Impact of the World Trade Organisation*, Oxford: Hart Publishing.

Harrison, James and Alessa Goller (2008), 'Trade and human rights: What does impact assessment have to offer?', *Human Rights Law Review*, **8**(4), 1–29.

Health Ministry of Peru (2005), *Evaluacion de los potenciales efectos sobre acceso a medicamentos del Tratado de Libre Comercio que se negocia con los Estados Unidos de America*, available at http://www.minsa.gob.pe/portal/Especiales/TLC-MINSA/EstudioTLCSalud.pdf (accessed 20 December 2009).

Heiskanen, Veijo (2004), 'The regulatory philosophy of international trade law', *Journal of World Trade*, **38**(1), 1–36.

Holguín Zamorano, Germán (2004), *La Bolsa y la Vida: Impacto de la Agenda Norte Americana para el TLC Sobre el Acceso a Medicamentos y la Salud Publica*, Bogota: Misión Salud.

Howse, Robert (2002), 'Human rights in the WTO: Whose rights, what humanity? Comments on Petersmann', *European Journal of International Law*, **13**(3), 651–9.

Human Rights Council (2011), 'Guiding principles on human rights impact assessments of trade and investment agreements', in *Report of the Special Rapporteur on the Right to Food* (Olivier De Schutter), A/HRC/19/59/Add.5.

Hunt, Paul and Gillian MacNaughton (2006), *Impact Assessments, Poverty and Human Rights: A Case Study Using the Right to the Highest Attainable Standard of Health*, Paris: UNESCO, available at http://www.who.int/hhr/Series_6_Impact%20Assessments_Hunt_MacNaughton1.pdf (accessed on 20 December 2009).

International Centre for Trade and Sustainable Development [ICTSD] (2007), 'Canada issues compulsory licence for HIV/AIDS drug export to Rwanda, in first test of WTO procedure', *Bridges Weekly Trade News Digest*, **11**(32), available at http://ictsd.org/i/news/bridgesweekly/6556/ (accessed on 20 December 2009).

Koskenniemi, Marti (2002), 'Fragmentation of international law? Postmodern anxieties', *Leiden Journal of International Law*, **15**(3), 553–79.

Koskenniemi, Marti (2009), 'The politics of international law – 20 years later', *European Journal of International Law*, **20**(1), 7–19.

Krikorian, Gaëlle and Dorota Szymkowiak (2007), 'Intellectual property rights in the making: The evolution of intellectual property provisions in US free trade agreements and access to medicine', *Journal of World Intellectual Property*, **10**(5), 388–418.

Lamy, Pascal (2003), *WTO Ministerial Conference (Cancun), Fifth Session*, 10 September, WT/MIN(03)/ST/5.

Lang, Andrew (2007), 'Re-thinking trade and human rights', *Tulane Journal of International and Comparative Law*, **15**(2), 335–414.

Médecins Sans Frontières (2006), 'Neither expeditious, nor a solution: The WTO 30 August decision is unworkable', available at http://www.msfaccess.org/resources/key-publications/key-publication-detail/index.html%3Ftx_ttnews%5Btt_news%5D=1256&cHash=e4416914cf (accessed on 20 December 2009).

Office of the High Commissioner for Human Rights [OHCHR] (2001), *The Impact of the Agreement on Trade-Related Aspects of Intellectual Property Rights on Human Rights, Report of the High Commissioner*, 27 June, E/CN.4/Sub.2/2001/13.

Osewe, Patrick L., Yvonne K. Nkrumah and Emmanuel K. Sackey (2008), *Improving Access to HIV/AIDS Medicines in Africa*, Washington: The World Bank.

Oxfam (2006), *Patents Versus Patents: Five Years after the Doha Declaration, Oxfam Briefing Paper 95*, available at http://www.oxfam.org.uk/what_we_do/issues/health/downloads/bp95_patents.pdf (accessed on 20 December 2009).

Pan American Health Organization (2004), *Modelo prospectivo del impacto de la propriedad intelectual sobre el acceso de medicamentos en Colombia*, report on file with author.

Pan American Health Organization (2005), *Impacto de fortalecer las medidas de Propriedad Intellectual como consequencia de la negociacion de un Tratado de Libre Comercio con los Estados Unidos*, report on file with author.

Proposal by the African Group (2001) (Bangladesh, Barbados, Bolivia, Brazil, Cuba, Dominican Republic, Ecuador, Haiti, Honduras, India, Indonesia, Jamaica, Pakistan, Paraguay, Philippines, Peru, Sri Lanka, Thailand and Venezuela), 4 October, IP/C/W/312, WT/GC/W/450.

Scott, Craig and Robert Wai (2004), 'Transnational governance of corporate conduct through the migration of human rights norms: The potential contribution of transnational "Private" Litigation', in Christian Joerges, Inger-Johanne Sand and Gunther Teubner (eds), *Transnational Governance and Constitutionalism*, Oxford: Hart Publishing, pp. 287–320.

Sekalala, Sharifah (2010), 'Third world access to essential medicines and the WTO General Council Decision 2003,' *Kings Law Journal*, **21**(1), 172–92.

Sell, Susan K. (2007), 'TRIPs-plus free trade agreements and access to medicines', *Liverpool Law Review*, **28**(1), 41–75.

Sleap, Bridget (2004), 'The most debilitating discrimination of all: Civil society's campaign for access to treatment for AIDS', in Paul Gready (ed.), *Fighting for Human Rights*, London: Routledge, pp. 153–73.

Sun, Haochen (2004), 'The road to Doha and beyond: Some reflections on the TRIPs Agreement and public health', *European Journal of International Law*, **15**(1), 123–50.

Thailand National Human Rights Commission [TNHRC] (2006), *Report on Results of Examination of Human Rights Violations*, report on file with author.

UN Special Rapporteur (2004), *Addendum, Mission to the World Trade Organisation*, 1 March (E/CN.4/2004/49/Add.1).

UN Special Rapporteur (2005), *Mission to Peru,* 4 February (E/CN.4/2005/51/Add.3).

Walker, Simon (2009), *The Future of Human Rights Impact Assessments of Trade Agreements*, Utrecht: Intersentia.

Williams, Andrew (2007), 'Human rights and law: Between sufferance and insufferability', *Law Quarterly Review,* **123**(Jan), 132–57.

World Trade Organization [WTO] (2001), *Brazil – Measures Affecting Patent Production*, Request for the Establishment of a Panel by the United States, WT/DS199/3, 9 January.

WTO (2003), *Intellectual Property Decision Removes Final Patent Obstacle to Cheap Drug Imports*, WTO Press Release, 30 August, Press/350.

WTO (2004), *The Future of the WTO: Addressing Institutional Challenges in the New Millennium: Report by the Consultative Board to the Director-General Supachai Panitchpakdi*, Geneva: World Trade Organisation.

WTO Council for Trade-Related Aspects of Intellectual Property Rights (2010), *Annual Review of the Decision of the Implementation of Paragraph 6 of the Doha Declaration on the TRIPS Agreement and Public Health*, IP/C/57.

6. Re-visiting the patents and access to medicines dichotomy: An evaluation of TRIPs implementation and public health safeguards in developing countries

Tahir Amin

1. INTRODUCTION

One of the key concerns surrounding the Agreement on Trade-Related Aspects of Intellectual Property Rights (TRIPs) was its potential impact on access to medicines (Correa, 2000, p. 35). Many developing and least-developed countries were required, for the first time, to implement a minimum level of patent protection for pharmaceutical chemical products. India, with the second highest HIV population globally and recognized as the pipeline of affordable generic drugs for the developing world, was confronted with numerous implementation challenges (Chaudhuri, 2005). Brazil and Thailand, which had invested heavily in their universal antiretroviral (ARV) access programmes for HIV/AIDS patients, faced rising costs of drug prices as patents came into play (Ford, Wilson, Chaves, Lotrowska and Kijtiwatchakul, 2007, pp. S21–9).

As a result, a vast amount of literature and public health commentary suggested how developing and least-developed countries could use the flexibilities within TRIPs to ensure patents not make medicines unaffordable (Musungu and Oh, 2005). However, pressure from developed countries, combined with a lack of political will or understanding of the issues in developing countries, has resulted in difficulties for many countries seeking to implement such flexibilities. Yet, despite these difficulties, there have been successes in developing countries implementing safeguards within their patent laws, which have subsequently been used to ensure continued access to affordable medicines.

The purpose of this chapter is to provide a comparative review and evaluation of the manner in which a selection of developing countries chose to implement TRIPs into their patent laws and how these policies straddle the patents and access to medicines dichotomy. The countries that form the basis of this study were selected based on the author's experience of working with international and local organizations on the respective local patent laws.

The chapter first provides a brief background on how the selected developing countries timed their implementation of pharmaceutical product patent protection in light of the transitional periods available under TRIPs. It then compares how these developing countries implemented their pharmaceutical product patent laws under TRIPs, with particular attention on India. Three key areas which potentially allow the most flexibility and strongest possible safeguards for public health needs within the boundaries of TRIPs – scope of patentability; opposition, observation, or revocation procedures to challenge patents pre-grant and post-grant; and compulsory or government use licensing – form the focus of the discussion.

After examining the *de jure* implementation of patent laws in these countries, attention is turned to how these new patent regimes are playing out *de facto*. Using case studies and actual evidence from the author's experience of ARV drug patenting in India, conclusions are drawn on the effectiveness of the legal safeguards used. The final section concludes by evaluating the implementation of TRIPs flexibilities and offering preliminary suggestions on how to build on some of the safeguards to ensure not only access to medicines, but also the improvement of patent quality and innovation in the pharmaceutical sector (Burke and Reitzig, 2007).[1]

2. BACKGROUND TO TRIPS IMPLEMENTATION

TRIPs came into force on 1 January 1995. Under Articles 65 and 66 of the Agreement, developing and least-developed countries were permitted transition periods within which to fully implement the minimum level of protection required for all intellectual property rights. Developing countries that did not yet provide product patent protection for pharmaceutical chemicals had until 1 January 2005 to do so.[2]

Although this transition period was available, developed countries had already been working hard to pressure developing countries to fully implement TRIPs standards sooner. Table 6.1 provides the year countries selected for this study implemented protection for pharmaceutical patents.

Table 6.1 *Year of implementation by developing countries of pharmaceutical product patent protection under the TRIPs transitional period*

Country	Year of implementing pharmaceutical patent protection under TRIPs
Mexico	1991
Thailand	1992
Brazil	1997
Philippines	1998
India	2005

Of all the developing countries that were members of the World Trade Organization (WTO) at the time TRIPs was signed, India waited until 1 January 2005 to commence examination and granting of pharmaceutical product patents. This delay was the result of a combination of factors, including internal disagreements between the coalition parties supporting the ruling government, a deliberate stalling tactic and active lobbying by a strong local generic pharmaceutical industry and civil society groups (Basheer, 2005). As will become apparent in the next section, whatever the reasons for the full use of the transitional period, India was able to use the delay to implement what could be considered some of the strongest safeguards to ensure that access to medicines would not be passed over for the sake of patents.

On the other side of the spectrum, in advance of the coming into force of the North American Free Trade Agreement (NAFTA) and TRIPs, Mexico shored up its patent laws to protect pharmaceutical chemical products in 1991. Thailand, under pressure from US trade sanctions, implemented protection for pharmaceuticals in 1992. Brazil, despite strong civil society and domestic industry resistance, succumbed to pressure from developed countries and introduced pharmaceutical patent protection from 1997 (Shadlen, 2009a). Notably, Brazil went TRIPs-plus by agreeing to allow 'pipeline' protection for patents on inventions that existed prior to the coming into force of TRIPs, provided such products were not already on the market (Brazilian Industrial Property Law, art. 230). The Philippines also implemented pharmaceutical product patents well before the end of the transition period. However, as prices on medicines soared in the Philippines to become some of the most expensive in Southeast Asia, the country 'rolled back' its TRIPs-plus patent laws to implement flexibilities to safeguard public health needs (World Health Organization and Health Action International, 2005).

With the exception of India, this small sample set of developing countries indicates the larger general trend that many developing countries failed to make full use of the transitional period for implementing pharmaceutical patent protection (Oliveira, Bermudez, Chaves and Velasquez, 2004).

3. DE JURE AND DE FACTO COMPARISON OF TRIPS IMPLEMENTATION AND PUBLIC HEATH SAFEGUARDS

This section reviews how selected countries implemented three key areas of TRIPs. The key areas are (1) scope of patentability, (2) opposition, observation, or revocation mechanisms, and (3) compulsory or government use licenses. These specific areas are selected as they potentially offer the strongest possible safeguards for public health needs within the boundaries of TRIPs. For each of these areas a brief comparison and analysis of the various provisions inserted into national patent legislation is provided. The chapter then turns to how each of these provisions is playing out post-implementation. In particular, it focuses on the author's experience of working with provisions in India's patent law and how they are being used to ensure access to medicines.

3.1 Scope of Patentability

Article 27.1 of TRIPs states that patents, subject to some exceptions, 'shall be made available for any inventions, whether product or processes, in all fields of technology, provided they are new, involve an inventive step [are non-obvious] and are capable of industrial application [utility]'. Included in the provision is the requirement that patents shall be made available without discrimination as to the field of technology.[3] This requirement ensures that pharmaceutical chemical products cannot be discriminated against and are entitled to patent protection under TRIPs.

One contentious issue is how countries interpret what an invention is without discriminating against a particular field. TRIPs does not provide a definition of the term 'invention'. A significant amount of literature exists arguing that developing countries are entitled to define 'invention' according to their particular social and economic needs (UNCTAD and

ICTSD, 2005, pp. 357–8). Indeed, given the marked levels of innovation within the pharmaceutical field, ranging from entirely new chemical compounds to low-hanging fruits such as polymorphs[4] and new dosage forms, there is undoubtedly scope within TRIPs for countries to define what the patentability criteria for such inventions should be.

Table 6.2 shows how the developing countries selected for this study chose to define invention and scope of patentability within their legislation. It is worth stating here that legislative provisions do not always determine what types of pharmaceutical chemical inventions will be permitted, as this is usually developed through implementing rules, national case law and patent office guidelines. Nevertheless, statutes do give an indication of how certain inventions will be perceived. More importantly, as will be discussed in the next section, the scope of patentability set out in legislative provisions can be a substantial aid to actors seeking to formally oppose patents. Provisions that help provide some definition of what constitutes an invention can also help national courts and patent offices determine their policies.

A comparison of the various provisions listed in Table 6.2 demonstrates India's progressive steps for defining what an invention is in the now universally famous Section 3(d) of the Indian Patents Act (Act). By importing a drug regulatory standard known as 'efficacy', India was determined to ensure that the common industry practice of secondary or follow-on patents (often termed 'evergreening') to extend patent life on existing drugs would not be permitted without there being a marked improvement in such products.

Unfortunately, the Act, which implements rules through a patent office practice manual for examiners, fails to provide any guidelines on how the term 'efficacy' should be defined.[5] It was for this reason that the Swiss pharmaceutical company Novartis brought a case against the Indian government. Novartis challenged the constitutional validity and lack of TRIPs compliance of the provision after its patent application for the drug Glivec had been refused for its failure to meet the efficacy standard.[6] The High Court of Madras not only dismissed Novartis' claims that the provision breached India's constitution for being arbitrary and vague, but also held that any grievance with respect to TRIPs compliance should be taken to the WTO Dispute Settlement Body. More significantly, the court held it was quite clear from the pharmaceutical industry's use of the term efficacy that it relates to the ability of a drug to produce the desired therapeutic effect. While this statement is technically *obiter dicta*, as will be seen in the following section, the various branches of the Indian patent office are now applying this definition. As a result, a number of follow-on patents that could potentially block more affordable generic medicines may not be granted.

Although there appear to be immediate positive effects from India's decision to implement a restricted scope of patentability, it remains to be seen how Section 3(d) will be applied in the future for new drug patents. The definition of efficacy as mentioned in the *Novartis* case may work for drugs relying on mailbox applications that were filed between 1995 and 2005.[7] This is because clinical data for such drugs are likely to be available to demonstrate whether there is an enhancement of efficacy over an existing form. Such an outcome may not be possible for follow-on patents of more recent new drug compounds, as clinical data are usually not available until 5–8 years after a patent application is filed.

Notably, the Philippines has also adopted a virtually identical provision to Section 3(d) of the Indian Patents Act. What is significant about the Philippines' decision to adopt such a provision is that it tightened the scope of patentability from the initial provision implemented under TRIPs, which permitted 'any technical solution and improvement'.

At the time of this writing, the Philippines is finalizing its implementing rules. It remains to be seen whether the Philippines defines efficacy in the same manner that is emerging in Indian case law. Other developing countries in Southeast Asia have also considered a similar provision (Prasad, 2007).

In comparison to India and the Philippines, Brazil's patent law defines an invention broadly to include 'any object of practical use … that involves an inventive act that results in a functional improvement in its use or manufacture'. Coupled with offering pipeline protection for pre-1995 patent inventions that were not mandated in TRIPs, on paper it seems Brazil has not utilized the flexibilities available in this area. Indeed, of the reported 1,182 pipeline patent applications filed it is believed that over 700 have been granted to date. These include key ARVs such as abacavir, amprenavir, atazanavir, efavirenz, ritonavir and lopinavir.[8] Reports also suggest that the Brazilian patent office, Instituto Nacional da Propriedade Industrial (INPI), has drafted guidelines that will permit patents on polymorphs and new uses of known drugs (Working Group on Intellectual Property of the Brazilian Network for the Integration of Peoples, 2008). By allowing such patents, Brazil's health budget, in particular its free ARV programme, could be stretched even more. Indeed, Brazil already pays significantly more for many of its ARVs than India and other developing countries (Ford, Wilson, Chaves, Lotrowska and Kijtiwatchakul, 2007, p. S28; Working Group on Intellectual Property of the Brazilian Network for the Integration of Peoples, 2008).

Table 6.2 Scope of patentability defined in patent laws

Mexico	Article 15 – Any human creation that allows matter or energy existing in nature to be transformed for use by man for the satisfaction of his specific needs shall be considered an invention. Article 16 – Inventions that are new, the result of inventive step and industrially applicable shall be patentable. Article 19 – Juxtaposition of known inventions or mixtures of known products, or alteration of the use, form, dimensions or materials thereof, except where in reality they are so combined or merged that they cannot function separately or where their particular qualities or functions have been so modified as to produce an industrial result or use not obvious to a person skilled in the art (Mexican Industrial Property Law, 1991).
Brazil	Article 8 – To be patentable an invention must meet the requirements of novelty, inventive activity and industrial application. Article 9 – An object of practical use, or part thereof, that involves an inventive act that results in a functional improvement in its use or manufacture. Article 10 – Discoveries, therapeutic or diagnostic methods for human use are not patentable (Brazilian Industrial Property Law, 1996).
India	Section 2(1)(ja) – Inventive step means a feature of an invention that involves a technical advance as compared to existing knowledge or having economic significance or both and that makes the invention not obvious to a person skilled in the art. Section 3(d) – The following are not inventions within the meaning of this Act – the mere discovery of a new form of a known substance which does not result in the enhancement of the known efficacy of that substance or the mere discovery of any new property or new use for a known substance or the mere use of a known process, machine or apparatus unless such known process results in a new product or employs at least one new reactant. *Explanation* – For the purposes of this clause, salts, esters, ethers, polymorphs, metabolites, pure form, particle size, isomers, mixtures of isomers, complexes, combinations and other derivatives of known substance shall be considered to be the same substance, unless they differ significantly in properties with regard to efficacy (Indian Patents Act, amended 2005).

Philippines	Section 22 – The following shall be excluded from patent protection – discoveries, scientific theories and mathematical methods and in the case of drugs and medicines the mere discovery of a new form or property of a known substance which does not result in the enhancement of the known efficacy of that substance, or the mere discovery of any new property or new use for a known substance or the mere use of a known process, unless such known process results in a new product or employs at least one new reactant. *Explanation* – For the purposes of this clause, salts, esters, ethers, polymorphs, metabolites, pure form, particle size, isomers, mixtures of isomers, complexes, combinations and other derivatives of a known substance shall be considered to be the same substance, unless they differ significantly in properties with regard to efficacy (Philippines Universally Accessible Cheaper and Quality Medicines Act, 2008).
Thailand	Section 3 – Invention means any innovation or invention which creates a new product or process, or any improvement of a known product or process. Sections 5 – A patent may be granted only for an invention, which is new, involves an inventive step and is capable of industrial application. Section 9 – The following inventions are not protected by this Act – methods of diagnosis, treatment or cure of humans (Thailand Patent Act, amended 1999).

There does appear to be some saving grace for Brazil. A few years ago, INPI refused to grant a patent on the much-needed ARV tenofovir disoproxil fumarate (Amin, 2009). Tenofovir disoproxil fumarate is a salt of the known compound tenofovir disoproxil and falls into a category termed 'selection patents'. Such patents are commonly granted in many countries. If INPI maintains its refusal, Brazil could see a more restricted scope of patentability and potentially save its free ARV programme millions of dollars.

Another important safeguard that was built into Brazil's patent law was the ability of its health regulatory body, Agência Nacional de Vigilância Sanitária (ANVISA), to make the final decision, also known as 'prior consent', on the grant of pharmaceutical patents (Basso, 2005). The controversial role of ANVISA in pharmaceutical patent determinations was arguably incorporated into law to curtail the abuse of the pipeline protection provision. This was a logical step as health agencies are uniquely positioned to assess if a pharmaceutical product had been marketed in Brazil. However, despite this being a strong safeguard in theory, disagreement between the INPI and ANVISA resulted in severe delays in patent decisions being issued. The result was that a number of generic companies were allegedly unwilling to enter the market due to the uncertainty over infringement if patents were eventually granted (Chaves, 2007; Shadlen, 2009b). Also notable was the grant of a number of pipeline patents, raising a question over ANVISA's effectiveness. Indeed, the political battle for the control of who examines pharmaceutical patents in Brazil resulted in an opinion of the Federal Counsel-General's Office (Advocacia-Geral da União), stating that ANVISA should no longer be able to examine the patentability criteria of a pharmaceutical patent application. While this opinion has yet to officially become law, ANVISA has stopped examining pharmaceutical patent applications, thus signalling the end of Brazil's use of this particular flexibility (Shadlen, 2011).

In contrast, Mexico has a very generous scope of patentability and fails to take into account any of the flexibilities within TRIPs. This may be attributed to the fact that Mexico is a signatory of NAFTA, albeit its patent law contains other provisions that may be considered to go beyond what is required under that Agreement (Mexican Industrial Property Law, 1991). As a result, many ARVs are patented in Mexico, which has arguably resulted in some of the highest prices in Latin America.

Should Section 3(d) of the Indian Patents Act serve public health needs, a number of countries could follow suit. This will also depend on how India's domestic pharmaceutical industry shapes up in the future. As more Indian companies are acquired, enter into agreements with transnational companies or pursue a R&D model, pressure from within India may emerge to change the law. For the short-term foreseeable future this is not likely to occur as public health issues continue to occupy the centre stage.

3.2 Oppositions, Observation and Revocation Procedures

TRIPs does not discuss the ability of countries to install pre-grant and post-grant opposition procedures within its patent laws. The patent systems in many developed countries, including the United Kingdom, and the European Patent Office permit third parties to: (a) file observations against the grant of a patent or (b) be party to a post-grant opposition or revocation action (UK Patents Act, 1977, ss 21, 72; European Patent Convention, 2000, arts 99, 115). Australia is one of the few developed countries that have a fully functioning pre-grant opposition procedure, whereby any person can challenge the grant of a patent on patentability grounds (Australian Patents Act, amended 1994, s 59). A number of developing countries have used the silence in TRIPs to install provisions that allow third parties to file observations or oppositions against the granting of a patent. These countries include Argentina, Indonesia, Pakistan and Vietnam.

Of the countries discussed in this chapter, only Mexico at the time of this writing does not have a mechanism for third parties to file pre-grant observations or oppositions (see Table 6.3). Presently, India has the most robust pre-grant opposition procedure. This is because of the various legal grounds available for opposing a patent and the unprecedented involvement of civil society groups utilizing the process. As of this writing, civil society groups have filed 15 pre-grant and two post-grant oppositions. It is estimated that out of almost 9,000 pharmaceutical patent applications that were in the mailbox, 200 (2 per cent) have been opposed (PhRMA, 2009, p. 57). This figure appears to confound theories put forward by industry that such procedures are being used in an abusive manner (PhRMA, 2009, p. 57).

The success of the opposition mechanism in India, in particular pre-grant opposition, has been aided by the availability of Section 3(d) of the Patents Act discussed above. For example, Boehringer Ingleheim's patent application for the paediatric drug nevirapine-hemihydrate claimed a storage benefit as a result of the new particle size stability for the known compound nevirapine. Following a pre-grant opposition by patient groups, the Delhi patent office found that storage benefit did not equate to a therapeutic benefit and, therefore, did not meet the efficacy standard (Amin, 2008b).

In other cases, applicants have withdrawn their applications following pre-grant oppositions. GlaxoSmithKline (GSK) withdrew the patent for the ARV abacavir, which allows Indian generic companies to continue manufacturing the drug for developing countries for a price around US$330 per patient per year (Amin, 2007). In anticipation of increased generic competition, GSK announced after the withdrawal of its application a 31 per cent price reduction for abacavir in developing countries (Alcorn, 2008). In Mexico, where abacavir is currently patented, the drug costs around US$2,600 per patient per year.[9] This story repeats itself for a number of other ARVs that are patented in Mexico and other Latin American countries.

Pre-grant oppositions have also been successful in extracting voluntary licenses from patent applicants in India. Gilead Sciences' two patent applications for tenofovir disoproxil and tenofovir disoproxil fumarate were both opposed before grant by patient groups and local generic companies. Within one week of the filing of the oppositions and before the issue of any decision, Gilead took the unprecedented step of issuing 11 voluntary licences to Indian generic manufacturers at a low royalty rate of 5 per cent. The result of this move meant that the price of the drug would be available in developing countries, including India, at US$207 per patient per year as opposed to a previous price of US$475. It should be noted here that the voluntary licences granted are still restrictive in that they block licensees supplying a number of developing countries, including Argentina, Brazil and China (I-MAK, 2006). Despite the issuing of the licenses, the patent applications were refused and are now under appeal. With competition from other manufacturers, it is expected the price of the drug will decrease further.

Despite the overall success of the pre-grant opposition mechanism, a number of newer ARV products have been granted patents. One of the reasons for this is the lack of transparency at the Indian patent office, as much of the information has only been recently made available in electronic form. Previously, the full specification and claims of the patents were not available online, making it difficult for potential opponents to find the correct application to oppose. It remains to be seen if patient groups and/or generic producers will file post-grant oppositions or revocation actions against these patents. This will likely depend on whether there are valid grounds to oppose. It will also depend on whether the World Health Organization recommends these new ARVs for national treatment programmes.

Oppositions or observations against patent applications have not been filed in abundance in Brazil, the Philippines and Thailand. Although there is a strong civil society in these countries, the specialized skill set and resources required to participate in such proceedings has made it difficult. Nevertheless, local groups in these countries are gearing up to take on the challenge of participating in the patent system.

The installation of pre-grant opposition procedures into patent law has several benefits. Removing patents that do not meet patentability requirements, or are excessively broad in scope, can allow for prices of drugs to become more affordable, and such procedures can encourage public participation in the patent system. Encouraging a more democratic patent system can also help to address information asymmetry, a significant problem in developing countries.

3.3 Compulsory Licensing and Government Use

Public health advocates have pushed hard for the use of compulsory licences in developing and least-developed countries since TRIPs was introduced. Paragraphs 5 and 6 of the Doha Declaration confirmed the availability of compulsory licensing as a flexibility within TRIPs. Paragraph 6 of the Doha Declaration was implemented by adding the proposed Article 31*bis* of TRIPs, which, if adopted, will ensure that members could export to other members with insufficient or no manufacturing capability of pharmaceutical products.

Table 6.3 Opposition, observation and revocation provisions

Mexico	Article 78 permits the invalidation action to be filed within five years of grant of a patent. The grounds for invalidation include a violation of the patentability criteria (Mexican Industrial Property Law, 1991).
Brazil	Article 31 permits interested third parties to submit documents and information to aid examination. Documents can be submitted between publication of the application and termination of the application. Article 51 allows an administrative nullity action to be filed by the patent office or any person having legitimate interest within six months of the date of grant of the patent. Article 56 allows a nullity action to be filed at any time during the term of a patent by the patent office or any legitimately interested party (Brazilian Industrial Property Law, 1996).
India	Section 25(1) – On publication of an application any person may file a representation of opposition against the grant of the patent. The grounds for opposition include that the invention: • lacks novelty; • lacks inventive step; • is not patentable under the Act; • does not sufficiently describe the invention or method by which it is to be performed; or • the applicant has failed to disclose information relating to the examination of the same or substantially similar application in another country. Section 25(2) – permits any interested person to file an opposition after the grant of a patent. The opposition must be filed within one year from the date of publication of grant of the patent. The grounds are the same as for pre-grant opposition. Section 64 – Any interested person, the Central Government or a party counter-claiming in an infringement action may file to revoke a granted patent (Indian Patents Act, amended 2005).
Philippines	Section 47 permits observations by any person in writing following publication of an application. Section 61 – [A]ny interested person may petition to cancel a patent on the grounds that the invention is not new, patentable or has insufficient disclosure (Philippines Intellectual Property Code, 1997).
Thailand	Section 31 permits an opposition to be filed before grant of an application on the grounds of lack of novelty, inventive step or the invention is not patentable under law. Section 54 allows any person to invalidate a granted patent on the grounds of a lack of novelty or inventive step or that the invention is not patentable under law (Thailand Patent Act, amended 1999).

Most developing countries have inserted some form of compulsory licensing into their laws (Musungu and Oh, 2005, pp. 31–2). Of the countries reviewed in this chapter (see Table 6.4), India and the Philippines have the most wide-ranging provisions for compulsory licensing or public non-commercial use (government use). Indeed, as part of its rolling back of intellectual property rights, the Philippines enacted compulsory licence provisions that virtually mirror India's. These include the right to issue compulsory licences where the public demand is not being met, the patented product is unreasonably priced or there is anti-competitive behaviour by the patentee.

India has what may be considered the most unique licensing provision in any patent legislation. Section 11(A)(7) enables enterprises that have invested in, produced and marketed a product that was filed as a mailbox application (during 1995–2005) to continue to do so. The patentee will not be entitled to enforce its patent rights, but only to receive reasonable royalty. This provision has yet to be contested. The reason for this is a number of the products that were in the mailbox and which Indian companies had been producing and marketing have been refused or have yet to be granted a patent.

At the time of writing, neither India nor the Philippines have issued a compulsory licence to date under their new laws. Where patents have been granted in India on key drugs, the Government of India has to date left it to the market, the patent office or the judiciary to decide on the outcome of access to affordable medicines.

The Indian generic manufacturer Natco Pharma Ltd attempted to utilize Section 92A of the Act to export the cancer drugs erlotinib and sunitinib to Nepal on the grounds of public health needs, as permitted under Paragraph 6 of the Doha Declaration. Although Section 92A of the Act does not expressly require the patent holder to be heard in such proceedings, the Delhi patent office held that in the interest of the principles of natural justice this was necessary.[10] This decision, alongside arguments that Nepal had failed to notify the TRIPs Council of its decision to import the drug and what the public health need was, caused Natco to withdraw its request (Unnikrishnan, 2008). To date, the difficulties in the practical implementation of Paragraph 6-type Doha compulsory licences has rendered this flexibility virtually void (Gupta, 2008; Médecins Sans Frontières, 2006).

Taking a more aggressive approach, the generic producer Cipla has proceeded to manufacture and market generic versions of the patented drugs erlotinib and the anti-infection drug valganciclovir (Mathew, 2008). In the interim hearing for infringement and revocation of the erlotinib patent, the Delhi High Court invoked a 'public interest' standard with respect to the pricing of the patented good when determining whether to grant the patent holder an interlocutory injunction (Amin, 2008a). On appeal, the decision of the High Court to refuse the interim injunction on the grounds of 'public interest' was subsequently upheld by the Supreme Court (Basheer, 2009). This matter is now in full trial and patent holders, patient groups and the Government will be watching events closely to see whether the judiciary will effectively be creating 'judge made compulsory licensing' (Basheer, 2008).

Despite the fact that most countries have some form of compulsory licensing, the mechanism requires strong political will due to the threat of trade sanctions or other economic threats by developed countries (Frenquest, 2008). As a result, only a handful of developing countries have invoked compulsory licensing to improve access to medicines (Musungu and Oh, 2005, pp. 37–46). Brazil and Thailand are two countries that have traversed this path.

Thailand's National Health Security Act 2002 aims to provide its citizens with universal access to essential medicines under one of three national public health insurance schemes. Rising costs of medicines and the inability to secure universal access compelled Thailand in 2006–2007 to issue three licences for public non-commercial use of the drugs efavirenz, lopinavir/ritonavir and clopidogrel.

Although public non-commercial use for public health needs by governments does not require prior negotiation with the patent holder under TRIPs, the Thai government attempted to negotiate favourable pricing with patent holders between 2004 and 2006 (Ministry of Public Health and the National Health Security Office of Thailand, 2007, p. 5). As negotiations were slow moving, the Thai government proceeded to issue 'government use' licences, providing a royalty of between 0.5 and 2 per cent of the sale value of the products licensed. On the drug efavirenz alone, generic versions of the drug cost half the price of the patented product, resulting in an estimated 20,000 new patients having access to the drug (Ministry of Public Health and the National Health Security Office of Thailand, 2007, p. 13). Since issuing the licence, the patent holder on efavirenz, Merck, has offered a more favourable price, closer to that of the generic version.

Brazil has on several occasions threatened the use of compulsory licences on ARVs to obtain price reductions from patent holders (International Centre for Trade and Sustainable Development, 2007). When Merck failed to agree on a price that matched the price that Thailand was paying for the generic version of efavirenz, Brazil followed Thailand by issuing a compulsory licence (ICTSD, 2007). Like Thailand, Brazil had previously attempted to negotiate a fairer price with Merck for two years, despite there being no requirement to do so under TRIPs.

Table 6.4 Compulsory and government use licensing provisions

Mexico	Article 70 – Any person may apply for a grant of a compulsory licence to use an invention which has not been used, unless there are justified reasons for such non-use. Requests can be made three years from the date of the grant of the patent. A compulsory licence will not be granted when the patent owner or its licensee has been importing the patented product or a patent obtained using the patented process.
	Article 72 – Prior to granting the first compulsory licence, the patent owner will be given the opportunity to make use of the patent within a one year period from the date of notification.
	Article 77 – For reasons of national emergency or security, including the outbreak of serious diseases declared as requiring priority by the General Health Council, the use of certain patents may be made by the means of the grant of licences of public utility in cases where, if such use were not made, the production, supply or distribution to the public of staple goods and services or medicines would be prevented, hindered or made more expensive (Mexican Industrial Property Law, 1991).
Brazil	Article 68 – Permits compulsory licence where: patentee is using the patent in an abusive manner, including abuse of economic power, for non-exploitation or lack of manufacture of the subject matter of the patent in Brazil, except where it is not economically viable then importation is permitted, and where commercialization does not meet market needs.
	Article 71 – In cases of national emergency or public interest where the patentee is not meeting the necessity (Brazilian Industrial Property Law, 1996).
India	Section 11(A)(7) – With respect to mailbox patents that are granted, enterprises that have made a significant investment, were producing and marketing the patented product can continue to do so and patentee will only be entitled to a reasonable royalty. No infringement proceedings will be permitted.
	Section 84 – Permits compulsory licence where reasonable requirements of the public not met, the invention is not available at a reasonable price, it is not being worked in the territory of India or there are anti-competitive grounds.
	Section 92 & 92A – Permits compulsory license in national or extreme emergencies or for public non-commercial use including for public health crises relating to AIDS, TB, malaria and other epidemics. Allows compulsory licences for export to any country with insufficient or no manufacturing capacity to address public health problems, provided a compulsory licence has been granted by such country or such country has provided notification to allow importation.
	Section 100 – Permits the Government at any time after an application has been filed to use an invention in exchange for adequate remuneration (Indian Patents Act, amended 2005).

Philippines	Section 74 – Permits exploitation by the Government or third party authorized by the Government without the patent owners agreement where: there is a public interest need, the patent holder has acted in an anti-competitive manner, demand is not being met and on reasonable terms as determined by the Department of Health, or there is a national or extreme emergency or reasons for public non-commercial use. Section 93 – Provides for compulsory licences on the same grounds as above. Section 93A – Provides for a special compulsory licence where on the recommendation of the Department of Health there will be permission to import patented drugs and medicines for domestic consumption provided adequate remuneration shall be paid to the patentee. Section 93A2 – Allows for a compulsory licence for the manufacture and export of drugs to any country having no or insufficient capacity to address public health problems (Philippines Universally Accessible Cheaper and Quality Medicines Act, 2008).
Thailand	Section 46 – Compulsory licences are available where the patentee fails to produce the patented product or process in the country without a legitimate reason or where the patented product is sold at unreasonably high prices or does not meet public demand. Section 52 – Permits the Government to exercise any right under a patent during an emergency. A fair remuneration will be paid to the patentee (Thailand Patent Act, amended 1999).

The use of compulsory licensing is still rare in the public health arena. This is despite the opinion of some commentators that the Doha Declaration gives countries the flexibility to determine what amounts to public health crises (Correa, 2002). Yet, the recurring issue with respect to the use of compulsory and government use licences is how to interpret the language of Paragraphs 5 and 6 of the Doha Declaration. By allowing each Member to determine what constitutes public health crises or need, it raises the question of whether diseases that are not considered epidemics or emergencies justify the use of compulsory licences. This was one of the main criticisms levelled by the pharmaceutical industry and developed countries at Thailand for issuing a compulsory licence for the drug clopidogrel, which is used to treat coronary artery disease.

Clearer guidelines couched in public health policy reasoning and not private rights are needed to help assess what constitutes public health crises for the purpose of compulsory licensing. This could include an epidemiological and prevention assessment rather than merely limiting the needs to major outbreaks. The downside to having such guidelines is they could be interpreted rigidly, thereby locking out other genuine public health needs. Until some clarification exists, countries seeking to utilize such flexibilities will continue to be pressured not to use such measures.

4. CONCLUSION

India, with the Philippines in pursuit, has led the charge in maximizing the TRIPs flexibilities available within the areas of patentability, opposition mechanisms and compulsory licensing. While some commentators see India's new patent regime, in particular Section 3(d), as a protectionist instrument that will discourage innovation and investment, others feel that India did not do enough to safeguard access to medicines (Bate 2007; Sridhar and Narrain, 2005).

Early analysis by the author suggests that a number of follow-on patents that would normally fall within the ambit of Section 3(d), or even under the grounds of obviousness, have been granted by the Indian patent office (The Register, 2008). On the other hand, where patents are challenged prior to grant, the patent office examination has been more transparent and rigorous, resulting in their refusal. This ensures legitimate competition in the marketplace, which usually means lower prices and increased access to medicines. These initial decisions suggest that informed participation by third parties during examination of a patent helps to improve patent quality and transparency at under-resourced developing country patent offices. Indeed, the issue of patent quality is not isolated to developing country patent offices and is also affecting the likes of the US Patent and Trademark Office and the European Patent Office (European Commission, Competition Directorate General, 2009; United States Government Accountability Office Report, 2006, pp. 33–5). As the discovery of new chemical entities and blockbuster drugs within the pharmaceutical field declines and industry focuses on lower hanging fruits of drug development and patent protection to protect markets, provisions like Section 3(d) alongside robust public participation mechanisms could help companies focus on more innovative new drugs.

This reasoning does not sit comfortably with everyone. INPI in Brazil believes that as its local pharmaceutical industry capability lies in developing follow-on inventions, a policy that benefits this practice is more feasible for its development agenda. As a result, patents on follow-on inventions, like polymorphs and salts of compounds, but without the heightened requirement of India's efficacy standard, are more likely to be permitted. Interest groups such as the US-India Business Council and Coalition for Healthy India (2009) are also pushing this view and for a withdrawal of Section 3(d) in India. As it stands, Brazil's policy reasoning may make it more difficult to ensure affordable access to medicines and more reliant on the onerous route of compulsory licensing.

It remains to be seen whether India maintains Section 3(d) in its current form. With a decision pending on Novartis's appeal to the Supreme Court concerning its rejected patent application for the drug Glivec, we could yet see another shift where Section 3(d) is more accommodating to incremental type patents. For the moment, the safeguards that India has built in are ensuring that patents must share the stage with public health demands. If provisions like Section 3(d) and pre-grant opposition mechanisms show over time that they improve the quality of patents but do not deter innovation, more countries like the Philippines could follow suit. This policy area will be closely studied going forward, as developing countries continue to grapple with the patents and access to medicines dichotomy.

Acknowledgements

The author would like to acknowledge Priti Radhakrishnan's contribution to the chapter.

NOTES

1. The term patent quality as discussed here covers the technological (economic) quality created by a patent's underlying invention (novelty, inventive step, sufficiency of disclosure and scope of claims to ensure only patents are granted for inventions with sufficient technological quality) and the legal quality created by a patent's reliability as an enforceable property right (the ability of a patent to sustain a legal challenge).
2. Article 65.4 of TRIPs provides: 'To the extent that a developing country Member is obliged by this Agreement to extend product patent protection to areas of technology not so protectable in its territory on the general date of application of this Agreement for that Member, as defined in paragraph 2, it may delay the application of the provisions on product patents of Section 5 of Part II to such areas of technology for an additional period of five years'.
3. See Articles 27(2) and (3) of TRIPs for exclusions from patentability.
4. Polymorphs are the different crystal arrangements of the same chemical composition. Different polymorphs will have different physical properties such as solubility, chemical stability and melting point.
5. The only supporting guidance that exists lies within the explanation that assists in the interpretation of Section 3(d), but which still fails to define efficacy.

6. *Novartis Application 1602/MAS/98* (unreported); *Novartis AG & Anr v Union of India & Othrs* (2007) 4 MLJ 1153.
7. Article 70.8 of TRIPs required countries that did not make available as of the date of entry into force of the Agreement patent protection for pharmaceutical and agricultural chemical products, a means by which applications for patents on such inventions could be filed. Applications filed under this 'mailbox' mechanism would entitle applicants to preserve both the novelty of the invention and the priority of the application as of the relevant filing and priority date.
8. Information provided by Associação Brasileira Interdisciplinar de AIDS (ABIA) at meeting on 'Examination of Pharmaceutical Patents: Arguing from a Public Health Perspective' attended by the author in Rio de Janeiro (18 November 2008).
9. Prices of ARVs available from the National Institute of Public Health Mexico, on file with author.
10. *Application for Compulsory Licence by Natco Pharma Ltd*, Patent No. 209251, Delhi Patent Office (unreported).

BIBLIOGRAPHY

Alcorn, Keith (2008), 'GSK cuts Abacavir price by 31% for developing countries', *Aidsmap*, 20 February, available at http://www.aidsmap.org/en/news/A26DDC35-2514-4C5F-BB01-7F40DD1D829C.asp (accessed 8 September 2010).

Amin, Tahir (2007), 'GSK withdraws its application for Abacavir in India', available at http://www.i-mak.org/i-mak-blog-updates/2007/12/9/gsk-withdraws-its-application-for-abacavir-in-india.html (accessed 8 September 2010).

Amin, Tahir (2008a), 'The battle for Erlotinib – High Court decision raises a number of procedural and practice issues', *I-MAK Blog*, available at http://www.i-mak.org/i-mak-blog-updates/2008/3/26/the-battle-for-erlotinib-high-court-decision-raises-a-number.html (accessed 8 September 2010).

Amin, Tahir (2008b), 'Delhi Patent Office refuses patent on pediatric Aids drug Nevirapine Hemihydrate', available at http://www.i-mak.org/i-mak-blog-updates/2008/6/21/delhi-patent-office-refuses-patent-on-pediatric-aids-drug-ne.html (accessed 8 September 2010).

Amin, Tahir (2009), 'Brazilian Patent Office issues final refusal for Tenofovir, but Gilead files divisional application', available at http://www.i-mak.org/i-mak-blog-updates/2009/7/14/brazilian-patent-office-issues-final-refusal-for-tenofovir-b.html (accessed 8 September 2010).

Australian Patents Act (amended 1994), Patents Act, 1990, No. 83 of 1990, as amended by Patents (World Trade Organization Amendments) Act, 1994, No. 154 of 1994.

Basheer, Shamnad (2005), 'India's tryst with TRIPs: The Patent (Amendment) Act, 2005', *The Indian Journal of Law and Technology*, **1**, 15–46.

Basheer, Shamnad (2008), 'Roche vs Cipla: Public interest imported into Indian jurisprudence', *Spicy IP Blog*, available at http://spicyipindia.blogspot.com/2009/04/roche-vs-cipla-did-judges-construe.html (accessed 8 September 2010).

Basheer, Shamnad (2009), 'Supreme Court dismisses Roche 'Tarceva' petition', *Spicy IP Blog*, available at http://spicyipindia.blogspot.com/2009/08/breaking-news-supreme-court-dismisses.html (accessed 8 September 2010).

Basso, Maristela (2005), 'Preliminary background paper on prior consent for pharmaceutical products by ANVISA in Brazil', available at http://www.wissensgesellschaft.org/themen/publicdomain/priorconsent.pdf.

Bate, Roger (2007), 'India's drug crossroads', *The New York Sun*, 26 January, available at http://www.nysun.com/opinion/indias-drug-crossroads/47445/ (accessed 8 September 2010).

Brazilian Industrial Property Law (1996), Lei N° 9279 de 14 de Maio de 1996 Regula direitos e obrigações relativos à Propiedade Industrial.

Burke, Paul F. and Markus Reitzig (2007), 'Measuring patent assessment quality – Analyzing the degree and kind of (in)consistency in patent offices' decision making', *Research Policy*, **36**,1404–30.

Chaudhuri, Sudip. (2005), *'The WTO and India's Pharmaceutical Industry: Patent Protection TRIPs and Developing Countries'*, New Delhi: Oxford University Press.

Chaves, Gabriela (2007), 'Case study on the use of TRIPs flexibilities in Brazil', available at http://www.utoronto.ca/cphs/China%20Conference/Chaves%20Presentation_Study%20on%20the%20Use%20of%20TRIPS%20Flexibilities%20in%20Brazil.pdf (accessed 8 September 2010).

Correa, Carlos M. (2000), *Intellectual Property Rights, the WTO and Developing Countries*, London: Zed Books.

Correa, Carlos M. (2002), *Implications of the Doha Declaration on the TRIPs Agreement and Public Health*, Geneva: World Health Organization.

European Commission Competition Directorate General (2009), 'Pharmaceutical sector inquiry report', available at http://ec.europa.eu/competition/sectors/pharmaceuticals/inquiry/index.html (accessed 8 September 2010).

European Patent Convention (2000), Convention on the Grant of European Patents, 5 October 1973, as revised by the Act revising Article 63 EPC of 17 December 1991 and the Act revising the EPC of 29 November 2000 and entered into force on 13 December 2007.

Fernquest, Jon (2008), 'US pharmaceutical lobby threatens to hit Thailand', *Economic Business Blog*, available at http://www.readbangkokpost.com/business/pharmaceutical_industry/us_pharmaceutical_lobby_threat.php (accessed 8 September 2010).

Ford, Nathan, David Wilson, Garbiela Costa Chaves, Michel Lotrowska, Kannikar Kijtiwatchakul (2007), 'Sustaining access to antiretroviral therapy in the less-developed world: Lessons from Brazil and Thailand', *AIDS*, **21**(Suppl 4), S21–9.

Gupta, Ekalavya (2008), 'Apotex ships drug under Doha licence', *Managing Intellectual Property*, 24 September, available at http://www.managingip.com/Article/2017247/Apotex-ships-drug-under-Doha-licence.html (accessed 8 September 2010).

I–MAK (2006), 'Analysis of Gilead Sciences voluntary license agreement', available at http://www.i-mak.org/storage/IMAK%20Analysis%20of%20Gileads%20example%20licence%20LPPD%20Advisor.pdf (accessed 8 September 2010).
Indian Patents Act (amended 2005), Indian Patents Act, No. 39 of 1970, as amended by The Patents (Amendment) Act, 2005, No. 15 of 2005.
International Centre for Trade and Sustainable Development [ICTSD] (2007), 'Brazil issues compulsory license for Aids drug', *Bridges Weekly Trade News Digest*, **11**(6), available at http://ictsd.org/i/ip/38960/ (accessed 8 September 2010).
Jurberg, Claudia (2008), 'Brazilian draft law would curb expanded patents on pharmaceuticals', *Intellectual Property Watch*, available at http://www.ip-watch.org/weblog/2008/12/02/brazilian-draft-law-would-limit-expansion-of-pharmaceutical-patents/ (accessed 8 September 2010).
Matthew, Joe C. (2008), 'Roche files two petitions against Cipla copycat drug', *Business Standard*, available at http://www.business-standard.com/india/news/roche-files-two-petitions-against-cipla-copycat-drug/335670/ (accessed 8 September 2010).
Médecins Sans Frontières (2006), 'Neither expeditious, nor a solution: The WTO 30 August decision is unworkable', available at http://www.msfaccess.org/resources/key-publications/key-publication-detail/index.html%3Ftx_ttnews%5Btt_news%5D=1256&cHash=e4416914cf (accessed 8 September 2010).
Mexican Industrial Property Law (1991), Ley de la Propiedad Industrial del 25 de junio de 1991.
Ministry of Public Health and The National Health Security Office of Thailand (2007), 'Facts and evidences on the 10 burning issues related to the government use of patents on three patented essential drugs in Thailand', available at http://www.bilaterals.org/spip.php?article7349 (accessed 8 September 2010).
Musungu, Sisule F. and Cecelia Oh (2005), *The Use of Flexibilities in TRIPs by Developing Countries: Can They Promote Access to Medicines?* Geneva: Commission for Intellectual Property Rights, Innovation and Health.
Oliveira, Maria A., Jorge Bermudez, Gabriela Chaves, German Velasquez (2004), 'Has the implementation of the TRIPs Agreement in Latin America and the Caribbean produced intellectual property legislation that favours public health', *Bulletin of World Health Organization*, **82**(11), 815–21.
Pharmaceutical Research and Manufacturers of America [PhRMA] (2009), 'Special 301 submission to USTR', available at http://www.phrma.org/files/attachments/PhRMA%20Special%20301%20Submission%202009%5B2%5D.pdf (accessed 8 September 2010).
Philippines Intellectual Property Code (1997), Republic Act No. 8293.
Philippines Universally Accessible Cheaper and Quality Medicines Act (2008), Republic Act No. 9502.
Prasad, Girish Chandra (2007), 'Copycats popping patent law pill', *The Economic Times*, 13 August, available at http://economictimes.indiatimes.com/News/News_By_Industry/Healthcare__Biotech/Pharmaceuticals/Copycats_popping_patent_law_pill/articleshow/2276358.cms (accessed 8 September 2010).
Shadlen, Ken (2009a), ' The politics of patents and drugs in Brazil and Mexico: The industrial bases of health policies', *Comparative Politics* **42**(1), 41–58.

Shadlen, Ken (2009b), 'The political contradictions of incremental innovation in late development: Lessons from pharmaceutical patent examination in Brazil', available at http://papers.ssrn.com/sol3/papers.cfm?abstract_id=1449086 (accessed 8 September 2010).
Shadlen, Ken (2011), 'The rise and fall of "prior consent" in Brazil', *The WIPO Journal*, **3**(1), 103–12.
Sridhar, V. and Siddharth Narrain (2005), 'A tempered patents regime', *Frontline*, **22**(8).
Thailand Patent Act (amended 1999), Patent Act, B.E. 2522 (1979), as amended by Patent Act (No. 3), B.E. 2542 (1999).
The Register (2008), 'EPO staff strike over patent quality', available at http://www.theregister.co.uk/2008/09/25/epo_staff_strike/ (accessed 8 September 2010).
UK Patents Act (1977), c. 37, as amended.
United Nations Conference on Trade and Development [UNCTAD] and ICTSD (2005), *Resource Book on TRIPs and Development: An Authoritative and Practical Guide to the TRIPs Agreement*, Cambridge, UK and New York, US: Cambridge University Press.
United States Government Accountability Office (2006), *New Drug Development: Science, Business, Regulatory and Intellectual Property Issues Cited as Hampering Drug Development Efforts*, Washington DC: GAO.
Unnikrishnan, C.H. (2008), 'Natco withdraws plea on making patented cancer drugs', Livemint, 28 September, available at http://www.livemint.com/2008/09/28214903/Natco-withdraws-plea-on-making.html (accessed 8 September 2010).
US-India Business Council and Coalition for Healthy India (2009), 'The value of incremental pharmaceutical innovation: Benefits for Indian patients and Indian business', available at http://dev.ahealthyindia.org/wpcontent/uploads/2010/03/USIBCIncrementalInnovationReportFinal.pdf (accessed 8 September 2010).
Working Group on Intellectual Property of the Brazilian Network for the Integration of Peoples (2008), '*Discussion of Polymorphs pits Ministers and Congress against the Brazilian Patent Office*', press note on file with author.
World Health Organization and Health Action International (2005), *Medicine Prices, Availability, Affordability and Price Components*, Geneva: World Health Organization and Health Action International.

7. Seizure of generic pharmaceuticals in transit based on allegations of patent infringement: A threat to international trade, development and public welfare

Frederick M. Abbott

1. INTRODUCTION

The European Union (EU) amended its border control regulations in 2003 in a way that allegedly signalled permission to EU patent holders to demand seizure of goods in transit through EU ports and airports. The precise intention of the EU Intellectual Property (IP) Border Regulation (Council Regulation 1383/2003, 2003) has been the subject of some controversy among European courts.[1] What has generated intense controversy, however, is the use of the regulation as the basis for seizure of pharmaceutical products alleged to be infringing 'local' patents on their way through European airports (ICTSD, 2009). Although the next steps at the intergovernmental level remain to be determined, the fundamental IP-related issues raised by the seizures are worthy of attention because of their long-term implications for the international economic system, economic development and public welfare.

2. THE PRINCIPLE OF INDEPENDENCE OF PATENTS

Implementation of the EU IP Border Regulation represents a challenge to fundamental ideas about the way the international intellectual property system operates. The Paris Convention on the Protection of Industrial Property incorporates 'independence' of patents as a core principle (Abbott, Cottier and Gurry, 2007; Paris Convention, art. 4*bis*: Patents: Independence of Patents Obtained for the Same Invention in Different

Countries). The principle is framed in terms of protecting national institutions and decision-making against intrusive determinations by foreign authorities. The principle of independence of patents preserves the sovereign authority of states to adopt and implement patent protections as they consider appropriate, within the framework of a general set of rules. Each member of the Paris Convention decides whether to grant or deny patent protection, and that determination is not dependent on decisions of foreign courts or administrative bodies. The principle of 'independence' is corollary to the 'act of state doctrine' in international law pursuant to which the courts in one country do not sit in judgment on the acts of foreign governments taken within their own territory based on considerations of comity and restraint.[2]

The principle of independence is sometimes equated with the 'territorial' nature of the international patent system. The Paris Convention does not prescribe the jurisdictional scope of patents, nor does it prescribe or define 'territoriality'. The scope, extension or limitation of patent jurisdiction is determined by national legislatures and courts within boundaries prescribed by public international law. Traditionally, national legislatures and courts have approached potential extraterritorial application of patent law with considerable caution, recognizing the problems that would arise in attempting to extend local control to economic activity taking place in other countries and fundamentally regulated by foreign legislatures and courts. (The territorial nature of the international patent system is recognized in the WTO Decision of 30 August 2003, at paragraph 6(i), and in the corresponding amendment to the Agreement on Trade-Related Aspects of Intellectual Property Rights (TRIPs Agreement), at the proposed article 31*bis*(3), each expressly referring to the 'territorial nature of … patent rights'.)

In recent years, some national courts have begun to move away from a rigid understanding of the 'territoriality' of patent law. In *NTP v Research in Motion*[3] (the *Blackberry* case), the US Court of Appeals for the Federal Circuit recognized that advances in technology may create situations in which an invention operates through actions carried out in more than one country, and that the issue of infringement within a country may not always be assessed only by examination of actions within that single national territory. A modest extension into extraterritorial application of patent law in this case was grounded in traditional international law concepts of jurisdiction, whereby an act undertaken outside the territorial limits of a state that has a direct and substantial effect within that state may lead its courts to take cognisance of those acts. In cases such as *Blackberry*, the infringement affects most directly and substantially the country where the allegedly infringed patent is held. Following the US Supreme Court decision in *Microsoft v AT&T*,[4] which stressed limitation of patent infringement to the national territory (and cautioned against extraterritorial extension), the Federal Circuit acknowledged a strong presumption against extraterritorial effect in excluding process patents from the scope of a US statutory prohibition on exporting infringement-capable components.[5]

It is an axiom of public international law that sovereign nations exercise exclusive control over activities taking place within their own territory (although international human rights law challenges certain aspects of that axiom) (compare UN Charter, art. 2). The European Union bases its exercise of jurisdiction over pharmaceutical products moving in transit through EU airports on its right as sovereign to control activity taking place within EU (and member state) territory. This extension of jurisdiction is said to be codified in EU customs regulations.[6]

Yet a corollary of the axiom of sovereign control over activities within the national territory is that states have the right to cede elements of exclusive control through international agreement and custom.[7] Thus, through a long history of international agreements and custom, states of the international community have adopted exceptions from exercise of jurisdiction in favour of immunity for diplomats, for naval vessels from *in rem* admiralty actions and for activities taking place on foreign operated military bases established under basing agreements.

3. THE WTO AND 'IN TRANSIT' GOODS

Since 1947, member states of the European Union have been members of the General Agreement on Tariffs and Trade (GATT), now the World Trade Organization (WTO). The European Union is a member of the WTO. The WTO provides the legal framework under which international trade is conducted. From its inception, the GATT/WTO has recognized in GATT Article V the principle of 'freedom of transit' for goods moving through ports and airports in international trade. This fundamental principle has been so widely and consistently implemented that there has been virtually no controversy about it in the history of the GATT/WTO, despite the fact that goods are constantly moving in transit through its members.[8] It is simply a 'given' in international trade law that the customs authorities of a country do not seize or detain goods passing through their ports and airports *en route* to foreign destinations without a good reason. Article V of GATT prohibits members from imposing unreasonable regulatory requirements on goods in transit.[9]

The TRIPs Agreement did not purport to modify the three core principles of the Paris Convention: national treatment, independence and right of priority (TRIPs Agreement, 1994, art. 2). The TRIPs Agreement obligates WTO members to extend patent subject matter coverage to all fields of technology (TRIPs Agreement, 1994, art. 27.1). But the authority to grant or deny patent protection remains with national patent offices of members based on relevant national legislation (TRIPs Agreement, 1994, arts. 1.1, 29, 62).

An inventor may lack patent protection in a WTO member for a number of reasons, including: (1) no patent was ever sought; (2) a patent has expired; (3) a patent application was rejected because the claimed invention was deemed not to meet the criteria of patentability; (4) the claimed invention did not constitute patentable subject matter under the law of the particular member – for example, computer software as such in Europe. India, as a case in point, was not required by the TRIPs Agreement to provide pharmaceutical product patent protection until 1 January 2005, and many pharmaceutical products patented in Europe are not patented in India.

Article 51 of the TRIPs Agreement obligates WTO members to adopt procedures allowing trademark and copyright owners to prevent counterfeit trademark and pirated copyright goods from entering national markets through detention at the border and notification by customs authorities. The TRIPs Agreement also allows members to adopt measures to prevent importation of goods 'infringing' other forms of intellectual property. Footnote 13 to that provision indicates that there is no obligation to provide anti-counterfeit or anti-piracy border procedures for parallel traded goods or 'goods in transit'. It was logical for the drafters of the TRIPs Agreement to frame these exceptions in such terms as 'no obligation' to provide measures, rather than as a bar or ban, because the drafters were not attempting to define the outer limits of IP protection.

In the case of parallel trade, it was understood that members might or might not provide border protection measures depending upon the local approach to the exhaustion question. At the time the TRIPs Agreement was negotiated, the practice of seizing goods in transit based on allegations of patent infringement was unknown; so members would not have contemplated such practice as an option when drafting the relevant provision. It places too much weight on footnote 13 to suggest that it was intended to authorize the seizure of patented goods in transit when the practice was almost certainly outside the contemplation of the drafters of the TRIPs Agreement.

4. RECENT EU DISPUTES

There have been a substantial number of recent cases in which EU customs authorities have acted to seize pharmaceutical products in transit between developing countries where there are no patents in force.[10] These seizures have been based on patents in force in the 'transit' EU member states. The customs authorities of the Netherlands have been the most aggressive. This is ironic since the Netherlands earlier acted as a champion of access to medicines for developing countries, and now appears to have retreated from its supportive posture.

The first case that received wide public attention was seizure by Dutch customs in December 2008 at Schiphol Airport of a shipment of losartan, a blood pressure medication, in transit from India to Brazil (Abbott, 2009). Losartan is not patented in India or Brazil, but Merck asserts patent rights in the Netherlands. In this case, lawyers acting on behalf of Merck demanded that the producer, Dr Reddy's, consent to destruction of the shipment. Merck eventually authorized release of the goods back to India in exchange for Dr Reddy's acknowledgment of its Dutch patent.

A second case involved a shipment of the antiretroviral medicine abacavir shipped from India by Aurobindo, where it is not patented, to Nigeria. GlaxoSmithKline claims patent rights in the Netherlands. In this case, GlaxoSmithKline advised Dutch customs authorities that it did not wish to initiate a legal action against the shipper, but Dutch customs authorities nevertheless referred the matter to a criminal prosecutor.[11] Remarkably in this case the goods had been purchased on behalf of UNITAID. Dutch customs authorities were interfering with a French-supported programme to supply generic antiretroviral medicines to Africa. Other recent cases involve seizure by Dutch customs authorities of a Cipla shipment of olanzapine en route from India to Peru, based on a Dutch patent asserted by Eli Lilly, and a shipment of clopidogrel en route from India to Colombia, based on a Dutch patent asserted by Sanofi Aventis (Miller and Anand, 2009).

The European Court of Justice (ECJ) in *Montex Holdings v Diesel*[12] raised serious doubt about whether seizure of IP-protected goods in transit and not intended for the European internal market was permissible. The Court of Justice noted that violation of the 1994 IP Border Regulation (Council Regulation 3295/94, 1994), the predecessor of the 2003 IP Border Regulation, was predicated upon infringement of an EU intellectual property right (in that case a trademark), and that the Trademark Directive (Council Directive 89/104, 1989) predicated trademark infringement on entry into the EU stream of commerce. The ECJ said that unless direct evidence of third-party action to place the goods into the EU stream of commerce was present, there could be no infringement under EU law; thus no seizure was authorized.

The High Court of England and Wales recently affirmed this line of reasoning in *Nokia v UK Customs*,[13] also with respect to trademarks, but on this occasion expressly interpreting the 2003 EU IP Border Regulation. Dutch authorities and pharmaceutical patent holders, on the other hand, have relied on a decision of the Court of The Hague in the Netherlands, *Sisvel v Sosecal*,[14] grounded in recital 8 of the 2003 IP Border Regulation. The Court of The Hague interprets the recital to establish a 'manufacturing fiction'. Using this 'fiction', an act of patent infringement takes place by 'use' of the patent for manufacturing in the Netherlands, even though it is absolutely clear that no such manufacturing takes place. It is a truly remarkable theory under which Dutch law is deemed to be violated by actions taking place in another country – for example, India – as if those actions had taken place in the Netherlands.

It is hard to imagine a greater departure from the principle of independence of patents than the 'manufacturing fiction' that is said to support a finding of infringement of a Dutch patent by an action in India. The absence of a patent in India where the manufacturing takes place (and which is independent of the Netherlands) is completely ignored. There is no direct or substantial effect on the Netherlands that might be deemed to constitute a reasonable substitute for actual manufacturing. There is no harm in or to the Netherlands unless one reaches to the farthest levels of attenuation (which the European Commission has historically rejected in the area of competition law) (Griffin, 1998).

It is also difficult to imagine what the international legal system will be like if the 'fictional acts' theory of jurisdiction becomes widely adopted. American manufacturers might be sued in Europe for violating EU environmental law standards when manufacturing in the United States in compliance with US environmental law. Chinese companies could be sued in the European Union for failing to provide EU-standard paid vacation for their workers on the fiction that they were manufacturing in France. A doctor performing a legal abortion in Germany could be prosecuted in Ireland on the theory that the abortion would have been illegal if performed in Ireland. An 18-year-old student drinking beer in Germany could be prosecuted in Florida because 21 is the legal drinking age in Florida. The concept of national sovereignty would be completely meaningless in this new 'fictional acts' environment.

The European Commission has sought to justify implementation of the 2003 regulation on grounds that it is seeking to further the legitimate public policy goal of preventing the circulation of 'counterfeit' drugs

(Mara, 2009). Since no one approves of counterfeiting, the Commission presumably considers that the public and legislators will ignore fundamental legal issues in favour of this 'public good'.

Patent infringement and drug counterfeiting are completely different acts and involve different legal concepts. In order to infringe a patent, the infringer must infringe on each and every claim of the patent. The producer of a 'patent infringing' drug should be producing the same thing as the patent holder or its licensee. Otherwise, there is no infringement. When a patent holder such as Merck alleges that Dr Reddy's is infringing its losartan patent, it is alleging that Dr Reddy's is producing the same drug as the one on which Merck holds its patent, but without its consent. Merck is not alleging that there is a risk to the public from a different or inferior product. The classic 'generic' pharmaceutical product is the same as the originator 'patented' product, produced by a third party, in a situation in which the patent does not apply.

The problem of 'counterfeiting' in the pharmaceutical sector is a problem of misidentified substandard drugs placed on the market without concern for the well-being of the public. In the sense of pharmaceutical regulation, a counterfeit substandard drug does not infringe a patent because it is not the same thing as the patented drug.

It is neither the responsibility nor the right of WTO members outside a country that has not granted patent protection to 'cure' that situation in favour of a local patent holder by disregarding the decisions taken by authorities in the country that has not provided protection. The European Union has elected to disregard the sovereign rights of foreign WTO members by refusing to give effect to their decisions as to patent status by the use of force – the seizure and detention by customs authorities of goods in transit. The allegations of infringement are purely for the convenience of a patent holder that happens to have chosen a particular transit country as a place to obtain a patent.[15] This is a form of 'long-arm' extension of jurisdiction that the European Union historically has claimed to abhor when adopted by US antitrust authorities (Griffin, 1998).

5. CONCLUSION

While the threat to the international economic system and foundations of international law are serious enough, an even more important negative consequence of the EU policy with respect to the seizure of generic pharmaceuticals in transit is the breach of the understanding reached at the WTO regarding access to medicines as embodied in the Doha

Declaration on the TRIPs Agreement and Public Health. There was a bargain reached at the conclusion of the GATT Uruguay Round of trade negotiations in 1993 that provided a 10-year transition period for countries such as India that did not provide pharmaceutical patent protection to institute that protection (Abbott and Reichman, 2003).[16] That bargain acknowledged that public health systems and patients throughout the developing world relied on countries such as India to provide low-cost generic versions of pharmaceutical products on patent in the developed countries, and that a rapid transition to globalized patent protection would have significant adverse effects on public health.

In good measure as a consequence of India's decision to take full advantage of the transition period, a significant part of the developing world can and does continue to rely on that country for the supply of low-cost generic medicines. The Doha Declaration was born out of frustration by developing countries with aggressive tactics employed by the pharmaceutical originator industry, the United States Trade Representative (USTR) and the European Commission that sought to eliminate through trade intimidation the flexibilities that had been negotiated and built into the TRIPs Agreement.

The Doha Declaration is an agreement among WTO members on interpretation of the TRIPs Agreement and provides that the Agreement does not and should not interfere with the right of members to protect public health. It further recognizes the objective of promoting 'access to medicines for all'. Seizure of generic drugs moving legitimately in transit is a frontal assault by the European Union on the object and purpose of the Doha Declaration. It is an effort to prevent developing countries from relying on the security of supply from Indian generic manufacturers, and to put them out of business (or force them into mergers with major originator companies). This cannot be justified as a means to control counterfeiting. If legitimate generic drugs are treated as counterfeit drugs the entire global public will suffer. Regrettably, the international patent system will again suffer a blow to its legitimacy.

Postscript

On 1 December 2011, the ECJ decided the joined cases of *Koninklijke Philips Electronics NV v Lucheng Meijing Industrial Co Ltd* (C-446/09) and *Nokia Corp v Her Majesty's Commissioner's of Revenue and Customs* (C-496/09). The court held that transit of goods through the territory of a country, without more, does not give rise to IP infringement. Infringement is assessed in countries where goods are placed on the market. The court rejected the manufacturing or production fiction.

The decision is grounded in the objectives of the European Union's common commercial policy. Goods may be detained based on evidence sufficient to establish suspicion of intent to fraudently divert to the EU market. Substantive infringement may be based on concrete evidence of that intent. The ECJ joined decision is consistent with and supportive of the approach taken in this chapter.

Acknowledgements

An earlier version of this chapter appeared as Abbott, Frederick M. (2009), 'Seizure of generic pharmaceuticals in transit based on allegations of patent infringement: A threat to international trade, development and public welfare', *WIPO Journal*, **1**(1), 43–50.

NOTES

1. *Montex Holdings v Diesel* (C–281/05) 2006 E.C.R. I–10881, interpreting 1994 predecessor to 2003 IP Border Regulation and holding that customs may not suspend transit of goods in commerce based on EU trademark absent direct evidence of third-party activity to place goods on market within a member state, even if goods were produced in contravention of trademark holder rights in a non-EU state; *Nokia v UK Customs* [2009] EWHC 1903 (Ch), holding that UK customs did not have authority under 2003 EU IP Border Regulation to detain fake goods in transit based on UK trademark holder claim where no direct evidence of third-party intention to place on market within EU, and rejecting Court of Hague analysis in *Sisvel v Sosecal* based on manufacturing fiction. Compare Court of Hague, Case 311378 KG ZA 08–617, *Sisvel v Sosecal*, 18 July 2008, holding that Netherlands customs authorities may suspend goods in transit based on allegation of infringement of Dutch patent based on 'manufacturing fiction' derived from recital of 2003 IP border regulation. See also Kuchar (2008) and Brink (2008), translating extracts from the *Sisvel* decision into English.
2. *Banco Nacional de Cuba v Sabbatino*, 376 US 398 (1964).
3. 418 F. 3d 1282 (Fed. Cir. 2005).
4. 550 US 437 (2007).
5. *Cardiac Pacemakers v St. Jude Medical,* 576 F. 3d 1348 (Fed. Cir. 2009).
6. See, for example, Council Regulation 2913/92 art. 3, defining the 'customs territory' of the Community as the territory of its member states.
7. See, for example, *The Case of the S.S. 'Lotus',* PCIJ, Judgment No. 9, PCIJ, Ser. A., No. 10, 1927.
8. See, for example, Note by WTO Secretariat, Article V of GATT 1994 – Scope and Application, TN/TF/W/2, 12 January 2005 (updating G/C/W/ 408, 10 September 2002). There is a recent WTO panel report, *Colombia – Indicative Prices and Restrictions on Ports of Entry*, Report of the Panel, 27

April 2009, WT/DS366/R. That report addresses an issue unrelated to the subject of this chapter, i.e., the point at which transit within a country removes goods from the protection of Article V.

9. The Panel in the *Colombia – Indicative Prices* case, at para. 7.387, noted: 'As its title indicates, Article V of the *GATT* 1994 thus generally addresses matters related to "freedom of transit" of goods. This includes protection from unnecessary restrictions, such as limitations on freedom of transit, or unreasonable charges or delays (via paras 2–4), and the extension of Most-Favoured-Nation (MFN) treatment to members' goods which are 'traffic in transit' (via paras 2 and 5) or 'have been in transit' (via para. 6)'.
10. See Miller and Anand (2009) and formal response by Dutch government on seizures and border measures in FTAs (to parliamentary questions), posted by Health Action International on IP-Health list server, 25 April 2009, available at http://lists.essential.org/pipermail/ip-health/2009-April/013674.html (accessed 8 September 2010).
11. See the Dutch Government's response to Parliamentary questions in a letter dated 7 May 2009 from the State Secretary for Finance to HAI Europe, copy on file with author.
12. *Montex Holdings v Diesel* (C–281/05) 2006 E.C.R. I–10881.
13. [2009] EWHC 1903 (Ch).
14. Court of Hague, Case 311378 KG ZA 08–617, *Sisvel v Sosecal*, 18 July 2008.
15. Imagine, for example, if the German computer software firm SAP sought to ship program disks from Heidelberg to Bogotá through Miami, and US Customs seized and detained the program disks because of an allegation of patent infringement by IBM based on a US software patent. Since the European Patent Office does not grant software patents, IBM presumably does not have protection in Europe. Would the European Union consider this a legitimate patent infringement action?
16. While the US Trade Representative eventually acknowledged the legitimacy of TRIPs flexibilities (as adopted by South Africa), the European Commission never did ('t Hoen, 2002, pp. 30–1).

BIBLIOGRAPHY

Abbott, Frederick M. (2002), 'The Doha Declaration on the TRIPs Agreement and public health: Lighting a dark corner at the WTO', *Journal of International Economic Law*, **5**(2), 469–505.

Abbott, Frederick M. (2009), 'Worst fears realised: The Dutch confiscation of medicines bound from India to Brazil', *Bridges Monthly*, **13**(1), 13–4.

Abbott, Frederick M. and Jerome H. Reichman (2003), 'The Doha round's public health legacy: Strategies for the production and diffusion of patented medicines under the amended TRIPs provisions', *Journal of International Economic Law*, **10**(4), 921–87.

Abbott, Frederick M., Thomas Cottier and Francis Gurry (2007), *International Intellectual Property in an Integrated World Economy*, New York: Aspen.

Agreement on Trade-Related Aspects of Intellectual Property Rights [TRIPs Agreement] (1994), 15 April.

Brink, Jens van den (2008), 'Comeback for the legal fiction of the anti piracy regulation?', *Kennedy Van der Laan Newsletter*, August, available at http://www.kvdl.nl/KVdL/en-GB/_main/News/Newsletter/Newsletter+August+2008/Anti+Piracy+Regulation_IP/default.htm (accessed 8 September 2010).

Council Directive 89/104 (1989), *To approximate the laws of the member states relating to trade marks*, 1989 OJ (L 40) 1.

Council Regulation 3295/94 (1994), *Laying down measures to prohibit the release for free circulation, export, re-export or entry for a suspensive procedure of counterfeit and pirated goods*, 1994 OJ (L 341) 8.

Council Regulation 1383/2003 (2003), *Concerning customs action against goods suspected of infringing certain intellectual property rights and the measures to be taken against goods found to have infringed such rights*, 2003 OJ (L 196) 7.

Griffin, Joseph P. (1998) 'Jurisdiction and enforcement: Foreign governmental reactions to U.S. assertions of extraterritorial jurisdiction', *George Mason Law Review*, **6**(3), 505–24.

ICTSD (2009), 'Access to medicines back on centre stage at the WTO', *Bridges Monthly*, **13**(1), 12, available at http://ictsd.org/i/news/bridges/44203/ (accessed 8 September 2010).

Kuchar, Barbara (2008), 'Comparative presentation of recent national court decisions in transit cases', PowerPoint presentation to the *INTA International Forum on Anticounterfeiting*, 4 December.

Mara, Kaitlin (2009), 'Generic drug delay called "systemic" problem at TRIPs Council', *Intellectual Property Watch*, 9 June, available at http://www.ip-watch.org/weblog/2009/06/09/generic-drug-delay-called-%E2%80%9Csyst em ic%E2%80%9D-problem-at-trips-council/ (accessed 8 September 2010).

Miller, John W. and Geeta Anand (2009), 'India prepares EU trade complaint', *Wall Street Journal*, 6 August.

't Hoen, Ellen (2002) 'TRIPS, pharmaceutical patents, and access to essential medicines: A long way from Seattle to Doha', *Chicago Journal of International Law* **3**(1), 27–46.

UN Charter (1945).

8. Patent licensing strategies for the research and development of pharmaceuticals in developing countries

Gail E. Evans

1. INTRODUCTION

More than 80 per cent of the world's population lives in developing countries where communicable diseases account for 50 per cent of the disease burden (WHO, 2008, Annex, p. 5). The opening recital of World Health Organization's (WHO) Global Strategy and Plan of Action on Public Health, Innovation and Intellectual Property (Global Strategy and Plan of Action) affirms the need to construct a sustainable basis for research and development (R&D) relevant to diseases that disproportionately affect developing countries (WHO, 2008). Regrettably, the factors that drive pharmaceutical innovation are often biased against the kinds of diseases that are disproportionately found in low-income countries.[1] Innovation to address diseases primarily affecting the poor is impeded by a combination of under-investment by the public sector and market failure (WHO, 2003, pp. 1–2; WHO Intergovernmental Working Group on Public Health, Innovation and Intellectual Property Rights, 2007, p. 6).

WHO Member States recognize that the global network of universities and publicly funded research institutions has a key role to play in the R&D of medicines for neglected diseases, frequently in partnership with the private sector (WHO, 2006, p. 3). The Bayh–Dole model of technology transfer[2] encourages such research institutions to seek patent protection for inventions made using public funds and to license those inventions to the pharmaceutical industry with the goal of promoting their commercialization and public availability (Arora and Fosfuri, 2003).[3]

However, in view of the long duration and high cost of innovation, when negotiating with a university, patentee pharmaceutical companies will normally seek an exclusive patent licence (European Commission, 2008, p. 55; OECD, 2004, p. 22). The grant of an exclusive licence confers powers on the licensee that are equivalent to those of the proprietor insofar as it permits only the licensee and persons authorized by the licensee to exploit the invention.[4] Under international patent law this gives the licensee exclusive rights of manufacture and sale of the invention for a 20-year term to the exclusion of the patentee.[5] An exclusive licence will also exclude the licensor from using the invention. For example, assume that in 2000, the University of Distopia received a patent for a new vaccine against tuberculosis. Two years later the university granted an exclusive licence to Pharmco to develop and test the product. In 2009, almost 10 years after obtaining the patent, the vaccine is given regulatory approval. On the one hand, without exclusive access to the technology, Pharmco might not be prepared to take the risk of investing the resources necessary to develop the vaccine into a marketable product. The major pharmaceutical companies consider the market exclusivity and higher prices made possible by patent protection particularly important, owing to the large investment in research and clinical testing required prior to sale, and because the actual manufacturing process is relatively cheap and easy to replicate.[6]

On the other hand, there is considerable debate about whether universities and public research organizations[7] (PROs) should grant Pharmco an exclusive licence, thereby potentially limiting further research and restricting dissemination of the technology (Commission on Intellectual Property Rights, 2006, p. 71). The problem is that an exclusive licence to Pharmco, without due consideration of future development, tends to inhibit the ability of PROs to have a meaningful role in monitoring the development and future use of health technology. A recent illustrative response is to be found in the proposed changes to the regulations accompanying South Africa's Intellectual Property Rights from Publicly Financed Research and Development Act (2008), which would see funding recipients having to ensure that, before granting an exclusive licence, the agreement contains terms requiring the licensee to provide a development plan and to ensure that the benefits of the intellectual property are reasonably accessible to the people of the Republic (South Africa Department of Science and Technology, 2009, p. 4, regs 8(3)(a) and 9(4)(a)).

As the South African proposal indicates, depending upon the goals and expectations with which the parties negotiate terms, there is considerable flexibility within the licensing agreement. The intersection of property and contract law provides an opportunity for university licensors in leading developing countries to reclaim the policy space needed in overcoming obstacles associated with pharmaceutical R&D. Given the importance of licensing to the development and availability of new products, licensing should be governed by terms that seek to meet commercialization benchmarks; to keep the licensed technology reasonably accessible to researchers; and to modify or terminate the contract if the public's reasonable healthcare needs are not met.

This chapter advances various licensing strategies that would allow PROs to negotiate with business partners in order to obtain the optimal development of pharmaceutical products. It aims to identify the goals of licensing policy for PROs in developing countries, and to examine the kinds of restriction and reservation clauses that PROs should consider including in patent licensing agreements. By such means, the author argues, developing countries can achieve a more appropriate balance between the needs of the pharmaceutical industry for patent protection and those of PROs to disseminate knowledge as broadly as possible among the research community.

In the exposition of this argument, this chapter is organized as follows: the first part examines various models of technology transfer from university to the business sector, in relation to patent licensing by universities in developing countries. Section 2 explains how public-private partnerships (PPP) for drug development with universities and health institutes in developing countries, has been facilitated by the restructuring of the pharmaceutical industry and the entry of new manufacturing companies from India and China. Section 3 explains how universities in developing countries might utilize a mix of exclusive and non-exclusive licences in order to promote R&D. Section 4 offers drafting guidelines for restriction clauses as to field of use, territory and rights to improvements, in the light of European competition law. Section 5 explains the legal status and importance of negotiating exemptions for research and experimental use. Section 6 provides guidance for the drafting of reservation clauses for publication and access rights to scientific data. The chapter concludes with a recommendation for a termination clause in the licensing agreement capable of preserving rights negotiated for the use and dissemination of research.

2. TECHNOLOGY TRANSFER FROM UNIVERSITY TO INDUSTRY IN THE DEVELOPING WORLD

The modern university has become an important source for the direct application of scientific research to identifiable and pressing needs in medicine and the health sciences, and for the patenting of those inventions. Today, PROs play a crucial role in promoting the R&D of pharmaceuticals at each stage of the process, from the exchange of scientific data[8] and personnel, to the facilitation of PPP for clinical trials and product manufacture (United National Health Internetwork Access to Research Initiative, various dates).[9] However, questions remain concerning the ostensible conflict of interests between the mission of PROs to conduct basic research in the public interest and those of the private sector to commercialize the results of publicly funded research. This debate becomes all the more acute in the case of developing countries, where questions arise as to the appropriate model for university-industry licensing. This chapter will begin with an appraisal of the Bayh–Dole model and its alternatives, before considering the relevance of these models to university-industry technology transfer in developing countries.

2.1 The Bayh–Dole Model

The United States Bayh–Dole Act of 1980[10] established the 'licensing' model of technology transfer from universities to the private sector. With the aim of encouraging the development of technologies based on university research, the Bayh–Dole legislation allows universities to patent inventions arising from publicly funded research. By this means, universities may retain ownership rights over government-funded research and license inventions on a non-exclusive or exclusive basis.[11] The Bayh–Dole model requires universities to establish a centralized technology transfer office (TTO) for the development and commercialization of research. The TTOs are responsible for evaluating inventions, filing for patent applications on behalf of the university and finding a suitable licensee within the business sector (OECD, 2003).[12]

The focus of the Bayh–Dole model is to transfer title from individual researchers to PROs.[13] It is a patent-centric model of R&D (Kesan, 2009), characterized by the diligent filing of applications and the retention of ownership rights for transfer to the private sector through licensing. The 20-year term of patent protection permits prices that are higher than the marginal price of manufacturing. This exclusivity is said to constitute an incentive for the initial R&D of new health products (Landes and Posner, 2003). The harm flowing from lessening competition by means of imitation is said to be outweighed by the advantage flowing from more innovation (AUTM, 2004, 2005, 2006, 2007a). When it comes to making investments in order to transform the university-generated knowledge about neglected diseases into a commercial application, the notional incentive becomes problematic.[14] The notion that patent protection would provide a financial incentive to drug firms to invest in treatments of tropical diseases has not materialized. The redistribution of resources to the private sector accompanied by the introduction of patents will not alone trigger the development of more drugs specifically related to the needs of the poor.[15] Even the relative boost in R&D for antiretroviral therapy is due to the fact that the HIV epidemic also involves developed countries. There is said to be a market failure for medicines in developing countries. Low-income countries do not constitute a market capable of inducing patent-driven investment.[16] In the majority of countries in Africa the profits have not existed to attract commercial development, and public funding for diseases has been difficult to obtain and sustain (World Bank, 2009a).

The Bayh–Dole model rests on the tidy hypothesis that innovation should spur a virtuous circle, generating revenue that can be applied to more basic research (Wasser, 1990). This combination raises concerns about the appropriate balance between pure and applied research. Concerns are expressed about the impact of rights to the exclusive use of patented medical technologies, as well as obligations to retain the confidentiality of research, on the public domain of science (Reichman and Uhlir, 2003, p. 320). The single-minded promotion of the downstream application of university research potentially conflicts with policies favouring full and open access to research data. Yet the open science model is considered to be one of the main reasons why research universities have been so important in the process of economic growth (Dasgupta and David, 1994; David, Mowery and Steinmueller, 1992). From the development of penicillin to the invention of recombinant DNA technology, research universities have spurred innovation. By its nature, the entrepreneurial model sparks misgivings that pressure to reap the financial fruit of patenting medical science will deflect universities from their traditional mission, the discovery and dissemination of new knowledge.

2.2 Variations of the Bayh–Dole Model

2.2.1 The EU innovation model

In 2004 the European Commission published a report on the management of intellectual property in PROs that recommended an innovation model of technology transfer in parallel with an open science model (European Commission, 2004, p. 11). The Report recognized that the US 'licensing' model was not entirely appropriate to the prevailing conditions for R&D in the European Union, primarily because of a more fragmented market and a lower density of research-based companies headquartered in

Europe. Instead, the Report advocated an interactive 'Innovation Model' in which the pure licensing model is supplemented by 'a more active policy of collaborative research with industry' and by 'a pro-active involvement in the creation of spinout companies' (European Commission, 2004, p. 1). Even so, the licensing and innovation models share a common character, in so far as they both advocate the PROs' ownership and strategic management of the intellectual property deriving from their research results.

Most OECD (Organization for Economic Co-operation and Development) countries have adopted 'Bayh–Dole style' models of technology transfer.[17] In the more technologically advanced developing countries there is also evidence that governments are willing to legislate to ensure that intellectual property resulting from publicly financed research is disclosed, appropriately protected and commercialized for the benefit of the nation. For example, India's Council of Scientific and Industrial Research pursues a policy of patenting inventions, and China also encourages patenting by its universities and research institutions (Commission on Intellectual Property Rights, Innovation and Public Health, 2006, p. 70). More recently, the South African Government has proposed the creation of a National Intellectual Property Management Office to oversee the transfer and commercialization of university research (South Africa Department of Science and Technology, 2009, p. 4, regs 4(1) and (2)). Nevertheless, in the case of middle-to-low-income developing countries questions concerning the feasibility of the Bayh–Dole model remain particularly pertinent.

2.2.2 The WIPO 'IP Hub'

For less-technologically-advanced developing countries, regional technology transfer hubs may prove a more viable model for strengthening R&D.[18] Developing countries, including Cameroon, Chad and Colombia, have benefited from a pilot project launched by the World Intellectual Property Organization (WIPO) in 2004, which established two networks of health research institutions in Africa and South America each with its own 'IP hub' (WIPO, 2006). Participating research institutions agree to common policies and to share technology transfer services in order to minimize costs and optimize resources through economies of scale. The 'IP hubs' offer intellectual property services, including managing and licensing patents owned by the research institutions and marketing the patent portfolio of the R&D network with a view to attracting further funding and promoting PPP.

3. PUBLIC-PRIVATE PARTNERSHIPS FOR RESEARCH AND INNOVATION

The WHO *Plan of Action on Public Health, Innovation and Intellectual Property* stresses the need for co-operation between public and private sectors to boost pharmaceutical innovation in developing countries and to facilitate the dissemination and use of R&D outcomes (WHO, 2008, p. 10, para. 30). This action is consistent with studies by the OECD which have concluded that greater use of PPPs can enhance the efficiency of innovation by securing private finance and expertise for the development of publicly funded research (Nwaka and Ridley, 2003; OECD, 2008; OECD, 2009, Annex 6.A1; Outterson, 2006). PPPs, varying from small groups to more complex consortia between PROs, international organizations and private companies, have become a major source of new drug development for developing countries. For example, the WHO's Special Programme for Research and Training in Tropical Diseases facilitates a partnership-oriented approach to drug discovery and development between public-sector organizations and private companies that permits projects to be launched with cost-effective budgets (WHO, various dates).

Scientific collaboration between PROs in developed and developing countries has been expanding since the 1980s. In addition, South-South collaboration is becoming an increasingly important element in R&D, providing opportunities for the development of pharmaceuticals that are tailored to meet local needs (Mazzoleni and Nelson, 2007; Osama, 2008).[19] PRO partnerships in Africa might include a mix of institutions with well-established research activities, as well as promising institutions that are developing their research potential. The way in which the Kenya Medical Research Institute (KEMRI) evolved is instructive for the development of PROs in other developing countries. It developed from a long-term partnership between KEMRI and the Wellcome Trust.[20] This partnership is fully integrated into the KEMRI research infrastructure. The KEMRI-Wellcome Trust partnership is embedded within Kilifi District Hospital, building its research programmes around local medical infrastructure and contributing to healthcare delivery. KEMRI has developed collaborative links with a large number of regional and international bodies including institutions such as National Institute of Medical Research in Tanzania and the British Medical Research Council.[21]

The example of KEMRI confirms the trend towards the locus of innovation in pharmaceuticals moving beyond the confines of central R&D laboratories of the largest companies and spreading outwards to

PROs, notably universities and their private-sector partners in the industry.[22] The contention that university patent ownership will facilitate technology transfer from universities to private firms begins to have some substance when we consider: first, the restructuring of the business model of the major pharmaceutical industry and, secondly, new entrants to pharmaceutical manufacturing from developing countries as potential business partners.

3.1 Restructuring Big Pharma's Business Model

The major pharmaceutical industry has acknowledged that the prevailing model, largely based on vertical or fully integrated pharmaceutical companies (FIPCO), is incapable of delivering sustainable growth. While the business climate for pharmaceutical companies has changed dramatically in the past five years, their business model has not kept pace. The pharmaceutical industry is facing a radical transition because the old business model shows diminishing returns.[23] Declining R&D productivity, rising costs of commercialization, increasing purchaser influence and shorter exclusivity periods have driven up the average cost of launching new products and reduced average expected returns on new investment.

The major pharmaceutical companies need a new business model to restore sound financial results. They are likely to transition to greater reliance on partnerships to manage risk and return, across both product pipelines and functions.[24] In the result, structural changes in the pharmaceutical industry portend a more favourable climate for PROs in leading developing countries to negotiate the terms of patent ownership and licensing. As 'Big Pharma'[25] expands and restructures on a global scale, for companies wishing to outsource research, universities in developing countries are potentially attractive options (Jack, 2009).[26]

3.2 New Pharmaceutical Manufacturers as Potential Business Partners

Moreover, as new pharmaceutical manufacturers enter the market from leading developing countries such as India and China, the ability of universities in Africa and Asia to find industry partners is likely to increase further.[27] Developing countries with significant national innovation capacity, such as India, now possess a patent system strong enough to attract foreign direct investment, access foreign technology and encourage local R&D.[28] The character of the Indian presence in Africa has the potential to assist product development. Whatever the infrastructural problems posed by the African continent, the increasing commercial activity of Indian pharmaceutical companies indicates their belief in the potential of the market and their ability to capture prospective profits. Indian pharmaceutical manufacturers are present in all the 53 markets of Africa,[29] supplying AIDS, malaria, anti-cancer and cardiac drugs, antibiotics and a variety of other products.[30] The prices are becoming more competitive as more Indian firms establish manufacturing capacities in countries such as Kenya and Zambia (Patwardhan, 2007).[31] They are also involved in technology transfer agreements with companies in Uganda, Nigeria, Gabon, Egypt, Morocco and Algeria. Yet other Indian companies, such as Flamingo, have formed joint ventures in African countries such as Ghana and Uganda with the aim of exploring the market (PricewaterhouseCoopers, 2007).

At the very least, the rationale that ownership by PROs, as opposed to individual researchers, provides greater legal certainty, lowers transaction costs and fosters more efficient channels for technology transfer, should be carefully considered in each case (Council on Governmental Relations, 1999). In fact, developing countries may find it more efficient for the government or a state-sponsored entity such as a trust or holding company to receive title to the intellectual property on behalf of academic inventors. For example, under South Africa's Intellectual Property Rights from Publicly Financed Research and Development Regulations, if a university chooses not to seek patent protection, the National Intellectual Property Management Office will have the right to reassess the decision and, if necessary, seek ownership of the research and patentable assets (South Africa Department of Science and Technology, 2009).

4. STRATEGIC PATENT LICENSING FOR ONGOING DRUG DISCOVERY

4.1 Utilizing Freedom of Contract

The intersection of intellectual property and contract law within the patent licensing agreement offers PROs the potential to reclaim a space for ongoing R&D into neglected diseases that may otherwise be eroded by the strength of patent law. In addition to the negative rights to exclude unauthorized uses under Article 28 of the WTO Agreement on Trade-Related Aspects of Intellectual Property Rights (TRIPs), the patentee also possesses the positive right to conclude licensing contracts.[32] Whereas the derogations from patent rights are narrow, when we turn from property rights to contract, the capacity of the parties to negotiate mutually acceptable terms begins to change. Within the normative framework of contract, there is an opportunity for the parties to implement their reasonable expectations. Contract allows the parties to set present values on probabilities of future outcomes. It requires a duty of good faith and fair dealing in negotiating the terms of the contract.[33]

Of course, the final terms of the licensing contract depend on the negotiating power the parties bring to the table. While PROs in developing countries may not have the financial strength of their business partners, the so-called flexibilities of the TRIPs Agreement, as affirmed by the Doha Declaration on the TRIPS Agreement and Public Health, may be invoked to support the continuation and dissemination of research.[34] Article 7 of the TRIPs Agreement echoes the International Covenant on Economic, Social and Cultural Rights,[35] insofar as the transfer of technology should be made 'in a manner conducive to social and economic welfare', free of conditions, and 'to the mutual advantage of producers and users of technological knowledge'.[36]

When a PRO negotiates with a private pharmaceutical manufacturer over the terms of a licensing agreement, the principle of freedom of contract provides a vehicle for addressing the parties' conflict of interests between the dissemination of research, and the need to recoup the costs of drug development. The process of offer and acceptance involves the quid pro quo of contract law and mutual assent of the parties to the agreement. When they are 'of one mind', intellectual property law becomes the background against which the parties negotiate and no longer the dominant factor in negotiations. Approaches to licensing, even for comparable technologies, can vary considerably from case to case based on circumstances particular to the parties, the invention and its commercial development. The absolute nature of the rights conferred on the patent holder may be organized to divide the fields of use of the invention, and to temper the prohibitions on third-party access and use of the invention with exclusive or non-exclusive licences.

4.2 Utilizing the Forms of Licensing

4.2.1 Exclusive, co-exclusive and non-exclusive licences

The capacity of licensing to accommodate the commercial exploitation of the patent and the dissemination of basic research lies in the dual nature of its character. A patent licence is not only a legal document, but also a way of doing business. Exclusive licences grant exclusive rights to produce and sell certain products in certain territories and markets during the term of the licence. An exclusive licence permits only the licensee and persons authorized by the licensee to exploit the invention. An exclusive licence will also exclude the licensor from using the invention. In this regard, the grant of an exclusive licence is similar to an assignment, since an exclusive licence confers powers on the licensee that are equivalent to those of the proprietor.[37] Unsurprisingly therefore, in the evaluation of the Bayh–Dole model, there is considerable debate about whether PROs should grant exclusive licences to the private sector for discoveries that have benefited from public funds. By definition, exclusive licences limit the diffusion of technologies. The drawback is that if the chosen licensee does not effectively promote or sell the invention, the patentee cannot then do so, nor can the patentee grant further licences to others.

Alternatively, 'co-exclusive' licences may be granted to a small, limited number of licensees. Such a licensing strategy has the advantage of permitting competitive product optimization by motivating a number of licensees to compete to achieve product development and market penetration or to develop a product that is an improvement over the original (AUTM, 2007b, p. 12). This strategy, in which a small pool of licensees conduct their R&D in parallel, is especially appropriate where there is a substantial unmet need for a particular product (such as an urgently needed vaccine). More specifically, such a strategy reduces the delay that might be involved in an exclusive licence, where a failure to develop the product will require the licensor to terminate the licence, negotiate a new licence and recommence product development (AUTM, 2007b, p. 12).

In contrast, a non-exclusive licence allows a PRO patentee to retain the right to exploit the licensed invention as well as the right to grant additional licences to third parties. Several licensees as well as the patent owner would have the right to use the patented technology. PROs should therefore consider the reasons for granting exclusive or non-exclusive licences, particularly in the light of the maturity of the technology and the organization's business strategy.

Generally, however, pharmaceutical innovation needs one company to invest heavily to commercialize the product. Pharmaceutical companies, when partnering with a PRO, will normally seek an exclusive patent licence to offset the high cost of innovation,[38] including the investment necessary to the performance of clinical trials. For their part, universities should strive to offset the impact that the exclusive licence may have on continuing research, unanticipated uses and future commercialization efforts. University licensors should endeavour to ensure that the agreement grants only those rights necessary to the development of a particular technology.

4.2.2 Hybrid licences

By way of compromise, the licensing contract between developing country PRO and industry partner may contain terms granting some rights on an exclusive basis and others on a non-exclusive basis. Hybrid licence grants can expand the range of creative possibilities for defining an exclusive licensee's rights (AUTM, 2007b, p. 13). The ability of the licensing contract to accommodate a variety of business models is reflected in the Lambert Model Contracts that were drafted for the use of PROs by university, business and industry stakeholders in the United Kingdom.[39] Each model contract represents a different approach to the management of intellectual property rights.

'Convertible exclusive' licences permit the licensor to grant an exclusive licence, either co-exclusive or non-exclusive, if a third party wishes to develop products not yet made available by the exclusive licensee, usually after the initial licensee has been given an opportunity to market the product within a limited timeframe (AUTM, 2007b, p. 13). More generally, over and above the failure to meet a product roll-out deadline, where the licensor agrees to an exclusive grant, it might possibly make the exclusivity subject to defeasance, in whole or in part, triggered by other performance shortfalls by the licensee, such as failure to meet performance or distribution requirements (Herzfeld and Bergovoy, 2007). If triggered, defeasance may take a variety of forms including the conversion of the entire licence grant from exclusive to non-exclusive; or the clawing-back of certain products or inventions from the exclusive licence grant, to either non-exclusive status; or total exclusion from the licence grant (Herzfeld and Bergovoy, 2007). In particular, a claw-back clause is normally used to remedy the licensee's failure to meet minimum net sales requirements (Herzfeld and Bergovoy, 2007). However, it might also be used in respect of any one of a number of performance requirements relating to drug development and distribution.

A 'non-exclusive exclusive' licence grant might begin with the classic non-exclusive language, but also undertake not to grant to third parties the right to sell like-products if the licensee complies with all the terms and conditions of the licence agreement (Herzfeld and Bergovoy, 2007). Usually, compliance is determined at the sole discretion of the licensor, which is to the advantage of licensor since there is no need to prove licensee default (Herzfeld and Bergovoy, 2007). Licensees are likely to favour a 'non-exclusive exclusive' grant over a standard non-exclusive grant, because it holds some degree of protection against competition (Herzfeld and Bergovoy, 2007).

Another variant within the hybrid licence includes a non-exclusive provision where it is not a breach if the licensor permits a third party to sell like-products, but in the event of such a grant, the licensor agrees to provide the licensee with a reduction in royalties or other previously defined remedies (Herzfeld and Bergovoy, 2007). Particularly when the licensor is seeking to get a new process used in a new geographical area by finding a manufacturing source there, a basic issue is likely to arise over exclusivity. It is usually a question of whether the licensee is to be guaranteed that neither the licensor nor other licensees will manufacture or sell, directly or indirectly, in its territory. A possible variation is the 'convertible non-exclusive' licence, where if additional expressions of interest are not received within a defined period of time, then a non-exclusive licence converts to exclusivity, at least within a particular territory or field of use (AUTM, 2007b, p. 12).

With a view to the promotion of research, PROs may utilize time-limited clauses in order to ensure that the duration of exclusivity is limited to the period necessary to afford licensees the competitive advantage afforded by early market penetration and to permit them to earn a reasonable return on their investment in R&D, following which the grant may convert to a non-exclusive licence, allowing competitors access to the market (AUTM, 2007b, p. 13). The period may vary from several years for the discovery of a drug that requires relatively little in product development to considerably longer intervals for drugs requiring many years of development and testing to obtain regulatory approval (AUTM, 2007b, p. 13).

5. PROMOTING DISSEMINATION USING RESTRICTION AND RESERVATION CLAUSES

The WHO Global Strategy and Plan of Action calls for 'the further development and dissemination of publicly or donor-funded medical inventions and know-how through appropriate licensing policies' (WHO, 2008, p. 30, para. 30, 2.4(d)). With the aim of reasserting their traditional commitment to open access and dissemination in the advancement of scientific research (National Institutes of Health, 1998), PROs should begin by setting out these core values in a mission statement. The traditional mission of the university is to serve society as a centre of higher learning, providing lasting benefits through the discovery of new knowledge and the dissemination of advanced knowledge. By way of illustration, the University of Cambridge's mission and core values speak specifically of the contribution the university can make to society through the pursuit, dissemination, and application of knowledge; the place of the university within the broader academic and local community; and creating opportunities for innovative partnerships with business, charitable foundations, and health care (University of Cambridge, various dates). Such a mission statement can then be incorporated in the recitals to the contract as a statement of what the licensing agreement hopes to achieve.

By such means, the contract provides a structure against which the core values of PROs in promoting the dissemination of research may be brought to bear on the bargain. The freedom of the licensing contract means that a developing country PRO has the opportunity to draft terms that allow it to reserve rights of access and use that are important for the dissemination and competitive commercialization of drugs and diagnostic tools. For instance, it might agree to place certain inventions in the public domain, or alternatively, to create mechanisms for sharing the results and exploitation of research. By utilizing in this way contractual terms that contain alternative arrangements, private and public partners can negotiate over alternative solutions to the dissemination of, and access to, knowledge.

5.1 Drafting Restriction Clauses on Field of Use, Territory and Term

The principle of freedom of contract provides the opportunity to define a space in which the value of basic research can be exempted in some measure from the restrictions associated with the exercise of patent rights. The licensing contract offers developing country PROs considerable advantages, not least the potential to control production, distribution in time and geographic area. To this end, the PRO, as licensor, can apportion particular uses of the patent, dividing use of the patent by territory and by the number of licensees. The parties may test their expectations by inserting performance milestones.

Universities in developing countries might deploy restrictions over field of use and territory terms in order to encourage development of the technology in hitherto under-served markets. A licence may be limited territorially or only for certain types of products covered by the patent. By this means, the licensee can be kept to its own territory simply by not granting it manufacturing or sales licences under the patents of other territories. Field-restricted licences therefore enable the grant of rights that cover only particular products that a licensee is able, and will accept a firm commitment to develop. This approach protects the licensee's investment in a product, while nevertheless allowing an opportunity for other parties who are not operating in the field of the exclusive licence grant to undertake product development (AUTM, 2007b, p. 12). A licence that extends to all fields of use for the term of the licensed patent may have negative consequences if the subject technology is found to have unanticipated utility. This possibility is of particular concern if the licensee is not able or willing to develop the technology in fields outside of its core business (AUTM, 2007b, p. 2).

5.2 Territorial Restrictions and Their Interface with Competition Law

If the university gives the licensee the security of exclusivity, it is normally on condition that it will respect the exclusivity of others, either licensor or exclusive licensee, in their territories (Cornish and Llewelyn, 2007, p. 284). The question then arises as to whether the licensee is to receive a guarantee that neither the licensor nor other licensees will manufacture or sell, directly or indirectly, into its territory (Cornish and Llewelyn, 2007, p. 284). For its part the licensee will be interested in ensuring protection of its investment, equipment, employees, distribution chains, advertising and other servicing that it may have to provide (Cornish and Llewelyn, 2007, p. 284). The greater the investment, the more likely the licensee will insist on territorial exclusivity in order to provide protection against potential price differences and the parallel importing that these may engender. However, such contractual terms will be enforceable only so long as the country of import neither treats an initial marketing outside its territory as exhausting patent rights, nor assumes that first sale abroad by one licensee implies a licence to export to other countries where parallel patents exist (Cornish and Llewelyn, 2007, p. 284).

In most countries, national patent laws will give the necessary protection. In the European Union, however, where the principle of the free movement of goods qualifies patent law, such terms may fall foul of competition law. The Commission opposes restrictions as to territory, considering the creation of a common market justifies treating a licence to manufacture in a Member State of the Community as a licence to sell in all (Cornish and Llewelyn, 2007, p. 292). The Community principle of the free movement of goods derives from Article 34 of the Treaty on the Functioning of the European Union (TFEU),[40] which prohibits quantitative restrictions on imports and all measures having an equivalent effect thereto between Member States of the European Union (Keeling, 2003, pp. 6–7). The exercise of a patent to block imports is considered a 'measure having an equivalent effect'. Article 36 provides that Article 30 shall not prevent the protection of intellectual property.

As a result we have a conflict between the free movement of goods across borders and the exercise of patent rights. Various attempts to use patents in the country of import to block parallel (unauthorized third-party) import of pharmaceutical products that were first placed on the market in another EU country have all foundered on the doctrine of exhaustion of rights. Generally speaking, the patent owner has the right to place the product first on the market within the European Economic Area (EEA), but not the right to block parallel imports from another EU Member State, where the product has been put on to the market in that Member State with the consent of the patentee.[41]

The principle of exhaustion that pertains throughout the European Union means that the licensor can still impose an obligation on a licensee not to sell licensed products outside its given territory, as long as the terms of the licence fall within the scope of the Technology Transfer Block Exemption (TTBE).[42] However, it is not possible for a licensor to impose an obligation on its licensee, in the nature of an exclusive licence with absolute territorial protection, to prevent customers of that licensee from selling goods in other EU Member States. Likewise, a licensor should not seek to prevent imports from its own customers or another licensee in another EU Member State.

In *L.C. Nungesser KG v Commission of the European Communities*,[43] the European Court of Justice (ECJ) ruled against an indiscriminate application of Article 81 of the Treaty Establishing the European Community, which prohibits agreements that have as their object the restriction of competition within the Single Market.[44] *Nungesser* concerned a licence for plant variety rights (PVRs) in a new form of maize seed. The developer of the new variety, INRA, a research institute financed by the French Ministry of Agriculture, had granted Nungesser, a German firm, an exclusive manufacturing and sales licence to cultivate and sell in the German market four varieties of its hybrid maize seeds. By way of exclusivity, INRA agreed that it would not grant further licences in the German territory and that it would try to prevent the seeds grown in France from being exported to Germany, except to Nungesser.

On the one hand, the court found that, to the extent that the agreement sought to confer absolute territorial protection on Nungesser, by requiring that parallel importers should be prevented from obtaining the seed in France and exporting it to Germany, it fell foul of Article 81(1) and could not be saved by the exemption in Article 81(3) (Cornish and Llewelyn, 2007, p. 292–3).[45] On the other hand, the court took into account the following factors: the agreement was in the nature of an open licence, insofar as it related solely to the contractual relationship between the owner of the PVR and the licensee; the agreement provided that neither

INRA nor its French licensees would themselves export to Germany; and that they would not compete with the licensee in the licensed territory of Germany. Based on those findings the court concluded that the agreement was compatible with Article 81(1) (TFEU, art. 101; Baches Opi, 2000, pp. 102–3; Cornish and Llewelyn, 2007, pp. 292–3). The exemption pertaining to open exclusivity was justified in view of the specific nature of the product in question. In view of the risk undertaken by INRA, involving years of high-risk investment and experimentation in a new technology, the court concluded that requiring the research institute to license the hybrid maize seed, without a period of territorial exclusivity, might discourage potential licensees, who would be deterred by the prospect of direct competition in the same product from other licensees. Such an outcome would be prejudicial to the dissemination of knowledge and techniques in the Community.[46]

Regarding territorial restrictions to encourage market entry, consistent with the decision in *Nungesser*, the Council Regulation 772/2004 on the Application of Article 81(3) of the Treaty to Categories of Technology Transfer Agreements (TTBER) takes account of whether the parties are competitors, and whether the licence constitutes a reciprocal or non-reciprocal agreement.[47] With regard to geographical limitations on production, these will be considered unacceptable divisions of markets where competitors enter into reciprocal agreements (Cornish and Llewelyn, 2007, p. 293). At the other end of the spectrum, if non-competitors are involved in a non-reciprocal agreement, the licence is normally acceptable (Cornish and Llewelyn, 2007, p. 293). In sum, in recognition of the need for a more specialized approach to the dynamics of technology transfer, the TTBER differentiates intellectual property licensing agreements between competitors and those between non-competitors, to the effect that agreements between competitors are considered to pose the greater risk to competition.

Likewise, restrictions on the sale of products are not permitted between competitors where the licensing arrangements are reciprocal (Cornish and Llewelyn, 2007, p. 293). In the case of a non-reciprocal agreement, however, they may simply undertake not to make active or passive sales in the other's territory (Cornish and Llewelyn, 2007, p. 293).[48] Nevertheless, in different Member States, the parties are free to engage in passive sales in the territories of other exclusive licensees.[49] The purpose of these criteria is to protect the investment of licensees. As the ECJ remarked in the case of *Nungesser*, no licensee would take the risk of launching the new product on a new market if it were not protected against direct competition from the IPR holder and from its other licensees.[50]

5.3 Improvement Clauses

Because medical technology is normally subject to ongoing R&D, if the PRO wants to continue to pursue a particular line of research, it is important to decide whether or not new information is to be fed back from licensee to licensor and vice versa. For example, in 2000, the Research Institute of Distopia (RID), lacking the funds to develop the antibiotic EPO (erythropoietin) granted Pharmco an exclusive worldwide licence to develop the product. However, RID subsequently found that by retaining rights to sell EPO only for the kidney dialysis market, it was restricted from entering the larger, more lucrative, non-dialysis market. In order to enter that market, RID developed an improved version of EPO, known as NESP, which, having a longer life than the original product, required less frequent dosing. In response Pharmco commenced legal action to prevent the commercialization of NESP, claiming that NESP was an improvement covered by the licensing agreement to which it had exclusive rights outside the dialysis market.[51] The patentee can obtain ownership or licence to any improvements made by the licensee if a right to improvements can be negotiated as a term of the licensing agreement. Thus, RID might have obtained ownership of, or licence to any improvements, had a right to improvements been negotiated as a term of the licensing agreement. Nonetheless, caution is necessary. Reservations regarding patent rights in any improvements appear to be a stipulation that is consistent with universities' core values to promote ongoing research.[52] Rights to improvements may prove problematic with respect to competition law (Binns and Driscoll, 1998, p. 98; Thorley, Miller, Burkill and Birss, 2006, paras 10–52). Let us take the case of a PRO that is attempting to patent and license an invention for the first time. Where the PRO licensor is involved in ongoing R&D, or the licensed technology is at an early stage of development, it is likely that improvements will be made to the process or product during the term of the licence agreement. Because novel technology is normally subject to further development, it is important to decide the extent to which new information is to be circulated between licensee and licensor. Further, if additional patent rights are acquired by one, the other party is likely to consider that it is entitled to no less than a non-exclusive licence to the improvement (Mendes, 2005, p. 17).

Sub-licensing is a further area where improvements are likely to be patentable or otherwise protectable. In this event, the licensor will want the right to use any such improvements developed by the licensee. This right might extend to the licensor being able to grant a sub-licence to other licensees in other territories and may involve the licensor using the improvements for other purposes. The patentee of the original invention will usually create a network of non-reciprocal licences, territory by territory (Cornish and Llewelyn, 2007, pp. 284 et seq.). Assuming that each licensee will likely discover improvements, the patentee will normally wish to maintain control over the technology by requiring not only that licensees keep it informed of any improvements, but also 'grant back' by assignment or exclusive licence follow-on patents and rights to know-how acquired by the licensee (Cameron and Borenstein, 2003, p. 22; Cornish and Llewelyn, 2007, pp. 254ff). However, each licensee will consider this arrangement to its benefit only to the extent that it feels that there is an exchange of equal advantage. In the contrary case, not only will it be disinclined to disclose improvements, it may be unwilling to discover improvements. In this situation, without a clear direction as to duration and termination of the licence, there may be difficulties about the obligations concerning improvements which one side owes to the other at the date of termination.[53]

Even though licensees will likely want an obligation to grant access to future improvements of licensed inventions, such an undertaking may effectively yoke academic research in a particular area to a particular industry partner (AUTM, 2007b, p. 4). This constraint would directly or indirectly diminish the capacity of the PRO and its scientists to garner alternative research funding and to engage in potentially fruitful collaborations with scientists employed by companies other than the licensee, perhaps having a chilling effect on collaboration with scientists in other research institutions (AUTM, 2007b, p. 4). Even worse, if rights to improvement affect inventions in other parts of the university, then scientists who did not benefit from the licensing of the original invention may nonetheless have their prospects restricted by an overly broad clause enabling the licensee to develop the technology.

The PRO should therefore aim to limit the licensing of 'future improvements'. When dealing with improvements, it is crucial that the contract defines the nature of an improvement and, thereby, what is covered by the licence and what constitutes a new, independently patentable technology.[54] The latter case, depending on the national law, may necessitate a new licence agreement.[55] Given the potential to reduce capacity, exclusive licensees should not receive rights to 'improvement' or 'follow-on' inventions without prior consent. As a matter of practice, the licensees' rights should be limited to existing patent applications and patents, and to no more than those claims in any continuing patent applications that are either completely supported by information in an existing application or patent, or entitled to the priority date of that application or patent (AUTM, 2007b, p. 4).[56] In the event a licensee is granted patent rights to improvements, it is essential to restrict the scope of the clause so that it does not affect unrelated research and is limited as to its future operation (AUTM, 2007b, p. 4). In addition, an improvements clause should be restricted to inventions that are owned and under the control of the licensor PRO (AUTM, 2007b, p. 4).

5.4 Grant-back of Improvements and EC Competition Law

Where a licensing agreement includes a grant back provision – that is, one which provides that any improvements developed by the licensee shall be granted back to the licensor to become the licensor's property – it may be considered anti-competitive. Article 5 of the TTBER sets out the excluded restrictions. If an agreement contains any of these restrictions, it is only the restriction in question that is excluded from the benefit of the block exemption, not the whole agreement (TTBER, 2004, art. 5, recital 14). Article 5(1) provides that the Article 2 exemption shall not apply to any of the following obligations contained in technology transfer agreements:

- any direct or indirect obligation on the licensee to grant an exclusive licence to the licensor or to a third party designated by the licensor in respect of its own severable improvements to or its own new applications of the licensed technology;
- any direct or indirect obligation on the licensee to assign, in whole or in part, to the licensor or to a third party designated by the licensor, rights to its own severable improvements to or its own new applications of the licensed technology;
- any direct or indirect obligation on the licensee not to challenge the validity of intellectual property rights which the licensor holds in the common market, without prejudice to the possibility of providing for termination of the technology transfer agreement in the event that the licensee challenges the validity of one or more of the licensed intellectual property rights.

Article 5(2) of the TTBER states that when the parties to a technology licence are non-competitors the block exemption is inapplicable to restrictions 'limiting the licensee's ability to exploit its own technology' or limiting the ability of either party to the agreement 'to carry out R&D, unless such latter restriction is indispensable to prevent the disclosure of the licensed know-how to third parties'.[57] Best practice is therefore to ensure that there is no licence term that may be considered incompatible with Article 81 of the EC Treaty in so far as it seeks to restrict competition within the Common Market by controlling not only what is made with the licensed technology, but also the use which is to be made of it subsequently.[58]

6. EXEMPTIONS FOR RESEARCH AND EXPERIMENTAL USE

As ongoing research may lead to new biomedical developments, it is important for the PRO to have the freedom to explore other applications of the research results. The law has traditionally exempted universities from paying fees for patented inventions they use in their own research, following the rationale that universities fulfil a public mission. For example, the UK Patents Act creates two general exceptions for private use and for experimental use (UK Patents Act, 1977, s 60(5)).[59] However, as more public research is carried out with business for the promise of monetary reward, the rationale for such exemptions has become less clear.

Cautiously, therefore, the WHO Global Strategy and Plan of Action calls upon Member States to 'consider, where appropriate, use of a "research exception" to address public health needs in developing countries consistent with the Agreement on Trade-Related Aspects of Intellectual Property Rights' (WHO, 2008, p. 12).[60] The circumspect wording of the appeal is undoubtedly due to the uncertain position regarding exemptions for research and experimental use in national patent laws. The extent and status of this exemption differs across countries and is often ill defined. Moreover, the patchwork of national research exemptions is being eroded by legal challenge.

Traditionally, patent laws admitted such an exception for experimental use for the non-commercial activities of the research scientist in a university or government laboratory. However, where the experimental use relates to the subject matter of patents over successful pharmaceutical products (e.g., Indian Patents Act, amended 2005, s 60(5)(b)), the exemption has proven increasingly controversial (Cornish and Llewelyn, 2007, pp. 254–5). Once it has been shown that a use has been carried out for an experimental purpose, it is necessary to show that the experiment relates to the subject matter of the patent. In the English Court of Appeal in *Auchincloss v Agricultural and Veterinary Supplies*,[61] Aldous L.J. said that the subject matter of the invention must be ascertained from the patent as a whole. For example, a third party who wishes to test a cure for cancer using a genetically modified mouse cannot rely on the defence of experimental use against a claim by the patentee of the mouse (Bentley and Sherman, 2002, p. 545). A researcher wishing to use diagnostic kits containing patented processes or products to test other subject matter will need to obtain a licence.

Recent developments within Contracting States to the European Patent Convention (EPC)[62] indicate that the exception may also apply to research that is carried out for profit. Such an interpretation may have been prompted by the arrangement of the exceptions in the domestic legislation of the EPC members.[63] However, it is necessary to distinguish between research which aims to improve the invention and unrelated research activities. Use of the invention for experiments on unrelated subject matter will be difficult to defend. Likewise the defence is unlikely to cover trials to see whether a third party can produce commercially, according to the patent. The English courts have, on occasion, been willing to entertain a broad interpretation of 'experimental'.[64] Yet it is unlikely that the research exemption will be held to apply where the defendant conducts none of the exploitation of technology for its own experimental purposes, but where the defendant, in each instance, is seeking to exploit and sell its technology to third parties.[65] In this respect, English law seems to have recently moved somewhat closer to the experimental use exception as it is applied in the United States.

Recent US jurisprudence, as exemplified by the case of *Madey v Duke University*,[66] favours a restrictive interpretation of the exemption. In *Madey* the US Court of Appeals for the Federal Circuit took a narrow view of acts done privately for experimental use such that use of patented technologies in the course of university research should be limited to strictly philosophical inquiry.[67] In the result, in view of the heterogeneous character of modern research funding, universities will largely be obliged to pay licensing fees for research inputs that are protected by law.[68]

Notwithstanding the attempt in *Madey* to distinguish between a university's 'legitimate business objectives' and commercial applications for the fruits of its academic research, at least two problematic situations may be identified. First, consider a situation where the defendant conducts tests and independently discovers beneficial properties of a substance which falls within the plaintiff's patent, but which differs from the product marketed by the plaintiff (Cornish and Llewelyn, 2007, p. 254). In such a case, experiments to legitimately discover further information about the properties of the defendant's substance will be permissible, but tests to provide further evidence of already known qualities fall outside the research exemption (Cornish and Llewelyn, 2007, p. 254). For example, in *Monsanto v Stauffer*,[69] Stauffer had developed a market variant of Monsanto's successful patented weed-killer 'Roundup', for which Stauffer established tests both inside and outside a research farm where interested parties could observe the results. The English Court of Appeal limited the interpretation of the word 'experimental' in accordance to its size, scale, recipient and methodology. Accordingly, the court allowed the defendant to continue its in-house experiments, but disallowed tests done outside a research farm on the basis that trials carried out in order to demonstrate to a third party that a product works cannot be regarded as acts done for experimental purposes.

Secondly, consider a situation where the defendant is testing for new uses and further information about the properties of a patented product, including the results of clinical trials with patients (Cornish and Llewelyn, 2007, p. 255). In 2004, the European Union introduced an extension of the experimental use exception to cover experimental testing for the purpose of seeking regulatory approval, thus bringing the position somewhat closer to that prevailing under the US Hatch-Waxman Act.[70] It is the accepted view that the purpose of Article 10(6) of the EU Medicinal Products for Human Use Directive[71] is to provide a 'Bolar'-type exemption from patent infringement in respect of experiments and trials, pre-clinical and clinical, conducted in pursuance of seeking regulatory approval for a generic or similar biological medicinal product. Nevertheless, care with drafting reservation clauses is particularly important in this area because it is not clear which 'trials and studies' are exempted. In particular, there is uncertainty regarding the application of the experimental use exception in Article 10(6) in cases where a third party wishes to conduct tests for the purposes of developing a new drug on the basis that the data may ultimately be used for an application for marketing authorization for that new drug.

There is likely to be greater uncertainty as to the scope of the experimental use exemption in the sphere of biotechnology, where it may be more difficult to draw a distinction between basic research and its commercial application (Cornish and Llewelyn, 2007, p. 255). It is important that this science, so vital to diagnostics and drug discovery, should remain open to experimentation and further progress.[72] The *Gowers Review of Intellectual Property*, commissioned by the UK Government, suggested that, in terms of a dividing line, the exception should only operate in those cases where licences of the existing patent are unlikely to be given – such as where a patentee is seeking to monopolize further experimentation (Gowers, 2006, pp. 45–76).

6.1 Draft Clauses for the Use and Practice of the Invention

6.1.1 Academic research

Consequently, it is advisable to prepare for the worst case, by considering the definitions of non-commercial use in light of *Madey*. Licensing contracts should seek to ensure that universities are reserving rights that are broader than those of an unlicensed party, and that activities held under *Madey* to constitute the university's 'legitimate business objectives, including educating ... students and faculty participating in [research] projects' are within the scope of reserved rights (AUTM, 2007b, p. 11). For example, for the purposes of such a clause 'Non-Commercial Research Purposes' should be defined to include:

> Use or practice of *licensed patent rights* for academic research and other not-for-profit or scholarly purposes which are undertaken at a non-profit or governmental institution that does not involve the production or manufacture of products for sale or the performance of services for a fee.
>
> Without limiting the foregoing:
>
> (i) 'academic research and other not-for-profit or scholarly purposes' includes, in non-limiting fashion, research that leads, or may lead, to patentable or unpatentable inventions that may be licensed or otherwise transferred, either directly or indirectly, to third parties; and
>
> (ii) neither (A) receipt of license revenues on account of such inventions or receipt of reimbursements for the costs of preparation and shipping of samples of materials provided to third parties as a professional courtesy, in response to post-publication requests or otherwise in accordance with academic custom nor (B) receipt of funding to cover the direct and/or indirect costs of research, shall constitute sale of products or performance of service for a fee. (AUTM, 2007b, p. 11)

In summary, in drafting reservation of rights clauses and associated definitions, it is important to keep in mind the relatively restricted scope of the research exemption.[73]

6.1.2 Rights to use

Similarly, universities should reserve the right to use or practise licensed inventions with a view to ensuring that other scholars are able to substantiate scientific data without concern for patents, and that scientists are able to publish the results of their research in theses, conference papers and peer-reviewed journals (AUTM, 2007b, p. 2). To this end, even when the invention is licensed exclusively to a commercial entity, PROs should nevertheless consider reserving rights in entire fields of use, for themselves and other non-profit research laboratories (AUTM, 2007b, p. 2). Such a general reservation should clearly articulate the scope of reserved rights to practise inventions and to use associated information and data for research and educational purposes, including research sponsored by commercial entities, and to transfer tangible research materials (such as biological materials and chemical compounds) and intangible materials (such as databases and know-how) to others in the non-profit and governmental sectors (AUTM, 2007b, p. 2; e.g., Gene Service, no date). For example, such a reservation clause should include a definition of non-commercial use, to read:

> The University reserves the rights, for itself and others, to
>
> (i) make and use, solely for Non-Commercial Research Purposes, the subject matter described and claimed in patent rights and covered by property rights; and
> (ii) provide to others the Biological Materials;

As used herein, the term 'Non-Commercial Research Purposes' means: Use of patent rights for academic research or other not-for-profit or scholarly purposes which are undertaken at a non-profit or governmental institution that does not use patent rights in the production or manufacture of products for sale or the performance of services for a fee (AUTM, 2007b, p. 2).

7. PUBLICATION AND ACCESS RIGHTS

In this section we consider how the terms of the licensing contract might preserve publication and access rights to the results of research and to new medical technologies. The global network of PROs shares a responsibility in advancing the medical knowledge of researchers in developing countries. One of the ways in which they can do this is by preserving open access to the results of scientific research.[74] The success of WHO's Access to Research Initiative 'HINARI' depends not only on major publishers enabling developing countries to access medical journals, but also on the extent to which PROs facilitate early publication.

However, since PROs began patenting the results of research, publication and access to scientific data connected with the subject matter of the patent have become a contentious issue. Pre-grant, as soon as the technology is identified for patent protection, the confidentiality needed to preserve the art in the invention comes into conflict with the goal of the PRO for the dissemination of research. Premature publication in articles, research papers and at conferences may destroy the novelty of a patentable invention.[75]

The licensing contract should reflect the necessary trade-off between the potential for future patent protection and the ability to freely publish the results of research. By way of compromise, the competing interests of the parties will typically be addressed by specifying withholding periods for publication; and providing industry partners with the opportunity to review any proposed publication, exclusive of the right to prohibit publication.

There is considerable scope for the self-regulation of publication in the licensing contract, as the following example illustrates:

> Nothing in this Agreement will be deemed to limit the right of the Institution to publish any and all technical data resulting from any research performed by the Institution relating to the Invention and to make and use the Invention, Licensed Product, and Licensed Services and to practice the Licensed Method and associated technology and allow other educational and non-profit institutions to do so for educational and research purposes (AUTM, 2007b, p. 10).

Apart from the problem of jeopardizing the novelty of the invention by early publication, there is a further issue, which is more difficult to address. There is considerably less awareness of what needs to be done in the period that starts with the first patent filing and ends, at most, one year later with the filing of follow-up applications. Researchers may well assume that having secured a priority date through a first application, they have effectively secured patent protection for an invention and that they are therefore free to publish their research. However, under European patent law, there are situations where such a publication may have adverse consequences for the patenting process.[76] If patentability of the original claims appears doubtful, the publication may need to be postponed in order to allow the filing of a follow-up application with additional features that were not disclosed in the priority application.[77]

Post-grant, the patentee will desire to maintain monopoly over the use of the invention. Instances of restricted access to proprietary research tools (for example, for genetic testing) risks slowing research and raising costs in developing countries (Heller, 1998, p. 626). It may potentially lead to a loss of expertise and information among other researchers. One notorious example is the monopoly Myriad acquired on BRCA1 and BRCA2 genes. The University of Utah, the National Institutes of Health (NIH) and the firm Myriad Genetics co-owned the BRCA1 patent covering the methods and materials used to isolate the gene associated with susceptibility to breast and ovarian cancer. In short, the initial US patent covered not only the DNA sequence of the genes, and therefore any reproduction, but also all diagnostic and therapeutic applications (Coriat and Orsi, 2005, pp. 1212–3). Initially, Myriad Genetics was not the sole beneficiary of the patent. By 1998, however, it succeeded in obtaining from rival patentees all the patents on the BRCA1 and BRCA2 genes. In turn, this gave Myriad unchallenged control over the main research materials concerning genes coding for breast and ovarian cancer susceptibility, thereby allowing it to make further discoveries and ultimately to file further patent applications as a result of such discoveries. In this case, the legal effect of Myriad's US patents was that it was able to monopolize the data collection, analysis and price of the genetic tests in that country (Coriat and Orsi, 2005, pp. 1212–3).[78]

By definition, exclusive licences limit the diffusion of medical technologies. In order to manage the potential conflict relating to the dissemination of knowledge and the commercialization of research, technology transfer officers should consider including clauses in licence agreements to protect access to the research tools for future research and discovery. The drafting of such an exclusive licence should specify that the licence is exclusive for the sale, but not use, of such products and services. By such means, the PRO seeks to ensure that it is free to license non-exclusively to others the right to use the patented technology (AUTM, 2007b, p. 5).

Further, recalling that patent law provisions concerning research exemptions differ across countries, to ensure that the conditions and cost of basic research remain manageable, technology transfer officers should seek to clarify the terms of access rights to research within the licensing contract. Negotiators should consider a series of contractual terms that are aimed at promoting the diffusion of university research. Where patent law allows, such provisions may include:

1. Providing for a grace period for protecting the PRO against a publication of the invention before the filing date. By such means, if a scientist wishes to publish the invention, he or she may do so, and the PRO may still validly file an application which will be considered novel despite the publication, provided that the filing is made during the grace period following the publication.[79]
2. Making a provisional filing of the patents on improvement with a one-year option for possible future filing, where the patent office allows.[80]

The provisional patent application keeps an option open to file patent applications internationally for one year. The one-year Paris Convention period may be used to conduct further development on the product and also to test the product in the marketplace to see if the product is successful and if it is worthwhile to proceed with the patenting procedure. At the end of the one-year Paris Convention period (Paris Convention, 1967, art. 4), the applicant may proceed to file complete patent applications in foreign countries of interest.

Alternatively, and to delay the costs of filing patent applications in the various countries, it is possible to file an 'international' patent application, or a Patent Cooperation Treaty (PCT) application.[81] A further advantage is that an international patent examiner conducts an independent novelty search and provides a written opinion on the patentability of the invention. The examination report can provide a good indication of whether it is worthwhile to proceed to file patent applications internationally.

8. TERMINATION AND CONCLUSION

This chapter has been premised upon the notion that the patent licensing contract is capable of creating some further space for the R&D of health products. Nevertheless, the asymmetrical relationship between property and contract can ultimately pose risks for the licensor, depending on the degree to which it may be considered in competition with the licensee. The PRO licensor therefore has an interest in protecting its intellectual property against internal attack from a licensee who decides to challenge the validity of the patent. The simplest means to guard against such a prospect is for the licensor to include a contractual provision indicating that, upon any challenge of the patented technology, the licensing agreement will be immediately terminated.[82] In such an event, the licensee would no longer be in a position to reap the benefits of the licence and the licensor could immediately look for another licensee.[83] Then again, since preserving the commercial relationship is important to a PPP, the licensor may prefer to add a clause providing pre-suit notification. This provision would give the licensor the opportunity to renegotiate the agreement or evaluate the strength of the licensee's claim.[84] The foregoing analysis has shown how patent licensing may offer a self-regulatory solution to the inherent tension between strong international patent protection and the norms of open science.[85] Owing to the conflict of interests associated with the transfer of technology from university to the business sector, it is necessary to safeguard the mission of universities to disseminate medical research for the public benefit. In order to address the interests of universities in developing countries in continued research into local diseases, as well as those of industry partners in minimizing the financial risks of product development, patent licensing agreements need to include appropriately tailored restriction and reservation clauses.[86] While many inventions do not merit the expense of filing for patent protection, those that do depend on technology transfer officers utilizing an appropriate mix of licences, and drafting terms that promote pharmaceutical R&D for the greater welfare of under-served patient populations.

NOTES

1. For example, maternal conditions are a major contributor to the global burden of disease, yet the pipeline of new drugs specifically for maternal health is less than 3 per cent of the pipeline in cardiovascular health (WHO, UNICEF, UNFPA and the World Bank, 2007; Zuniga and Guellec, 2009).
2. US Bayh-Dole Act of 1980, Pub. L. No. 96–517, § 6(a), 94 Stat. 3015, 3019–28 (1980) (codified as amended at 35 USC §§ 200–12 (2006)).
3. A patent licence is a contract by which the patent holder (the licensor) authorizes another party (the licensee) to use its invention under certain, normally financial, conditions.
4. An '"exclusive licence" means a licence from the proprietor of or applicant for a patent conferring on the licensee ... to the exclusion of all other persons (including the proprietor or applicant), any right in respect of the invention to which the patent or application relates': UK Patents Act, 1977, s 130.
5. Article 28 of TRIPs, which concerns the rights conferred on the patentee, stipulates that during the term of the patent, any person imitating the invention not having the consent of the patent holder, is committing an act of infringement.
6. In the chemical and pharmaceutical industries patent licensing tends to be as high as 80 per cent (Zuniga and Guellec, 2009, p. 8).
7. This chapter is concerned primarily with research universities and research centres funded by public funds (collectively public research organizations or PROs).
8. Further on the importance of dissemination, see WHO (2005a, 2005b) and practical initiatives such as the United Nations Health Internetwork Access to Research Initiative (various dates), a project to make scientific journals accessible.
9. See also the resolutions of the Fifty-Eighth World Health Assembly aiming, *inter alia*, to foster public-private partnerships in R&D (WHO, 2005a, 2005b).
10. Pub. L. No. 96–517, § 6(a), 94 Stat. 3015, 3019–28 (1980) (codified as amended at 35 USC §§ 200–12 (2006)). See generally Council on Government Relations (1999).
11. 'It is the policy and objective of Congress to use the patent system to promote the utilization of inventions arising from federally supported research or development ... [and] to promote the collaboration between commercial concerns and non-profit organizations, including universities'. 35 USC § 200 (2006).
12. Larger universities will have an R&D department or knowledge transfer office as well as a company that provides commercialization services to the university. As a department or institute does not have legal personality,

incorporation is the most effective means of ensuring that the PRO has the legal capacity to assume ownership and control of intellectual property.

13. Note that generating revenue for universities was not the actual goal of the Bayh-Dole Act, which requires that the profits accruing to the beneficiary non-profit organizations 'be utilized for the support of scientific research or education': 35 USC § 202(c)(7) (2006).
14. Between 1975 and 1996, R&D for diseases in developing countries has declined rather than increased. Of the new chemical entities developed between 1975 and 1996, only 11 were for the treatment of tropical diseases (Trouiller and Ollario, 1999, p. 61).
15. On addressing the lack of R&D for neglected diseases, see Drugs for Neglected Diseases Initiative (various dates).
16. For tropical diseases affecting 90 per cent of the world population, only 10 per cent of the research is allocated to them (UK Parliamentary Office on Science and Technology, 2005).
17. The OECD has 31 members, the majority of whom are developed countries, for a current list, see http://www.oecd.org/countrieslist/0,3351,en_33873108_33844430_1_1_1_1_1,00.html (accessed 8 September 2010).
18. Two 'IP hubs' were established in Colombia (SECOPI) and the Economic Community of Central African States (SECOVIPI), using local researchers, lawyers and managers selected among the 130 persons that had been trained by WIPO. With the support of SECOPI in Colombia, patents have been filed nationally and through the Patent Cooperation Treaty on a kit for the diagnosis of various cancers. With the support of SECOVIPI, the participating research institute in Gabon has also filed patent applications for plant extracts to produce drugs against cancer (WIPO, 2007).
19. A number of scientific organizations, such as the Academy of Sciences of the Developing World (TWAS), the Consortium on Science, Technology and Innovation for the South (formerly the Third World Network of Scientific Organizations), the African Union (AU) and the Organization of the Islamic Conference's (OIC) Standing Committee on Science and Technology (COMSTECH), are promoting South-South research collaboration by means of policy interventions and initiatives. Developing countries of similar economic standing are also increasingly building bilateral and multilateral collaborations, such as the India–Brazil–South Africa Collaboration.
20. KEMRI received an award for Quality Scientific Research and excellent management in the International Quality Summit Awards Ceremony in 2007 in New York (BioChem Solutions, no date).
21. Local and regional collaborators include universities, hospitals, government agencies such as the Kenyatta National Hospital, the Suez Canal University-Egypt; Noguchi Memorial Institute of Medical Research, Ghana; the Ethiopia Health and Nutrition Research Institute; Makerere University Medical School; University of Zambia Medical School; and the Medical Research Council of South Africa. International collaborators include the WHO; Japan International Cooperation Agency (JICA); Walter Reed Army

Institute of Medical Research (WRAIR); United States Agency for International Development (USAID); and the Royal Tropical Institute, Amsterdam. See KEMRI (various dates). Of note also is the Centre for Health Policy and Strategic Studies in Lagos, Nigeria, founded in 1995. Among Nigeria's Medical Schools, the University of Ibadan and the College of Medicine at the University of Lagos are particularly active in R&D.

22. The OECD Science, Technology and Industry Scoreboard 2007 analyses shares of NPL (non-patent literature) in citations across patent classes in order to provide insights into the technologies that are closer to scientific R&D and thus more dependent on the progress of scientific knowledge. Indicated patent concentrations in the biotechnological and pharmaceutical industries are consistent with other observed patterns of science-industry linkages in these fields (OECD, 2007).
23. For a discussion of the need for change based on the instability of the revenue stream for the development and marketing of innovative products, see von Braun and Pugatch (2005).
24. Gilbert, Henske and Singh (2003) explain that the blockbuster business model that underpinned the major pharmaceutical companies' success is irreparably broken.
25. The phrase 'Big Pharma' is commonly used to refer to pharmaceutical companies such as GlaxoSmithKline with revenue in excess of $3 billion, or R&D expenditure in excess of $500 million: see House of Commons Select Committee on Health (2005).
26. GlaxoSmithKline has announced it will reinvest a fifth of any residual profits made in developing countries in improving local health care, and share with other researchers the intellectual property on any of its experimental chemical compounds that could treat 'neglected' developing world diseases (Jack, 2009). See also Asakawa and Som (2008), discussing the growing trend of foreign research and development investment in China and India. Further concerning the move by Big Pharma to outsource R&D to developing countries (PricewaterhouseCoopers, 2007).
27. See World Bank (2009b), explaining how China and India's economic rise over the last two decades has accelerated their trade and investment flows with the Middle East and North Africa. The major strengths the Indian pharmaceutical industry has to offer PROs in developing countries include a cost-competitive manufacturing base that extends to clinical studies; extensive skills in chemistry and process development; the ability to manufacture over 50 per cent of the bulk drugs needed for its pharmaceutical production activities locally; the emergence of a promising biotechnology industry; the availability of local scientists and R&D personnel of a high scientific quality; and a wide network of organizations performing various aspects of pharmaceutical R&D (Sampath, 2005).
28. Ranbaxy is but one Indian pharmaceutical company that announced plans to spin off its drug-discovery division to a new subsidiary, to be called Ranbaxy Life Science Research that will enable the company to create intellectual property at a faster pace while also positioning for future expansion (Grover, 2008). Further, concerning the capacity of developing

countries with innovation capacity to access foreign technology, see Agarwal, Gupta and Dayal (2007) and Barton and Emanuel (2005).

29. The Indian pharmaceutical company Cipla has a presence in all the 53 markets of Africa. See Patwardhan (2007), explaining how Indian pharmaceutical companies consider the potential demand for drugs within Africa as an opportunity not to be ignored.
30. India is the preferred country to source pharmaceuticals especially ARVs and anti-malarials because of its competitiveness. India's full compliance with the TRIPs Agreement will only affect medicines patented since 2005, but the impact will be sizeable, as it will affect disease categories that show a high speed of new product development due to emerging resistance, including ARVs, anti-malarials and TB drugs, as well as new drug classes such as those for cancer and diabetes which have little therapeutic substitution (Sampath, 2005).
31. Further, Ranbaxy Laboratories acquired Be-Tabs Pharmaceuticals, the largest manufacturer of penicillin formulations in South Africa (Hindu Business Line, 2007).
32. For example, Section 30(4)(b) of the UK Patents Act 1977 provides that 'a licence may be granted under any patent or any such application for working the invention which is the subject of the patent or the application'. See further Jones (1993).
33. See de Larena (2007), discussing the intersection of normative values between intellectual property and contract law.
34. See especially Article 8 of TRIPs art. 8, providing that 'Members may, in ... their laws and regulations, adopt measures necessary to protect public health'. See to the same effect, para. 4 of the Declaration on the TRIPs Agreement and Public Health: 'We agree that the TRIPs Agreement does not and should not prevent members from taking measures to protect public health'.
35. See Articles 2(1) and 23 of International Covenant on Economic, Social and Cultural Rights, concerning the obligation of State Parties to afford less-developed nations technical assistance and cooperation.
36. On the current balance of rights and obligations, see United Nations High Commissioner for Human Rights (2000).
37. Exclusive licensees can sue infringers in their own right: see, eg, UK Patents Act (1977, s 67(1)).
38. Exclusivity is also important to university spin-offs in the biomedical field because both rely on protected intellectual property as their main asset in raising capital for development (OECD, 2004, p. 22).
39. Stakeholders included the UK University Research & Industry Links (AURIL), the Confederation of British Industry (CBI) and the Small Business Service (SBS): see Lambert Working Group on Intellectual Property (2005).
40. Formerly Article 28 of the Treaty Establishing the European Community (TEC). See also Article 101 TFEU (ex Article 81 TEC) prohibiting all agreements between undertakings which may affect trade between Member States and which have as their object or effect the restriction of competition within the internal or single market.

41. In *Centrafarm BV v Sterling Drug* (C–15/74) 1974 E.C.R. 1147, the ECJ held that the owner of the patent in Holland could not use its patent to block imports of drugs which had been put on the market in the UK with its consent under the protection of its UK patent; see also *Merck Inc v Stephar BV* (C–187/80) 1981 E.C.R 2063. Regarding trademarked pharmaceuticals, see *Boehringer Ingelheim KG and Boehringer Ingelheim Pharma GmbH & Co KG v Swingward* (C–348/04) 2007 E.C.R. I–3391. The ECJ held there that rules allowing trade mark owners to object to parallel imported pharmaceuticals within the European Economic Area (EEA) apply to re-labelled, as well as re-boxed, products.
42. Council Regulation 772/2004, On the Application of Article 81(3) of the Treaty to Categories of Technology Transfer Agreements, 2004 OJ (L 127) 11 (TTBER) provides block exemptions (or safe harbours) for IP licensing agreements, ensuring that certain technology transfer agreements are automatically exempt from the application of Article 81(1) of the EC Treaty (Article 101(1) TFEU) which prohibits anti-competitive agreements. Note that the technology transfer agreement must concern the production or supply of goods (Recital 7). Note further that R&D agreements are not covered by the TTBE, but by Council Regulation 2659/2000, On the Application of Article 81(3) of the Treaty to Categories of Research and Development Agreements, 2000 OJ (L 304) 7.
43. (C–258/78) 1982 E.C.R. 2015.
44. As of 1 December 2009 the Lisbon Treaty came into force within the European Union. As a result the numbering of the Articles that relate to the single market and competition has changed. See Article 101 TFEU (ex Article 81 TEC).
45. Article 101(3) TFEU (ex Article 81(3) TEC) provides by way of exception that 'the provisions of paragraph 1 may, however, be declared inapplicable in the case of: any agreement … between undertakings', which contributes to promoting technical or economic progress and 'which does not afford such undertakings the possibility of eliminating competition in respect of a substantial part of the products in question'.
46. *L.C. Nungesser KG v Commission of the European Communities* (C–258/78) 1982 E.C.R. 2015 at [57].
47. The test of whether an agreement may benefit from the block exemption is whether the parties to the agreement fall within specified market share thresholds. Where the parties are competitors, the threshold is reached if their combined market share is 20 per cent or more. Where they are not, the threshold is only crossed if either of them separately has a 30 per cent share or more: see TTBER art. 3. There is reciprocity when each party is licensing competing technologies to the other. For the definitions of reciprocal and non-reciprocal agreements: see TTBER art. 1(c)–(d).
48. Active sales by the licensee are made by actively approaching individual customers inside another distributor's exclusive territory by, for instance, direct mail or visits or other promotions specifically targeted at that customer group; whereas sales in response to unsolicited requests from individual customers are considered passive sales: see Commission Notice, Guidelines on Vertical Restraints, 2000 OJ (C 291) 1–44, para. 50.

49. See, for example, Commission Notice, Guidelines on the Application of Article 81 of the EC Treaty to Technology Transfer Agreements, 2004 OJ (C 101), paras 63, 64, 77.
50. *L.C. Nungesser KG v Commission of the European Communities* (C–258/78) 1982 E.C.R. 2015 at [44].
51. Regarding the dispute between Amgen, a start-up biotechnology company, and Ortho Pharmaceutical, a subsidiary of Johnson & Johnson, over erythropoietin alfa (EPO) and the improvement, a hyperglycosylated analogue of EPO known as NESP, see Dow and Quigley (2004).
52. The standard improvement clause in a patent licence would stipulate: 'If during the continuation of this Agreement the Owner shall develop or discover any improvement to any of the Inventions (Improvement), the Owner shall promptly notify the Licensee and provide full details to the Licensee', see Commission Notice, Guidelines on Vertical Restraints, 2000 OJ (C 291) 1, para. 50.
53. See generally *National Broach v Churchill Gear* [1965] RPC 516 CA.
54. Where the nature of the licensed subject matter leaves any room for uncertainty, the licensor may be advised to add an exclusionary clause pointing out that 'improvement' does not include developments to materials or processes useful in practising the inventions of the licensed patents, but which do not themselves infringe the licensed claims of the licensed patent (Einhorn and Parker, 1968, para. 6A03[c]).
55. Under US patent law, if the licensee participated in the improvement enough to qualify as a named inventor he will have the right of use regardless of a licence. 35 USC § 262 (2006).
56. Note that the 'priority date' or the date of filing of the first application marks the point at which the patent will be examined for novelty, both at home and in the case of subsequent foreign applications (Paris Convention, 1967, art. 4).
57. The Commission may withdraw the benefit of the block exemption pursuant to Article 29(1) of Regulation 1/2003 where it finds that a technology transfer agreement has certain effects which are incompatible with the conditions laid down in Article 81(3) of the EC Treaty (TTBER art. 6, recital 16).
58. *Intel Corp v Via Technologies Inc* [2002] EWCA Civ 1905 per Morritt V.C. at 72.
59. Both Article 69 of the European Patent Convention and the Protocol on the Interpretation of Article 69 specify that the scope of the right is determined by the terms of the claims. See also European Patent Convention (1973, art. 27(b)); Council Agreement 89/695 Relating to Community Patents, [1989] OJ (L 401) 1, and Article 9(b) of the draft Community Patent Regulation of 2004 which states that a 'Community Patent shall not extend to acts done for experimental purposes relating to the subject matter of the patented invention'. Proposal 10786/00 for a Council Regulation on the Community Patent art. 9(b), 2000 OJ (C 337).
60. Concerning the use of research exemptions, see also Commission on Intellectual Property Rights, Innovation and Public Health (2006, pp. 68–9).
61. [1999] RPC 397 CA (Civ Div).

62. Article 64(3) of the EPC provides that any infringement of a European patent shall be dealt with by national law. Therefore no provision regarding defences to infringement is found in the EPC. For a current list of Contracting States, see http://www.epo.org/about-us/epo/member-states.html#contracting (accessed 8 September 2010).
63. Most Contracting States have introduced a uniform, general non-industry specific experimental use exception in their patent statutes. For example, Sections 60(5)(a) and (b) of the UK Patents Act refer to an act which is 'done privately and for purposes which are not commercial', followed immediately by reference to an act which 'is done for experimental purposes relating to the subject-matter of the invention'. See also Cornish and Llewelyn (2007, p. 254).
64. See *Monsanto v Stauffer Chem. Co* [1985] RPC 515 CA (Civ Div); *Smith Kline & French Laboratories Ltd v Evans Medical Ltd* [1989] F.S.R 513 Ch D. The court in the latter case observed that 'what is or is not an experiment must depend upon the facts of each case but can include experiments designed with a commercial end in view'.
65. *Inhale Therapeutic Systems Inc v Quadrant Healthcare Plc* [2002] RPC 21 Ch D.
66. 307 F. 3d 1351 (Fed. Cir. 2003).
67. The later concept reflects the common law experimental use exception, considered to have originated in the remarks of Justice Story that the legislature could not have intended to punish those who undertook 'philosophical experiments' with protected items: *Whittemore v Cutter* 29 F. Cas. 1120, 1121 (C.C.D. Mass. 1813).
68. Similarly see *Merck KGaA v Integra LifeSciences I, Ltd*, 545 US 193 (2005), where the US Supreme Court held academic research too remote from the regulatory filing process to fall within the scope of the exemption allowable under the safe harbour provision of the Hatch-Waxman Act, also known as the Drug Price Competition and Patent Term Restoration Act of 1984, 35 USC § 271(e)(1) (2006).
69. [1985] RPC 515.
70. The Hatch-Waxman Act allows generics to win FDA marketing approval by submitting bioequivalence studies. Manufacturers of generic pharmaceuticals are permitted to use the technology of a patented pharmaceutical to perform work that would assist in the marketing or regulatory approval of the generic product, while the patent is in force. The 'Bolar' provision then allows the generic producer to market and manufacture their goods as soon as the patent expires. It also grants a period of additional marketing exclusivity to make up for the time a patented pipeline drug remains in development. This extension cannot exceed five years, and it is in addition to the 20-year exclusivity granted by the issuance of a patent.
71. 'Conducting the necessary studies and trials with a view to the application of paragraphs 1, 2, 3 and 4 and the consequential practical requirements shall not be regarded as contrary to patent rights or to supplementary protection certificates for medicinal products'. Council and European Parliament Directive 2004/27, amending Directive 2001/83 on the Community Code Relating to Medicinal Products for Human Use, 2004 OJ (L 136) 6,

art. 10. This provision was implemented in Section 60(5) of the UK Patents Act. Note the Directive introduced an eight-year data exclusivity period with an additional two years of market exclusivity so that a generic product is not marketed until 10 years have elapsed from the initial authorization of the reference product.

72. In *Madey* the court held that Duke University could not rely on the experimental use exception as it had used Madey's patents to further its business, one of providing education. In an unsuccessful attempt to have the decision overturned by the Supreme Court, Professor Sarnoff and others filed an *amicus curiae* brief, arguing that the Federal Circuit's narrow interpretation of the experimental use exception impeded the 'Progress of Science and useful Arts' (US Constitution, art. I, § 8, cl. 8). Insofar as under that interpretation, most basic research would be seen as furthering a business purpose, rather than strictly philosophical inquiry. Scientists would therefore need to license essential patented technologies and other research inputs, see Sarnoff (2005).
73. Sarnoff and Holman (2008) discuss a variety of alternatives to the experimental use and regulatory approval exceptions that could facilitate access and continued use of patented technologies in scientific research and commercial development.
74. The OECD's 'Principles and Guidelines for Access to Research Data from Public Funding' serve to stress the importance of publication and access to scientific research in meeting the challenges of health care, see OECD (2007).
75. The requirements of patent law for novelty and non-obviousness involve searching for *prior art,* i.e., earlier publications that show the invention is not new or obvious. See *Massachusetts Institute of Technology v AB Fortia* 774 F. 2d 1104 (Fed. Cir. 1985).
76. Regarding the underlying legal principles European Patent Office Enlarged Board of Appeals, see European Patent Office, DG3: DBA case G 0003/93 EBA (16 August 1994).
77. Paying a filing fee during the priority application leads to the EPO issuing a search report and a written opinion, which may provide the applicant with advanced notice of the doubtfulness of patentability: see European Patent Office (2005).
78. Note also the difficulties Myriad Genetics experienced in attempting to dominate the European market. The grant of three patents on BRCA genes by the European Patent Office (EPO) to the company provoked significant controversy: see Matthijs (2006, p. 99).
79. For example, US law provides for a 'grace period' of one year prior to the date of application: see 35 USC § 102 (2006) (Conditions for Patentability; Novelty and Loss of Right to Patent). Disclosures by the inventor during the 'grace period' do not have a patent-defeating effect. In contrast, other patent laws, including that in the EPC, have an 'absolute novelty' requirement such that any disclosures, including those by an inventor himself, made prior to the date a patent application is filed, are considered prior art.
80. For example, in South Africa it is possible to file a provisional patent application, a complete patent application, or a Patent Cooperation Treaty

(PCT) international patent application which also designates South Africa. If the idea has not been finalized in detail then a provisional patent application is usually the first step in obtaining patent protection while having 12 months during which to conduct further experiments and make further improvements (South African Institute of Intellectual Property Law, various dates).

81. The main advantage of filing a PCT application is that the deadline for filing patent applications in countries or territories of interest is delayed by a further 18 months. The cost of filing a PCT application typically ranges from £4,000–£6,000.
82. Article 5(1)(c) of the TTBER states that the exemption will not apply to 'any direct or indirect obligation on the licensee not to challenge the validity of intellectual property rights which the licensor holds in the common market, without prejudice to the possibility of providing for termination of the technology transfer agreement in the event that the licensee challenges the validity of one or more of the licensed intellectual property rights'.
83. On the enforceability of such a provision, see *Lear v Adkins*, 395 US 653 (1969).
84. See, for example, the Drug Price Competition and Patent Term Restoration Act (Hatch Waxman Act), 21 USC § 301 (1984), which provides for a notification process similar to that by Generic Drug Manufacturers under Section 505(j), para. IV.
85. Concerning the need for R&D that also facilitates access to technologies for health, see WHO (2003, pp. 2–3).
86. An express reservation of rights in a licensing agreement can ensure that the PRO's institutional objectives to support humanitarian applications of its technology are not inhibited by an overly broad definition of the licensee's rights (Bennett, 2009).

BIBLIOGRAPHY

Agarwal, Sumit P., Ashwani Gupta and Rajeshwar Dayal (2007), 'Technology transfer perspectives in globalizing India (drugs and pharmaceuticals and biotechnology)', *Journal of Technology Transfer*, **32**(4), 397–423.

Arora, Ashish and Andrea Fosfuri (2003), 'Licensing the market for technology', *Journal of Economic Behavior & Organization*, **52**(2), 277–95.

Asakawa, Kazuhiro and Ashok Som (2008), 'Internationalization of R&D in China and India: Conventional wisdom versus reality', *Asia Pacific Journal of Management'*, **25**(3), 375–94.

Association of University Technology Managers [AUTM] (2004), *FY 2004 Licensing Survey*, Deerfield, Illinois, USA: AUTM.

AUTM (2005), *FY 2005 Licensing Survey*, Deerfield, Illinois, USA: AUTM.

AUTM (2006), *FY 2006 Licensing Survey*, Deerfield, Illinois, USA: AUTM.

AUTM (2007a), *FY 2007 Licensing Survey*, Deerfield, Illinois, USA: AUTM.

AUTM (2007b), 'In the public interest: Nine points to consider in licensing university technology', available at http://otl.stanford.edu/documents/whitepaper-10.pdf (accessed 20 July 2009).

Baches Opi, Sergio (2000), 'The approaches of the European Commission and the US antitrust agencies towards exclusivity clauses in licensing agreements', *Boston College International and Comparative Law Review*, **24**, 85–144.

Barton, John H. and Emanuel J. Ezekiel (2005), 'The patents-based pharmaceutical development process: Rationale, problems, and potential reforms', *Journal of American Medical Association*, **294** (16), 2075–82.

Bennett, Alan B. (2009), 'Reservation of rights for humanitarian uses', in Anatole Krattiger (ed.), *Executive Guide to Intellectual Property Management in Health and Agricultural Innovation: A Handbook of Best Practices*, Oxford, UK, Rio De Janeiro, Brazil, Davis and Ithaca, USA: MIHR, Oswaldo Cruz Foundation and bioDevelopments-International Institute, pp. 41–5.

Bentley, Lionel and Brad Sherman (2002), *Intellectual Property Law*, Oxford: Oxford University Press.

Binns, Richard and Bryan Driscoll (1998), 'Intellectual property issues in R&D contracts, *Pharmaceutical Science and Technology Today'*, **1**(3), 95–9.

BioChem Solutions (no date), 'Product development', available at http://www.biochemsolutionsinc.com/development.php (accessed 20 July 2009).

Cameron, Donald M. and Rowena Borenstein (2003), 'Key aspects of IP Licence agreements', delivered at Key Business Agreements Seminar, Canadian Institute, Toronto, 30 September, available at http://www.jurisdiction.com/lic101.pdf (accessed 26 June 2009).

Commission on Intellectual Property Rights, Innovation and Public Health (2006), *Public Health, Innovation and Intellectual Property Rights*, Geneva: World Health Organization.

Coriat, Benjamin and Fabienne Orsi (2005), 'Are "strong patents" beneficial to innovative activities? Lessons from the genetic testing for breast cancer controversies', *Industrial and Corporate Change*, **14**(6), 1205–21.

Cornish, William and David Llewelyn (2007), *Intellectual Property: Patents, Copyrights, Trademarks and Allied Rights*, London: Sweet and Maxwell.

Council on Government Relations (1999), *The Bayh–Dole Act: A Guide to the Law and Implementing Regulations*, New York and Washington DC: COGR.

Council Regulation 772/2004 [TTBER] (2004), *On the application of Article 81(3) of the treaty to categories of technology transfer agreements*, 2004 OJ (L 127) 11.

Dasgupta, Partha and Paul A. David (1994), 'Toward a new economics of science', *Research Policy*, **23**(5), 487–521.

David, Paul A., David Mowery and Edward Steinmueller (1992), 'Analysing the economic payoffs from basic research', *Economics of Innovation and New Technology*, **2**(1), 73–90.

de Larena, Lorelei R. (2007), 'License to sue?' FSU College of Law, Public Law Research Paper No. 279, 2 October, available at http://ssrn.com/abstract=1018715 (accessed 26 June 2009).

Dow, Kenneth J. and Traci Dreher Quigley (2004), 'Improvements for handling improvement clauses in IP licenses: An analytical framework', *Santa Clara Computer & High Technology Law Journal*, **20**, 577–600.

Drugs for Neglected Diseases Initiative (various dates), 'Overview', available at http://www.dndi.org/index.php/overview-dndi.html?ids=1 (accessed 20 July 2009).

Einhorn, Harold and Thomas J. Parker (1968), *Patent Licensing Transactions*, 2 vols., New York: Matthew Bender.

European Commission (2004), 'Management of intellectual property in publicly-funded research organizations: Towards European guidelines', Working paper EUR 20915.EN, available at http://ec.europa.eu/research/era/pdf/iprmanagementguidelines-report.pdf (accessed 25 June 2009).

European Commission (2008), 'Pharmaceutical sector inquiry: Preliminary report', available at http://ec.europa.eu/competition/sectors/pharmaceuticals/inquiry/index.html (accessed 25 June 2009).

European Patent Convention (1973), Convention on the Grant of European Patents, 5 October.

European Patent Office (2005), 'The patent process', available at http://www.epo.org/about-us/office/annualreports/2005/business-report/patent-process.html (accessed 26 June 2009).

Gene Service (no date), 'Material transfer agreements for the supply of biological matter', http://www.geneservice.co.uk/products/mtas/ce_acad_mta_USA.pdf (accessed July 20, 2009).

Gilbert, James, Preston Henske and Ashish Singh (2003), 'Rebuilding Big Pharma's business model', *Invivo: The Business and Medicine Report*, **21**(1), 1–10.

Gowers, Andrew (2006), 'Gowers review of intellectual property', available at http://webarchive.nationalarchives.gov.uk/+/http://www.hm-treasury.gov.uk/d/pbr06_gowers_report_755.pdf (accessed 20 July 2009).

Grover, Nalin (2008), 'Ranbaxy to demerge R&D unit into a subsidiary', *Economic Times*, 20 February, available at http://www.stockwatch.in/ranbaxy-demerge-drug-discovery-unit-stock-surges-5-2468 (accessed 20 July, 2009).

Heller, Michael A. (1998), 'The tragedy of the anticommons: Property in the transition from Marx to markets', *Harvard Law Review*, **111**, 621–86.

Herzfeld, Oliver and Richard Bergovoy (2007), 'Trademark licensing made easy: Part I', *Managing Intellectual Property*, available at http://www.managingip.com (accessed 26 June 2009).

Hindu Business Line (2007), 'Ranbaxy concludes Be-Tabs buyout in South Africa', *Hindu Business Line*, 9 May, available at http://www.thehindu businessline.com/bline/blnri/2007/05/09/stories/2007050904010200.htm (accessed 20 July 2009).

House of Commons Select Committee on Health (2005), 'Fourth report session 2004–2005 H.C. 42-I', available at http://www.publications.parliament.uk/pa/cm200405/cmselect/cmhealth/42/4205.htm (accessed 26 June 2009).

Indian Patents Act (amended 2005), Indian Patents Act, No. 39 of 1970, as amended by The Patents (Amendment) Act, 2005, No. 15 of 2005.

Jack, Andrew (2009), 'GSK limits drug prices in poor nations', *Financial Times*, 14 February.

Jones, Phillip B.C. (1993), 'Violation of a patent license restriction: Breach of contract or patent infringement?', *IDEA: The Journal of Law and Technology*, **33**(3), 225–40.

Keeling, David T. (2003), *Intellectual Property Rights in EU Law: Free Movement and Competition Law*, Oxford: Oxford University Press.

KEMRI (various dates), 'Collaborators and partners', available at http://www.kemri.org/index.php/features-mainmenu-27/typography-mainmenu-33 (accessed 21 July 2009).

Kesan, Jay P. (2009), 'Transferring innovation', *Fordham Law Review*, **77**, 2169–225.

Lambert Working Group on Intellectual Property (2005), 'Model agreements', available at http://www.innovation.gov.uk/lambertagreements/index.asp?lvl1=2&lvl2=0&lvl3=0&lvl4=0 (accessed 26 June 2009).

Landes, William M. and Richard A. Posner (2003), *The Economic Structure of Intellectual Property Law*, Cambridge, MA, USA: Harvard University Press.

Matthijs, Gert (2006) 'The European opposition against the BRCA gene patents', *Familial Cancer*, **5**(1), 95–102.

Mazzoleni, Roberto and Richard R. Nelson (2007), 'Public research institutions and economic catch-up', *Research Policy*, **36**(10), 1512–28.

Mendes, Philip (2005), 'Licensing and technology transfer in the pharmaceutical industry', in World Intellectual Property Organization and International Trade Centre, *Exporting Pharmaceuticals: A Guide for Small and Medium-Sized Exporters*, Geneva: WIPO Publishing, available at http://www.wipo.int/export/sites/www/sme/en/documents/pdf/pharma_licensing.pdf (accessed 20 July 2009).

National Institutes of Health (1998), 'Report of the national institutes of health working group on research tools', available at http://www.nih.gov/news/researchtools/index.htm (accessed 26 June 2009).

Nwaka, Solomon and Robert G. Ridley (2003), 'Virtual drug discovery and development for neglected diseases through public-private partnerships', *Nature Reviews Drug Discovery*, **2**, 919–20.

OECD (2003), 'Turning science into business, patenting and licensing at public research organizations', available at http://www.oecd.org/document/61/0,3343,en_2649_34269_2513917_1_1_1_1,00.html (accessed 25 June 2009).

OECD (2004), 'Patents and innovation: Trends and policy challenges', available at http://www.oecd.org/dataoecd/48/12/24508541.pdf (accessed 25 June 2009).

OECD (2007), 'OECD principles and guidelines for access to research data from public funding', available at http://www.oecd.org/dataoecd/9/61/38500813.pdf (accessed 26 June 2009).

OECD (2008), 'Public-private partnerships, in pursuit of risk sharing and value for money', available at http://www.oecd.org/document/27/0,3343,en_2649_33735_40757595_1_1_1_1,00.html (accessed 20 July 2009).

OECD (2009), 'Economic policy reforms 2009, going for growth', available at http://www.oecd.org/document/33/0,3343,en_2649_34325_41935009_1_1_1_37443,00.html (accessed 20 July 2009).

Osama, Athar (2008), 'Opportunities and challenges in south-south collaboration', *Science and Development Network Policy Brief*, 14 May, available at http://www.scidev.net/en/science-and-innovation-policy/south-south-cooperation/policy-briefs/opportunities-and-challenges-in-south-south-collab.html (accessed 26 June 2009).

Outterson, Kevin (November 2006), 'Access to global disease innovation', available at http://www.who.int/phi/public_hearings/first/15Nov06KevinOutterson.pdf (accessed 26 June 2009).

Paris Convention for the Protection of Industrial Property [Paris Convention] (1967), 20 March 1883, as revised at Stockholm on 14 July.

Patwardhan, Nandini (2007), 'India on African safari', *Express Pharma*, available at http:/www.exprarmaonline.com/20070630/market01.shtml (accessed on 20 July 2009).

PricewaterhouseCoopers (2007), 'Gearing up for a global gravity shift: Growth, risk and learning in the Asia pharmaceutical market', available at http://www.pwc.com/extweb/pwcpublications.nsf/docid/76DEF9E310AB1DCD802572DF002C5ECA (accessed 20 July 2009).

Reichman, Jerome H. and Paul Uhlir (2003), 'A contractually reconstructed research commons for scientific data in a highly protectionist intellectual property environment', *Law and Contemporary Problems*, **66**, 315–462.

Sampath, Padmashree Ghel (2005), *Economic Aspects of Access to Medicines Post-2005*, Tokyo, Japan: United Nations University-INTECH, available at http://www.who.int/intellectualproperty/studies/PadmashreeSampathFinal.pdf (accessed 26 June 2009).

Sarnoff, Joshua D. (2005), 'Brief of Amicus Curiae Consumer Project on Technology and Public Knowledge in Support of Petition for Writ of Certiorari', No. 02–1007, available at http://www.cptech.org/ip/briefs/madeyduke-cptech-pk.pdf.

Sarnoff, Joshua D. and Christopher M. Holman (2008), 'Recent developments affecting the enforcement, procurement, and licensing of research tool patents', *Berkeley Technology Law Journal*, **23**, 1299–365.

South Africa Department of Science and Technology (2009), *Intellectual Property Rights from Publicly Financed Research and Development Regulations*, Pretoria: Government Gazette.

South African Institute of Intellectual Property Law (various dates), 'What is a patent?', available at http://www.saiipl.org.za/introductio-patents.htm (accessed 26 June 2009).

Thorley, Simon, Richard Miller, Guy Burkill and Colin Birss (2006), *Terrell on Patents*, 16th edn, London: Sweet and Maxwell.

Trouiller, Patrice and Pierro Ollario (1999), 'Drug development output from 1975 to 1996: What proportion for tropical diseases?', *International Journal of Infectious Diseases*, **3**(2), 61–3.

UK Patents Act (1977), c. 37, as amended.

UK Parliamentary Office of Science and Technology (2005), 'Postnote no. 241: Fighting diseases of developing countries', available at http://www.parliament.uk/documents/upload/POSTpn241.pdf (accessed 25 June 2009).

United Nations Health Internetwork Access to Research Initiative (various dates), 'A project to make scientific journals', available at http://www.who.int/hinari/en/ (accessed 25 June 2009).

United Nations High Commissioner for Human Rights (2000), 'Intellectual property rights and human rights', Sub-Commission on Human Rights resolution 2000/7, available at http://www.unhchr.ch/Huridocda/Huridoca.nsf/0/c462b62cf8a07b13c12569700046704e?Opendocument (accessed 20 July 2009).

University of Cambridge (various dates), 'Mission and core values', available at http://www.admin.cam.ac.uk/univ/mission.html (accessed 26 June 2009).

von Braun, Joanna and Meir P. Pugatch (2005), 'The changing face of the pharmaceutical industry and intellectual property rights', *Journal of World Intellectual Property*, **8**(5), 599–623.

Wasser, Henry (1990), 'Changes in the European University: From traditional to entrepreneurial', *Higher Education Quarterly*, **44**(2), 110–22.

World Health Organization [WHO] (2003), *Fifty-Sixth World Health Assembly: Report by the Secretariat. Intellectual Property Rights, Innovation and Public Health*, A56/17.

WHO (2005a), *Fifty Eighth World Health Assembly: Report of the Secretariat eHealth*, A58/21.

WHO (2005b), *Fifty Eighth World Health Assembly. eHealth*, WHA58.28.

WHO (2006), *Fifty-Ninth World Health Assembly: Public Health, Innovation, Essential Health Research and Intellectual Property Rights: Towards a Global Strategy and Plan of Action*, WHA59.2427.

WHO (2008), *Sixty-First World Health Assembly: Global Strategy and Plan of Action on Public Health, Innovation and Intellectual Property*, WHA61.21.

WHO (various dates), 'Special programme for research and training in tropical diseases *(TDR)*', available at http://apps.who.int/tdr (accessed 20 July 2009).

WHO Intergovernmental Working Group on Public Health, Innovation and Intellectual Property (2007), 'Draft global strategy and plan of action on public Health, innovation and intellectual property, mapping the funding for research and development for neglected diseases, 28 August', A/PHI/IGWG/2/INF.DOC./2, available at http://apps.who.int/gb/phi/pdf/igwg2/PHI_IGWG2_ID2-en.pdf (accessed 20 July 2009).

WHO, UNICEF, UNFPA and the World Bank (2007), 'Maternal mortality in 2005: Estimates developed by WHO, UNICEF, UNFPA and the World Bank', available at http://www.who.int/reproductivehealth/publications/maternal_mortality_2005/(accessed 25 June 2009).

World Intellectual Property Organization [WIPO] (2006), *Research Networks and Intellectual Property 2004–2006*, Geneva: WIPO Publication, available at http://www.wipo.int/freepublications/en/intproperty/921/wipo_pub_921.pdf (accessed 20 July 2009).

WIPO (2007), 'Project boosts strategic use of intellectual property by health research institutes in developing countries', *WIPO Press Release*, 25 September, available at http://www.wipo.int/pressroom/en/articles/2007/article_0068.html (accessed 20 July 2009).

World Bank (2009a), *Africa Development Indicators 2008/9*, Washington DC: World Bank, available at http://siteresources.worldbank.org/EXTSTATINAFR/Resources/ADI-200809-essay-EN.pdf (accessed 20 July 2009).

World Bank (2009b), *Strengthening China and India's Trade and Investment Ties to the Middle East and North Africa*, Washington DC: World Bank.

Zuniga, Maria Pluvia and Dominique Guellec (2009), *Who Licenses Out Patents and Why? Lessons from a Business Survey*, Paris, France: Organisation for Economic Co-operation and Development.

9. Increasing access through incentives for innovation: The Health Impact Fund

Laura Biron

1. INTRODUCTION

The global pharmaceutical industry should be driven by two overarching goals: to create innovative medicines that improve global health and to enable people all over the world to access these products once developed. At present, there is widespread recognition that these twin goals – valuable innovation and widespread access – are not being met (Morgan, 2006). The most profitable research efforts for pharmaceutical companies are not those with the most therapeutic value. Moreover, when valuable drugs do exist, firms often price them out of the reach of many who need them in order to guarantee returns for expenditure on R&D. In the wake of global pandemics such as HIV/AIDS, the prevalence of neglected diseases in developing countries and the disproportionate spread of pharmaceutical R&D expenditure relative to the Global Burden of Disease (GBD), there is widespread agreement that something needs to be done to realign the industry's goals.

This chapter outlines a proposal called the Health Impact Fund (HIF) (Hollis and Pogge, 2008) which is designed to stimulate therapeutically valuable innovation and simultaneously achieve widespread access. The HIF offers to reward pharmaceutical innovators directly on the basis of health impact, whilst also requiring them to sell their products at low prices to enable access. Health impact would be rewarded globally at an equal rate, making it profitable for innovators to develop medicines to treat the poor, amongst whom the greatest health impacts are waiting to be realized. The most striking feature of the HIF is that it is an optional pay-for-performance scheme for new pharmaceuticals; it pays firms directly on the basis of performance in terms of health impact, and it is an option that firms can choose to pursue alongside the current patent system.

The chapter proceeds as follows. To begin, it explains the background problem the HIF seeks to address, first in terms of the disproportionate spread of the GBD relative to pharmaceutical research and development, and then in terms of the impact of the World Trade Organization's Agreement on Trade-Related Aspects of Intellectual Property Rights (TRIPs) on the widespread availability of essential medicines in poor countries and in terms of the lack of incentives for pharmaceutical companies to reduce the GBD. It goes on to outline the mechanism of the HIF in some depth: its health impact measurement system, funding mechanism and governance structure. It finishes by outlining the positive features of the HIF, along with its expected beneficiaries, and calls upon policymakers and others to assist its creators in refining it into a workable improvement to the existing rules governing the development, distribution and price of new medicines.

2. BACKGROUND: A GROWING GLOBAL DISEASE BURDEN AND A FAILING SYSTEM OF PHARMACEUTICAL INNOVATION

Some 18 million human beings die each year from diseases that are preventable, curable or treatable. This is equivalent to 50,000 avoidable deaths per day, or one-third of all human deaths. Understandably, these diseases put great strains on the economies of many poor countries, and this in turn perpetuates their members' ill health. In addition to being widespread, the GBD is disproportionately spread, with people of colour and children heavily overrepresented (UNICEF, 2003) – women and girls, in particular, within these categories (UNDP, 2003). But by far the most significant determinant of the GBD is poverty. Nearly all of the avoidable mortality and morbidity occur in poor countries and especially among their poorest inhabitants (WHO, 2004). Worse still, not only is the GBD disproportionately spread, but global pharmaceutical R&D is equally disproportionate; only 10 per cent of all pharmaceutical research focuses on diseases that account for 90 per cent of the GBD (WHO, 2004). Despite the great advances in medical progress seen over the last century, the reality is that relatively few poor people benefit from such innovations.

The link between better access to medicines and the reduction of poverty has long been recognized by policymakers, and is enshrined in the Millennium Development Goals (MDG). Goal 8, Target 8.E of the MDG lays down the following objective: 'In cooperation with pharmaceutical companies, provide access to affordable essential drugs in developing countries' (UN, various dates). But the key question facing governments and policymakers is: how can such an objective be made compatible with the market-based pharmaceutical patent system? Despite the health-improving potential of pharmaceuticals, drug firms do not currently focus enough of their research efforts on innovations that have the largest global health impact, and the price of the innovations they do bring to market is crucially dependent on the purchasing power of the affluent. This problem is importantly linked to the pharmaceutical patent system.

The patent system is designed, in part, to correct the following economic problem with innovation that applies in the context of public goods. There is very little incentive to conduct pharmaceutical research in a free market system since, with no mechanism in place to prevent copying, competitors are able to copy or retro-engineer the invention, driving down the marginal cost of its production. The result is that the innovator is unable to profit from its successes. Patent rules – globalized through TRIPs – are granted to inventor firms as a way of correcting this market failure. The patent grants inventors temporary monopolies on their inventions, usually for 20 years from the time of filing a patent application. This solution, though it corrects the first market failure, unfortunately creates another market failure. During the patent's life, the sale price of the invented medicine is far above its marginal cost of production. This impedes sales to a certain class of buyers who are unable to pay the monopoly price, even though they are often able and willing to pay more than its marginal cost of production. These potential transactions are known as 'deadweight losses'.

Prior to the TRIPs Agreement, signed at the end of the Uruguay Round of Trade Negotiations in 1994, developed countries typically had the broadest and most restrictive patent laws, providing strong protection for the manufacture and sale of a wide range of patented products, whereas most developing countries benefited from thriving generics industries. But this situation changed when a powerful alliance of industries (including the pharmaceutical industry) pressured the governments of richer countries to impose the rules of the TRIPs Agreement on all WTO member states, with the poorer countries agreeing to institute TRIPs-compliant IP regimes within a certain number of years of the agreement (Drahos and Braithwaite, 2002). Thus, although patent systems are still set down by and enforced domestically, patent law has effectively become globalized through adherence to the TRIPs Agreement.

Even though the TRIPs Agreement contains provisions for governments to issue compulsory licences on patented products in cases of medical emergency (TRIPs, 1994, art. 31(b)), a debate continues over the effectiveness of such measures for ensuring widespread access to drugs (e.g., Ford, 1999). Moreover, even when compulsory licences can be issued on existing patented drugs, there remains the problem of providing incentives for new drug development to tackle the growing GBD (WHO, 2009). More generally, Thomas Pogge (2008) identifies the following seven problems with the globalized pharmaceutical patent system, all of which the HIF attempts to address:

1. *High prices.* When a medicine is under patent, it is sold at the profit-maximizing monopoly price, which is largely determined by the purchasing power of the affluent. This means that those who are unable to pay the monopoly price are excluded from purchasing the medicine.
2. *Neglect of diseases concentrated among poor.* The patent system does nothing to address the so-called 10–90 gap, according to which only 10% of all pharmaceutical research focuses on diseases that account for 90% of the GBD. This is largely because innovators will only steer their research efforts towards commercially valuable innovations, whilst the GBD is concentrated amongst the poor.
3. *Bias towards symptom relief.* Under the existing monopoly patent regime, symptom-relieving medicines are by far the most profitable, and are therefore more attractive to pharmaceutical companies than curative or preventative medicines. But curative and preventative medicines have greater long-term health impact.
4. *Wastefulness.* Innovators must currently bear the cost of filing and monitoring multiple patents, which is often an administratively burdensome process.
5. *Counterfeiting.* Large profit margins encourage the illegal manufacture and sale of medicines across borders.
6. *Excessive marketing.* When pharmaceutical companies can maintain a very high mark-up on their products, they find it rational to attempt to increase sales volume by influencing both physicians' prescription decisions and consumer demand for certain medications.
7. *The Last Mile Problem.* The present regime provides no incentives for innovators to ensure that people actually benefit from the medicines they use. Thus, even when life-saving drugs do exist, companies do not take measures to ensure that they are used properly, in the right dosage, and according to the needs of the patient.

Each of these problems has provoked ideas and initiatives by academics, NGOs, governments and international agencies, resulting in a wave of initiatives and proposals designed to improve the fairness of the patent system. Some proposals, like differential pricing (Danzon and Towse, 2003) and patent pools (UNITAID, 2009), focus on the access problem. Others, like medical innovation prizes (Love and Hubbard, 2007) and advanced market commitments (GAVI Alliance, various dates), focus on the innovation problem. The proposal under consideration here – the HIF – is designed to tackle both problems simultaneously, tying the best of these ideas into a comprehensive policy package. As will be explained below, the HIF does not look to pharmaceutical companies for philanthropy. Instead, the idea is to offer them the opportunity for market-based rewards for the contribution their products make to improving global health.

3. THE MECHANISM OF THE HEALTH IMPACT FUND

The essence of the HIF is to offer firms a share of a fixed fund, underwritten by governments, for each of 10 years in proportion to the share of health impact of their registered product out of all products registered with the fund. As an example of how this would work in practice, let us imagine that all products registered with the fund were estimated to have saved 20 million Quality-Adjusted Life Years (QALYs). A registered product that had saved two million of these QALYs would receive 10 per cent of the fund (Hollis and Pogge, 2008, pp. 13–8). It is expected that this calculation would be performed annually, and each registered product would receive a payment for 10 years following market approval of their product.

In order for a firm to be eligible for the reward, they would be required to sell their product worldwide at a specified low price, which would likely be roughly equal to the average cost of manufacturing it. Other requirements on the company include providing sales data for assessing the product's health impact, paying a yearly fee to cover the costs of health impact assessment, and preauthorizing the HIF to sublicense the relevant patents to generic firms following the end of the reward period. But the fundamental point to bear in mind when thinking about these requirements is that the HIF is still an optional mechanism for innovators; firms could choose whether to register any particular product for health impact rewards or to exploit their monopoly pricing privileges in the traditional way. It is therefore likely that if the HIF were implemented, certain currently undervalued innovations would become profitable, whilst the products that work well under the current patent system would remain largely untouched.

When assessing health impact, the HIF would estimate the difference between (1) the actual health status of people who consumed the registered product and (2) the estimated health status of those people, had they not had access to the registered product, or to any other products introduced less than two years before the registered product. That is, the HIF would estimate the incremental health impact of each product registered with it, setting the counterfactual baseline at the set of technologies two years before the registered product became available. The incremental health impact of each product would be estimated each year for 10 years during which the firm would be eligible for payments and, in each of those years, the firm would receive a share of the available funds.

4. MEASUREMENT: QUALITY-ADJUSTED LIFE YEARS

To measure health impact, the HIF would use the standard measure of health impact, the QALY. For the purposes of the HIF, a drug that extended a person's life by 10 healthy years would be recognized as having created 10 QALYs, since both the quality and quantity of life lived would be factored into the measurement. The health impact of a product would be evaluated without any reference to the wealth or income of the population in which it was introduced, and it would be aggregated globally in order to assess the drug's total health impact in each year. The health impact would be deemed to have occurred at the time the medicine was consumed. Thus, even if some of the 10 extra years of life fell beyond the end of the medicine's specific reward period, the company would nonetheless receive 10 years' worth of reward.

Of course, one of the significant challenges posed by the implementation of the HIF is that assessing the incremental effect of health on the average consumer in terms of QALYs is difficult and in some cases controversial (Murray, Salomon, Mathers and Lopez, 2002). One reason for the difficulty is that there are often limited data available about certain diseases and even certain populations, particularly in less-developed countries, which often makes evaluations of global health impact incomplete. That being said, there is widespread agreement that better data surveillance is needed to measure global health impact, regardless of whether a HIF is ever implemented (Lopez, 2005). Moreover, the HIF actually encourages firms to use their available resources to help accurate data measurements to be carried out, particularly since firms are required to provide information about their sales, and comparative data on the effectiveness of their products, in order to produce requisite evidence for obtaining payments from the HIF.

Despite the incentives the HIF offers for companies to improve data measurement, though, there is little doubt that the difficulty of rewarding them on the basis of health impact is significant. Nonetheless, Aidan Hollis and Thomas Pogge point out that the health systems of most developed countries rely on various assessments of drug effectiveness, particularly when health insurers – both state and private – are determining access to certain drugs (Hollis and Pogge, 2008, pp. 31–4). Quite often, drugs are listed on the formulary of an insurer only after an assessment is carried out comparing the drug's effectiveness to its price. The judgement of cost-effectiveness required by the HIF is in fact very similar to the judgement made by such insurers. There are two important differences, however. First, unlike the payments made by insurers, the payments made by the HIF are conditional on incremental improvement over alternative products. Second, the HIF relies on data derived from actual uses of the product; most insurers make their decisions based on preliminary information from clinical trials. But these differences should not be too surprising. After all, the HIF must ensure that only those products that actually are shown to be improvements on alternatives receive a reward based on health impact. Likewise, it seems right to think that companies should only receive payments on the basis of actual health impact, as opposed to estimated impact, since otherwise the incentives to ensure their drugs reach patients are largely removed, let alone the important data-gathering incentives already discussed above.

5. FUNDING

Let us now consider how the HIF would be funded, since this question naturally arises when first encountering the proposal. Funds for the HIF would be provided by partner countries on the basis of an agreement made by their governments. Of course, the greater the support a country offered, the more attractive the fund would be to innovators, making it more effective in encouraging widely accessible innovations. Whilst the system could be scaled up as larger funding became available – this, indeed, is one of the attractive features of the proposal – Hollis and Pogge suggest a reasonable starting level of six billion US dollars per year (Hollis and Pogge, 2008, pp. 43–4). They estimate that, at this scale, the HIF could support the development of about two new drugs per year, sustaining a stock of about 20 medicines.

The HIF would require substantial government funding, then, and partner countries would need to commit to financial support for at least 12 years into the future at any time, so that innovators would have some guarantee about expected payments. For reasons of fairness, the contributions of partner countries would also need to be proportional to their respective gross national incomes. On this point, Hollis and Pogge suggest that an ideal structure would involve countries committing a fixed share (0.03 per cent) of their annual gross national income, so that the HIF could grow in proportion to their economies. This approach would ensure there is parity between the contributions of the different funding partners.

Although the proposed size of partner contributions to the HIF would likely exceed their international development budgets, it seems more proportionate when compared with their overall annual expenditures on pharmaceuticals. Assume countries representing one-third of the global product agree to underwrite the HIF, each country would need to contribute 0.03 per cent of its gross national income (GNI) in order to reach the minimum $6 billion fund size. For affluent countries with GNI per capita of around $40,000 per annum, committing 0.03 per cent of GNI would constitute a contribution of $12 per citizen per year – as compared to average annual per capita expenditure on pharmaceuticals of $413 in the OECD (Organization for Economic Co-operation and Development) countries. In the context of overall spending on pharmaceuticals, this amount does not seem significant. Moreover, Hollis and Pogge point out that the actual net cost of the HIF to OECD citizens might well be lower than $12, because of the savings they would go on to realize on HIF-registered drugs. It is also worth pointing out that these small net costs would bring much larger benefits, because global economic performance would be improved as a result of the stimulation of widely accessible new medicines.

6. GOVERNANCE

Now that we have considered funding, it is important to outline the governance structure of the HIF. The administrative structure of the HIF would consist of three main branches: the technical branch, the audit branch, and the assessment branch. The *technical branch* would determine standards for the assessment of health impact, ensuring consistent expectations across different countries and across diseases, particularly with regards to data interpretation. To ensure the integrity of this process, a separate *audit branch* would be established. The Board of Directors of the HIF would bear ultimate responsibility for overseeing the auditing process. The Board would include representatives of each contributing country, with a voting representation based on their contribution share. This representation would be required to ensure that the measurement and auditing processes were supported by the funding partners.

In addition, the HIF would have a substantial *assessment branch*, specializing in undertaking continuous evaluation of the health impacts of registered medicines, as discussed above. This would be an expensive feature of the fund, but the costs would in part be covered by the fees innovators pay when registering with the fund. Moreover, it would provide a fair and reasonable way for determining the reward for a given product, and it would be an extremely valuable resource for medical practitioners, giving them more accurate information about the actual effectiveness of particular drugs. And at an even broader level, the data provided would help poor country governments, international agencies, NGOs and development aid ministries in gathering vital data for the promotion of international development.

7. SUMMARY: CHARACTERISTICS OF THE HEALTH IMPACT FUND

The HIF offers innovative firms the option of being directly rewarded based on their contribution to global health, without impeding access through high prices. It would therefore be able to achieve the twin goals of stimulating pharmaceutical innovation in the most important therapeutic areas *and* enabling widespread access. The HIF offers innovators the option of being rewarded for the global health impact their products achieve, even if most of the people consuming their products are poor and can only afford medicines priced near cost. This opens up a range of diseases and treatments, which so far have been of only marginal interest to investors, since under the current system they have little prospect of benefiting from sales to the poor. The intuitively compelling approach of the HIF therefore has many attractive characteristics, including:

1. *Social value of products.* The HIF mechanism offers incentives for innovation that are directly proportional to the social value of the innovation, as measured by health impact. This is in stark contrast to the approach of the patent system, which measures the value of an innovation in terms of people's willingness to pay. Thus, the HIF, unlike the patent system, actually aligns socially desirable innovation with profit.

2. *Low drug prices.* Because the HIF requires products to be sold at a globally uniform low price, it eliminates the need for high drug prices, which currently prevent important drugs from being accessible to the poor. But it is also worth pointing out that the savings from low drug prices will accrue to everyone, rich and poor alike.
3. *Reduced incentives for counterfeiting.* Because the price of HIF medicines is low, incentives for counterfeiting are reduced. Counterfeit drugs harm manufacturers and even patients when they fail to contain the correct ingredients, and the HIF directly tackles these problems through its pricing mechanism.
4. *Scalability.* The HIF is scalable in two ways: first, if it works well, it can be expanded by increasing the amount of funding available; second, it could apply initially to certain ring-fenced disease areas, such as communicable diseases, and then branch out to allow other disease areas to come within its reach.
5. *Last mile problem.* The HIF addresses the last mile problem – getting drugs to the people who need them. As stated above, the present regime provides no incentives to ensure that medicines actually reach patients, and are properly used by them. But in the HIF system, innovators are financially motivated to encourage appropriate use of their products among both the rich and the poor, since the amount of health impact will depend on the number of people who are using the medicine effectively.
6. *Economic benefits.* The economic benefits of the HIF are global, just like its scope. Thus, citizens of all countries would benefit directly from lower drug prices and industry focus on achieving actual health impact. Citizens of developing countries would benefit directly from improved health, but this would lead to indirect global benefits in terms of economic growth and reduction in the development and spread of harmful pathogens.
7. *Reduction in waste.* The HIF would reduce wasteful expenditures by pharmaceutical companies on promotional activities and litigation, which would allow such companies to focus their spending more directly on innovation.
8. *Globally uniform price.* The HIF requires a uniformly low price for all its products, whilst offering companies direct payment based on health impact. This means that innovative companies can make money in poorer countries, since they can afford to charge the low prices that are required to generate substantial sales, whilst at the same time being paid directly on the basis of health impact.

8. THE BENEFICIARIES OF THE HEALTH IMPACT FUND

Now that we have outlined the mechanism of the HIF in some depth, it is important to state who its main beneficiaries are, and to explain the proposal's attractiveness to them. First and perhaps most importantly for the purposes of the practical implementation of the fund, *innovative companies* would benefit from the HIF because they could profitably introduce important new medicines that are needed by patients who cannot pay high prices. Because the HIF is a supplementary system to the patent system, it does not in any way reduce the profits of pharmaceutical companies, nor does it reduce their capacity for funding research. Rather, it simply gives them an additional 'track', an opportunity to profit by developing high-impact medicines. Firms would not be required to charge high prices to poor people, but they could still recover the costs of research and development, provided the products in question were effective in their target areas. From the perspective of pharmaceutical companies, the HIF seems to create a win-win situation.

Another reason for the HIF's attractiveness to innovative companies is that it is designed to use market forces to set the rate of payment made to innovators: the more patented medicines that are registered with the HIF, the lower the payment for any given health impact would be. Market forces would also determine the sales volumes of registered medicines, thus greatly reducing the monopoly price distortions typical of pharmaceutical markets (Hollis, 2007). The HIF provides a method for determining payments to innovators that is more transparent than the current mechanisms used by state and private insurers. Moreover, the HIF administrators would not intervene in the funding of research, but would only reward successful products based on their assessed health impact.

Of course, it is not just innovators who would benefit from the HIF, although pharmaceutical companies are the stakeholders that would initially need the most persuading. *Patients* – especially those in the developing world – would benefit through access to new drugs at low prices. Properly funded, the HIF would make a huge difference to the health care of the world's poor. It would achieve this difference in three ways. First, the poor would have immediate access to currently available high-impact medicines that would otherwise have been sold under the monopoly pricing system. Second, the poor would have immediate access to some other high-impact new medicines that would not have been developed without the incentives provided by the HIF. Third, the poor would greatly benefit from a newly created motive of pharmaceutical firms: to ensure appropriate use of their products, thereby ensuring the long-term benefits of medicines are achieved.

Finally, by supporting the HIF, *governments* in all countries would reap large cost savings on medicines as well as substantial reductions in the human and economic burdens of disease. And they would be able to harness the power that pharmaceutical companies have on health policy in order to realize these goals. After all, pharmaceutical companies influence greatly the practice of health care in affluent countries, not only through the diseases they research, but through their interactions with national health systems, insurance companies and legislators. The HIF enables the profits made on pharmaceutical products to be aligned with the health impacts they actually achieve, making the companies' aims compatible with those of policymakers and legislators.

9. DIFFICULTIES AND STEPS FORWARD

This chapter is not put forward as a 'sales pitch' for the HIF, nor should it give the reader the impression that the HIF is a fully polished policy proposal. In fact, part of the aim of this chapter is to generate interest in the HIF whilst it is still in its early stages of development and to encourage academics and policymakers to consider its advantages whilst also raising awareness of possible obstacles to its implementation. For example, as mentioned above, there is the problem of ensuring that efficient and reliable data can be gathered to make accurate health impact measurements. Second, and related, there is the problem of developing a fair and effective currency for 'exchanging' QALYS to dollars. Third, there is a question about the scope of the proposal, and whether it should apply only to patented medicines, or more generally to all interventions that can be shown to have a health impact. This relates to another problem, which regards the question of whether or not patent registration should be a requirement of registration with the HIF. The HIF team has published a series of working papers on these and related topics (Bollyky, 2009; Mendel and Hollis, 2009; Syed, 2009).

Of course, the HIF proposal was originally developed before the global recession, and it is natural to wonder whether it is still an attractive policy proposal, in light of the foreseeable government spending cuts that lie ahead. Although it is too early to say whether the global financial crisis will ultimately prevent governments from making financial commitments to the HIF, it certainly has not led to a decline of interest in the proposal. Pogge and Hollis have spent a great deal of time over the past two years presenting the central ideas of the HIF to policymakers in the

United States, the United Kingdom, Germany, Norway, India and China. As stated above, the HIF is premised on cost-effectiveness, and it has the potential to reduce a great deal of waste in the patent system. For these and other reasons, the proposal should strike governments as a sustainable supplement to a system of innovation that has proved thus far unsustainable.

For the HIF to become a reality, the proposal will need to be studied, challenged, refined, and considered from a variety of perspectives, and consultation with its various stakeholders (companies, governments, insurers, epidemiologists, ethicists, NGOs, lawyers, economists, doctors) is needed to strengthen it. This process has already begun, and the HIF team is currently looking to pilot both the health impact metric and the incentive mechanism. In addition to further research on the technical aspects of the proposal, it is also necessary that governments begin making commitments to support the HIF, once they are satisfied that the proposal has sufficient traction. The HIF is a fair and cost-effective proposal for stimulating research and development of life-saving medicines. It would make advanced medicines available to all at competitive prices, and it would simultaneously provide sufficient rewards for innovators. There is therefore much to be gained and very little to lose from exploring its potential to the full.

Acknowledgements

This chapter was originally presented as a paper on behalf of Thomas Pogge and the HIF team at the 'Global Governance of HIV/AIDS: Intellectual Property and Access to Essential Medicines' Conference held at the University of Liverpool in October 2008. I have been a member of the HIF team since 2007, and I would like especially to thank Thomas Pogge and Aidan Hollis for leading the project and working to produce the 2008 policy book, which this chapter summarizes. The reader is encouraged to consult this book for further elaboration of the HIF proposal, and to visit the website at http://www.healthimpactfund.org/ for details of its latest developments.

BIBLIOGRAPHY

Agreement on Trade-Related Aspects of Intellectual Property Rights [TRIPs] (1994), 15 April.

Bollyky, Thomas (2009), 'The relationship of the health impact fund and its registrants', *IGH Discussion Paper no. 2*, available at http://www.yale.edu/macmillan/igh/files/DP3_Bollyky.pdf (accessed 8 September 2010).

Danzon, Patricia and Adrian Towse (2003), 'Differential pricing for pharmaceuticals: Reconciling access, R&D and patents', *AEI-Brookings Joint Center Working Paper No. 03–7*, available at http://papers.ssrn.com/sol3/papers.cfm?abstract_id=422821 (accessed 8 September 2010).

Drahos, Peter and Braithwaite, John (2002), *Information Feudalism*, London: Earthscan Publications.

Ford, Sara M. (1999), 'Compulsory licensing provisions under the TRIPs Agreement: Balancing pills and patents', *American University International Law Review*, **15**, 941–74.

GAVI Alliance (various dates) 'Information on advanced market commitments (AMCs)', available at http://www.gavialliance.org/vision/policies/in_financing/amcs/index.php (accessed 8 September 2010).

Hollis, Aidan (2007), 'Drugs for neglected diseases: New incentives for innovation', in Frank A. Sloan and Chey-Ruey Hsieh (eds), *Pharmaceutical Innovation: Incentives, Innovation and Cost-benefit Analysis in International Perspective*, Cambridge: Cambridge University Press, pp. 75–90.

Hollis, Aidan and Pogge, Thomas (2008), *The Health Impact Fund: Making New Medicines Accessible for All*, New Haven: Incentives for Global Health.

Lopez, Alan D. (2005), 'The evolution of the global burden of disease framework for disease, injury and risk factor quantification: Developing the evidence base for national, regional and global public health action', *Globalization and Health*, **1**(5), 1–8.

Love, Jamie and Tim Hubbard (2007), 'The big idea: Prizes to stimulate R&D for new medicines', *Chicago-Kent Law Review*, **82**(3), 1519–54.

Mendel, Joy and Aidan Hollis (2009), 'The health impact fund and traditional medicines', *IGH Working Paper no. 8*, available at http://www.yale.edu/macmillan/igh/files/DP8_Mendel_and_Hollis.pdf (accessed 8 September 2010).

Morgan, Maxwell R. (2006), 'Medicines for the developing world: Promoting access and innovation in the Post-TRIPs environment', *University of Toronto Law Review*, **65**, 45–112.

Murray, Christopher J.L., Joshua A. Salomon, Colin D. Mathers and Alan D. Lopez (eds) (2002), *Summary Measures of Population Health: Concepts, Ethics, Measurement and Applications*, Geneva: WHO.

Pogge, Thomas (2008), 'Access to medicines', *Public Health Ethics*, **1**(2), 73–82.

Sell, Susan (2001), 'TRIPs and the access to medicines campaign', *Wisconsin International Law Journal*, **20**, 481–522.

Syed, Talha (2009), 'Should a prize system for pharmaceuticals require patent protection for eligibility?', *IGH Discussion Paper no. 2*, available at http://www.yale.edu/macmillan/igh/files/DP2_Syed.pdf (accessed 8 September 2010).

UN (various dates), *MDG Monitor: Goal 8 – Develop a Global Partnership for Development*, available at http://www.mdgmonitor.org/goal8.cfm (accessed 8 September 2010).

UNDP (2003), *Human Development Report 2003*, New York: Oxford University Press, available at http://hdr.undp.org/en/media/hdr03_complete.pdf (accessed 8 September 2010).
UNICEF (2003), *The State of the World's Children 2003*, New York: UNICEF, available at http://www.unicef.org/sowc03/ (accessed 8 September 2010).
UNITAID (2009) *The Medicines Patent Pool Initiative*, available at http://www.unitaid.eu/images/projects/PatentPool/pp_factsheet_april2010_web.pdf (accessed 8 September 2010).
World Health Organization [WHO] (2004), *The World Health Report 2004*, WA540.1, Geneva: WHO Publications, available at http://www.who.int/whr/2004 (accessed 8 September 2010).
WHO (2009), *Sixty First World Health Assembly: Global Strategy and Plan of Action on Public Health, Innovation and Intellectual Property*, WHA61.21, available at http://www.who.int/phi/implementation/phi_globstat_action/en/index.html (accessed 8 September 2010).

10. Building IPC4D to promote access to essential medicines

Peter K. Yu

1. INTRODUCTION

On 6 December 2005, shortly before the World Trade Organization (WTO) Ministerial Conference in Hong Kong, WTO member states agreed to accept a protocol of amendment to the Agreement on Trade-Related Aspects of Intellectual Property Rights (TRIPs Agreement). This proposed amendment sought to provide a permanent solution to implement paragraph 6 of the Doha Declaration on the TRIPS Agreement and Public Health (Doha Declaration). If ratified by two-thirds of the WTO membership by December 2013, the proposed Article 31*bis* of the TRIPs Agreement will allow countries with insufficient or no manufacturing capacity to import generic versions of on-patent pharmaceuticals.[1]

To facilitate the supply of essential medicines to countries with insufficient or no manufacturing capacity, the proposed amendment creates a special arrangement not only for the affected countries, but also for those belonging to a regional trade agreement. Such an arrangement allows less developed countries – including both developing and least developed countries – to aggregate their markets to generate the purchasing power needed to make the development of an indigenous pharmaceutical industry attractive (Yu, 2007b, p. 848). The provision also paves the way for the development of regional supply centres, procurement systems, and patent pools and institutions, while facilitating technical cooperation within the region (Abbott and Reichman, 2003, pp. 973–7; Musungu, Villanueva and Blasetti, 2004, pp. xv–xvi).

Unfortunately, because Article 31*bis* specifically requires that least developed countries make up at least half of the membership of any beneficiary regional trade agreement, the provision would benefit only a limited number of less developed countries, predominantly those in Africa. Even worse, the interpretation of the provision remains contested within the WTO. While the European Union 'insisted that the [provision] should be limited to what is effectively sub-Saharan Africa', less developed countries in Asia, the Caribbean, and South America embrace a much broader interpretation of Article 31*bis* (Abbott and Reichman, 2003, p. 945).

In light of the limited benefits of the proposed amendment to the TRIPs Agreement, this chapter explores how greater collaboration among less developed countries can promote access to essential medicines in the less developed world. The chapter begins by explaining how building intellectual property coalitions for development (IPC4D) can help less developed countries strengthen their collective bargaining position, influence negotiation outcomes, and promote effective and democratic decision making in the international intellectual property regime. It then discusses four coordination strategies that can be used to develop these coalitions. The chapter concludes with a discussion of the various challenges confronting the creation and maintenance of these coalitions.

2. INTELLECTUAL PROPERTY COALITIONS FOR DEVELOPMENT

IPC4D is a concept that can take many different forms – blocs, alliances, regional integration, or other cooperative arrangement. The resulting coalitions have several attractive features. By bringing countries together, the coalitions can achieve leverage that does not exist for each less developed country on its own. If used strategically, they will enable less developed countries to shape a pro-development agenda, articulate more coherent positions, or even establish a united negotiating front. The coalitions will also help less developed countries establish a more powerful voice in the international debates on public health, intellectual property, and international trade. In doing so, countries will be able to develop treaties and policies that promote access to essential medicines in the less developed world.

Moreover, from the standpoint of international relations, the creation of IPC4D will help many less developed countries combat the external pressure that each country will face on a one-to-one basis from the European Union, the United States, or other powerful trading partners (Bird and Cahoy, 2008, p. 317). With the appropriate arrangements, these coalitions may even facilitate the transfer of technology from the haves to the have-nots, targeting a major weakness of the current international intellectual property regime (Yu, 2008, pp. 368–9).

If regional coalitions are set up – such as through regional economic integration; the institution of regional organizations, mutual recognition systems, or procurement systems; the facilitation of regional cooperation in research and development; or the creation of regional competition enforcement mechanisms – there may be additional benefits. As Sisule Musungu, Susan Villanueva, and Roxana Blasetti (2004, p. xiv) have noted in a South Centre study:

> A regional approach to the use of TRIPS flexibilities will enable similarly situated countries to address their constraints jointly by drawing on each others' expertise and experience and by pooling and sharing resources and information. This approach has several advantages. First, it creates better policy conditions for addressing the challenges of implementing TRIPS flexibilities, which can be daunting for each individual country. Second, a common approach to improve access to essential medicines will enhance the efforts by developing countries to pursue common negotiating positions at the WTO and in other multilateral negotiations such as those on a substantive patent law at the World Intellectual Property Organization (WIPO). In addition, a regional approach coincides with the objective of enhancing South-South cooperation on health and development.
>
> Consequently, if strategically utilized, regional South-South frameworks will significantly help developing countries devise ways by which national constraints in the use of TRIPS flexibilities can be overcome.

Likewise, two political scientists remind us that '[s]hared historical experiences among states of a particular region develop over time … and the cultural affinities which facilitate commerce are more likely with neighbouring peoples than with those from afar' (Coleman and Underhill, 1998, p. 1). It is, therefore, no surprise that Amrita Narlikar (2003, p. 155) finds 'coalitions that utilize regionalism as a springboard for bargaining [to] be … "natural coalitions"'.

Indeed, regional coalitions can serve as a fairly effective strategy to promote access to essential medicines in the less developed world. As stated further in the South Centre study (Musungu, Villanueva and Blasetti, 2004, pp. 35–6):

> [a] regional approach can provide incentives for establishing or developing regional pharmaceutical production and help expand research capabilities. In addition, higher effective demand for the same medicines due to climatic conditions and other geographical reasons, as well as cultural aspects, will result in lower consumer drug prices due to increased economies of scale in procurement and distribution. Other important benefits include: the costs associated with adapting medicines to the region may be offset/lowered due to increased economies of scale; stronger local technological capacities/domestic innovation resulting from the pooling of adequate resources including financing, and human capital and physical capital will be stimulated. Finally, a regional approach can also help to improve cross-border disease control.

While IPC4D have many attractive features, building these coalitions is important for four additional reasons. First, the WTO has dominated current international intellectual property discussions, and group representation of less developed countries is particularly deficient in this international trading body. As Sonia Rolland (2007, p. 483) noted, '[a]lthough the organization operates on a one-country-one-vote basis and on a consensus mechanism ... developing countries still find themselves in a relatively marginalized position and experience difficulties in linking their development agenda to multilateral trade negotiations'. Collective bargaining is therefore greatly needed.

Second, there is a rare and unprecedented opportunity for less developed countries to reshape the intellectual property debate. At the WTO ministerial conferences in Doha, Cancún, and Hong Kong, less developed countries have built considerable momentum in pushing for reforms that would recalibrate the balance of the international trading system. In October 2007, WIPO also adopted a development agenda, including 45 recommendations that range from technical assistance and capacity building to norm setting and public policy and from technology transfer to assessment, evaluation, and impact studies (WIPO, 2007). In light of these developments, greater collaboration would help less developed countries take advantage of this momentum while protecting the gains they already have obtained in recent negotiations.

Third, and related to the second, after the conclusion of the Doha Development Round of Trade Negotiations, if at all, development issues may not feature as prominently in the WTO negotiations as in the current round. Indeed, without the urgency created by the September 11 tragedies, the fatalities caused by the 2001 anthrax attacks in the United States, and the United States' resulting general interest in working more closely with the less developed world, one has to wonder whether the Doha Round could have been negotiated as far as it has gotten (Amoore, Germain and Wilkinson, 2003, p. xiii). Thus, if less developed countries want to continue their success in future rounds of trade negotiations, they need to significantly increase their collective bargaining leverage.

Finally, the international intellectual property regime has slowly expanded to cover issue areas that are traditionally covered by other international regimes or fora, creating what I have termed the 'international intellectual property regime complex' (Yu, 2007c, pp. 13–21).[2] As a result of its complexity and fragmentary nature, this conglomerate regime is likely to harm less developed countries more than it has harmed developed countries (Benvenisti and Downs, 2007). The growing complexities have also upset the existing coalition dynamics between actors and institutions within the international trading system, thus threatening to reduce the gains made by less developed countries through past coalition-building initiatives (Yu, 2007c, pp. 17–8).

3. COORDINATION STRATEGIES FOR DEVELOPING IPC4D

To help develop IPC4D, this section discusses four different coordination strategies: (1) the initiation of South-South alliances; (2) the facilitation of North-South cooperation; (3) joint participation in the WTO dispute settlement process; and (4) the development of regional or pro-development fora. It also explains the need for, and benefits of, each strategy. Since these four strategies are not intended to be mutually exclusive, countries seeking to strengthen their bargaining position are encouraged to maximize the impact by using a combination of these strategies.

3.1 South-South Alliances

Since the failure of the fifth WTO Ministerial Conference in Cancún (Cancún Ministerial) in 2003, the United States has initiated a divide-and-conquer strategy that seeks to reward countries that are willing to work with the United States while undermining efforts by Brazil, India, and other G-20 members to establish a united negotiating front for less developed countries (Yu, 2006a, p. 403). Although the United States had begun negotiating new bilateral and regional trade agreements before the failed ministerial conference, these agreements have been increasingly used as a means to isolate uncooperative less developed countries. As Robert Zoellick (2003), the former US Trade Representative, wrote in the *Financial Times* shortly after the Cancún Ministerial, the United States will attempt to separate the 'can-do' countries from the 'won't-do' countries and 'will move towards free trade with [only] can-do countries'.

This isolation strategy is not new. It was used by the United States to increase its bargaining leverage during the negotiations of the TRIPs Agreement. At that time, the United States used Section 301 provisions to isolate major opposition countries, such as Argentina, Brazil, India, Japan, Mexico, South Korea, and Thailand (Yu, 2004, p. 413). South Korea, for example, was threatened with sanctions for inadequate protection for computer programs, chemicals, and pharmaceuticals as well as in the areas of copyrights, patents, and trademarks (Watal, 2001, p. 18). Likewise, the US trade representative included on the Section 301

Priority Watch List or Watch List half of the 10 hardliner countries that refused to expand the mandate of the General Agreement on Tariffs and Trade to cover substantive intellectual property issues, namely Argentina, Brazil, Egypt, India, and Yugoslavia (Drahos, 2002, p. 774).

If less developed countries are to counterbalance the United States' divide-and-conquer strategy, lest more TRIPs-plus standards be developed at both the multilateral and regional levels, they need to initiate a combine-and-conquer strategy. Simply put, they need to build more coalitions within the less developed world. A successful example was the development of the G-20 during the Cancún Ministerial. Although its success was short-lived, the group was instrumental in preventing the WTO member states from reaching agreement on such issues as investment, competition policy, government procurement, and trade facilitation. Its success eventually led to the premature ending of the ministerial conference and the Bush administration's change of focus from multilateral negotiations to bilateral, plurilateral or regional agreements.

Today, there is a tendency to view these non-multilateral agreements with scepticism, partly as a result of their wide and controversial uses by the European Union and the United States to ratchet up global intellectual property standards. However, it is important to distinguish these North-South agreements from the more favourable South-South agreements. Non-multilateral agreements are not always destructive to the international intellectual property regime. Depending on their terms, South-South agreements may serve as an effective way to build coalitions within the less developed world. They may also promote multilateralism by fostering common positions among participating countries.

3.2 North-South Cooperation

Although the WTO and the international intellectual property regime remain heavily state-centred, the participation of non-state actors (such as multinational corporations and NGOs) and sub-state agents has grown considerably. During the Cancún Ministerial, 'most high-profile NGOs, such as Greenpeace, Oxfam, and Public Citizen, explicitly backed the developing countries' stand and heavily criticized developed countries, in particular the US and the EU, for a lack of consideration for their poorer trading partners' (Cho, 2004, p. 235). While '[s]ome operated as think tanks in supporting the agenda of developing countries, … [o]thers issued statements expressing political support for the demands of the G20' (Hurrell and Narlikar, 2006, p. 424).

In addition, sub-state agents have become increasingly active. As Chris Alden (2007, p. 29) has noted with respect to China's government and business ties in Africa, Chinese provincial and municipal authorities have undertaken major initiatives to establish formal and informal ties in South Africa, the Democratic Republic of Congo, Namibia, Angola, and Nigeria. Since the late 1990s, there has also been an interesting emergence of non-national systems, such as the adoption of the Uniform Domain Name Dispute Resolution Policy (UDRP) by the Internet Corporation for Assigned Names and Numbers (ICANN), a private not-for-profit corporation in California (Yu, 2007a, pp. 88–91).

Thus, instead of focusing on state-to-state relationships, less developed countries need to better understand the importance of and challenges to working with NGOs and sub-state agents and within non-national systems. They also 'need to work consistently with US and European political allies to alter the US and European domestic political contexts' (Shaffer, 2004, p. 479). With the changing contexts, these allies will be able to obtain more support within the domestic deliberative processes in developed countries – comparable to the support they have already received within their own countries or in the less developed world. As Gregory Shaffer (2004, p. 480) elaborates:

> Domestic and international non-governmental advocates, such as ACT UP, Doctors Without Borders, and Oxfam, ... raise fundamental moral issues to hold US and EC political leaders accountable. They also harness the public's self-interest over the cost of prescription drugs and public officials' struggles to finance health care commitments within the United States and Europe themselves.

Even if these countries are unable to obtain their desirable policy outcomes through the political processes in the developed world, their foreign allies may be able to significantly reduce the political pressure developed countries will exert upon their less developed counterparts. As Shaffer (2004, pp. 479–80) continues:

> If developing countries cannot neutralize the clout of large pharmaceutical firms in the formation of US and European positions, then developing countries will face the full brunt of US and European coercion in the negotiation and enforcement of pharmaceutical patent rights. In a world of asymmetric power, developing countries enhance the prospects of their success if other US and European constituencies offset the pharmaceutical industry's pressure on US and European trade authorities to aggressively advance industry interests.

Despite the importance of cultivating allies in other countries, this point is sometimes lost on less developed countries, whose 'domestic lobbies have played a much smaller role in determining foreign economic policy than in the developed democracies' (Narlikar, 2003, p. 4).

To date, there has been significant collaboration between policymakers in less developed countries and NGOs in both developed and less developed countries. Intergovernmental and non-governmental organizations that have been active in the public health area include ACT UP (AIDS Coalition to Unleash Power), Health Action International, Health GAP (Health Global Access Project), the International Centre for Trade and Sustainable Development (ICTSD), Knowledge Ecology International (formerly the Consumer Project on Technology), Médecins Sans Frontières (MSF), Oxfam, the South Centre, the Third World Network, the Trade Law Centre for Southern Africa (tralac), and the Treatment Action Campaign, among others. As these North-South alliances are built and strengthened, they will be able to push for policies that will support greater access to essential medicines in less developed countries.

Academics and the media in the North can also play important roles. For example, academics and their institutions have helped identify policy choices and negotiating strategies while developing technical capacity in less developed countries. Likewise, less developed countries can increase their leverage and negotiating outcomes if they are able to 'capture ... the attention of the mass media in industrial countries and persuade ... the media to reframe the issue using a reference point more favorable to the coalition's position' (Odell and Sell, 2006, p. 87). As John Braithwaite and Peter Drahos (2000, p. 576) surmise, '[h]ad TRIPS been framed as a public health issue, the anxiety of mass publics in the US and other Western states might have become a factor in destabilizing the consensus that US business elites had built around TRIPS'.

In addition, commentators have underscored the need to design and stimulate alliances between generic manufacturers in the developed and less developed worlds. With caution, cooperation between brand name and generic manufacturers can also be beneficial, although commentators are generally wary of such cooperation. If developed properly, these two sets of alliances 'can provide efficiencies, foster dynamic competition, enhance their competitive ability and benefit consumers' (Rosenberg, 2006, p. 76). To obtain maximum benefits, these alliances can be set up not only within the less developed world, but also between the developed and less developed worlds – perhaps with the assistance of intergovernmental and non-governmental organizations. It may also be helpful for public authorities in less developed countries to coordinate strategies with the private generic pharmaceutical sector (Shaffer, 2004, p. 481).

Finally, North-South cooperation can go beyond a specific field. For instance, it may be useful to develop cross-discipline cooperation linkages between health and medical experts in the North and intellectual property offices in the South. As commentators have noted, the participation of health officials and ministries in trade negotiations is scant and inadequate (Musungu, Villanueva and Blasetti, 2004, p. 77).

In a recent article, Professor Drahos (2008) advocated coordination between patent offices and health and medical experts in making assessment of an invention's contribution to innovation and health welfare. Drawing on experience of ANVISA, the Brazilian National Health Surveillance Agency, he explained that these experts are likely to be in a much better position than patent examiners to make such an assessment. While there is no doubt that the Brazilian model and greater cooperation between patent offices and health experts will benefit many less developed countries, such a model is not limited to the country or the region. Greater cooperation between intellectual property offices in the South and health and medical experts and related NGOs in the North is likely to be equally, or if not more, fruitful.

3.3 The WTO Dispute Settlement Process

One of the major features of the WTO is its mandatory dispute settlement process. Although the United States and the European Union had used the process predominantly in the first few years of the WTO's existence, especially when the disputes involved the TRIPs Agreement, less developed countries have begun to use the process more actively in recent years (Davey, 2005, pp. 17 and 24). While Brazil and India initially used the process primarily against less powerful WTO member states, such as Argentina, Turkey, Mexico, Peru, and Poland, they have started to use the process more aggressively against powerful WTO member states, such as the European Union and the United States.

Today, globalization and international trade have deeply affected domestic policies, and an active participation in the WTO dispute settlement process is of paramount importance to WTO member states. By participating in it, countries can help develop WTO jurisprudence in a way that can shape the ongoing negotiations in the areas of international trade, intellectual property, and even public health. Gregory Shaffer (2004, p. 470) describes such participation as negotiation 'in the shadow of' the WTO dispute settlement process. As he explains:

> Participation in WTO judicial processes is arguably more important than is participation in analogous judicial processes for shaping law in national

> systems. The difficulty of amending or interpreting WTO law through the WTO political process enhances the impact of WTO jurisprudence. WTO law requires consensus to modify, resulting in a rigid legislative system, with rule modifications occurring through infrequent negotiating rounds. Because of the complex bargaining process, rules often are drafted in a vague manner, thereby delegating de facto power to the WTO dispute settlement system to effectively make WTO law through interpretation.
>
> As a result of the increased importance of WTO jurisprudence and the rigidity of the WTO political process, those governments that are able to participate most actively in the WTO dispute settlement system are best-positioned to effectively shape the law's interpretation and application over time.

Shaffer's approach makes a lot of sense. After all, there is no indication that the WTO dispute settlement panels are biased toward stronger protection of intellectual property rights. In the decisions issued thus far, the panellists have focused narrowly on the language of the TRIPs Agreement, taking into consideration the recognized international rules of interpretation, the context of the TRIPs negotiations, and the past and subsequent developments of relevant treaties. In *Canada – Patent Protection of Pharmaceutical Products* (WTO, 2000a, para. 7.26), the panel even referred favourably to the limitations and public interest safeguards contained in the TRIPs Agreement. As the panel declared, '[b]oth the goals and the limitations stated in Articles 7 and 8.1 must obviously be borne in mind when [examining the words of the limiting conditions in Article 30] as well as those of other provisions of the TRIPS Agreement which indicate its object and purposes'.

Moreover, as I have noted elsewhere in the context of the United States' recent WTO dispute with China over the lack of intellectual property enforcement, the European Union and the United States did not win all of the disputes 'litigated' before the Dispute Settlement Body (Yu, 2006b, pp. 939–40). In June 2000, for example, the United States lost its dispute with the European Communities over Section 110(5) of the US Copyright Act, which enables restaurants and small establishments to play copyrighted music without compensating copyright holders (WTO, 2000b). In a subsequent ruling, a WTO panel found inconsistent with the TRIPs Agreement Section 211(a)(2) of the US Omnibus Appropriations Act of 1998, which prohibits the registration or renewal of trademarks previously abandoned by trademark holders whose business and assets have been confiscated under Cuban law (WTO, 2002).

In addition, the WTO panel curtailed the ability of the US administration to pursue retaliatory actions before exhausting all remedies permissible under the WTO rules, even though it nominally upheld Sections

301–310 of the US Trade Act of 1974 (WTO, 1999). The Caribbean islands of Antigua and Barbuda also successfully challenged US laws on Internet and telephone gambling in *United States – Measures Affecting the Cross-Border Supply of Gambling and Betting Services* (WTO, 2004).

While many of the United States' losses before the WTO Dispute Settlement Body have come at the hand of the European Union, the WTO dispute settlement process is not only reserved for use by powerful WTO member states. The last dispute has shown that, in the WTO process, even two tiny Caribbean islands can prevail over a trading giant like the United States. One can imagine how effective the use of this process can be when less developed countries team up with others as co-complainants or third parties. On the one hand, such a collective effort can pull together scarce economic and legal resources to defend laws that seek to exploit the flexibilities provided by the TRIPs Agreement and that are explicitly affirmed by paragraph 5 of the Doha Declaration. On the other hand, less developed countries can use these resources to design effective strategies to challenge non–TRIPs compliant legislation in developed countries.

Compared with the uncoordinated arrangement where each country has to file a separate complaint, or join the complainant as a third party, the collaborative strategy has at least five benefits. First, countries will be able to significantly reduce the costs of WTO litigation, thus lowering the threshold for determining whether it would be worthwhile to file a WTO complaint. Shaffer's (2004, p. 473) analysis has shown how it may not be worthwhile for a small or poor country to file a WTO complaint even when there is a high economic stake. Based on 2004 figures, he found that 'an average WTO claim cost … in the range of US$300,000–400,000 in attorneys' fees'. Although a potential loss of US$200,000 in trade may be highly important to the economy of a small, poor country, such a loss does not always justify taking the case to the WTO Dispute Settlement Body or defending it there. Instead, these countries often give up their valid claims (Shaffer, 2004, p. 472). If they are sued, they often settle the claims either by abandoning legal or policy experiments that are permissible under the WTO agreements, or by transplanting laws from abroad against their wishes and to their detriment.

Such an outcome is particularly problematic from the standpoint of the TRIPs negotiations. One of the primary reasons why less developed countries reluctantly agreed to increase intellectual property protection is the ability to use the WTO dispute settlement process as a bulwark against developed countries' coercive, and often unilateral, tactics. As some less developed countries pointed out at the time of the negotiations, it would be pointless for them to join the WTO if the United States were able to continue imposing unilateral sanctions despite their membership (Yu, 2006a, p. 372). Unfortunately, the high start-up costs required by the WTO dispute settlement process have made it very difficult for less developed countries to benefit from the hard-earned bargains they won through the WTO negotiations.

More problematically, the lack of participation by some less developed countries in the WTO dispute settlement process can hurt the protection of other less developed countries. As Shaffer (2004, p. 465) reminds us, '[w]ho participates in the institutional process affects which arguments will be presented, which, in turn, affects how the competing concerns over patent protection, public health, and market competition will be weighed'. Thus, if the WTO rules are to be shaped to advance the interests of the less developed world, greater participation by less developed countries in the WTO dispute settlement process is needed.

Less developed countries can also benefit from the additional expertise and resources provided by other less developed countries. Instead of spending a substantial amount of money on outside counsel or spending even more in developing local expertise, less developed countries can take advantage of cost-sharing arrangements and devote more resources to improving the living standards of their nationals (Shaffer, 2004, p. 475). If these countries team up with countries such as Brazil, China, or India, they can benefit from even more sophisticated expertise. Since the latter are active litigants in the WTO dispute settlement process, over the years they have developed considerable expertise that can be shared with other less developed countries.

Moreover, as repeat players in WTO litigation, less developed countries will benefit from the economies of scale in deploying legal resources (Shaffer, 2004, p. 474). They are also more likely to possess the mindset to plan legal strategies that will help them advance the interests of the less developed world and strengthen their overall legal positions, rather than strategies that seek to win only one case at a time (Shaffer, 2004, p. 470). In doing so, these countries can use the WTO dispute settlement process effectively to shape both the judicial interpretation and the future negotiation of the TRIPs Agreement in a pro-development manner. They may even be able to regain the momentum that less developed countries lost during the negotiations of the TRIPs Agreement due to their limited understanding of intellectual property rights and weak bargaining power. Thus far, the European Union and the United States have been able to advance their commercial interests through the WTO dispute settlement process because they are the predominant users of this process (Shaffer, 2004, p. 470). If less developed countries are to curtail the developed countries' ability to advance these interests, they need to make greater strategic use of the WTO dispute settlement process.

A further benefit of this collective approach is that less developed countries do not need to worry as much about the backlash they might encounter should they individually file a WTO complaint against the European Union or the United States. As William Davey (1987, p. 71) has noted, when countries do not face each other often as adversaries in the WTO process, 'initiation of a complaint would be something of a slap in the face. The ignominy of a loss would also loom larger'. By taking collective action, many otherwise infrequent players in the WTO dispute settlement process will become more frequent players. As they become involved in more complaints against the European Union or the United States and, as each of these parties has its share of wins and losses, the impact of a WTO dispute on diplomatic relations will be greatly reduced (Yu, 2006b, p. 945).

Finally, less developed countries may not 'have the diplomatic or economic muscle to ensure that the decision is implemented' even if they win their case (Davey, 1987, p. 90). Indeed, as Davey (1987, p. 102) points out, there is a good chance that 'even massive retaliation by a small country would be unnoticed by a larger one'. Thus, by uniting together, less developed countries may be able to have more leverage at the enforcement level by increasing the economic impact of trade countermeasures permitted by the WTO dispute settlement panel.

3.4 Regional or Pro-development Fora

Regional or pro-development fora are particularly effective means for coordinating efforts by less developed countries in the areas of public health, intellectual property, and international trade. These fora will provide the much-needed focal points for countries to share experience, knowledge, and best practices and to coordinate negotiation and litigation strategies (Musungu, Villanueva and Blasetti, 2004, pp. xiv–xv; Narlikar, 2003, p. 206; Shaffer, 2004, p. 478). Through these fora, less developed countries can '(i) raise political awareness of certain members … (ii) help define the agenda, prior to the actual negotiations … and (iii) achieve particular regulatory outcomes on a particular issue or economic sector or sub-sector … and defend interests in dispute settlement' (Rolland, 2007, p. 499).

In addition, these fora allow countries to reframe issues 'in a way that eases impasses' (Odell, 2006, p. 16), thereby providing a mechanism to balance interests internal to the group. In doing so, conflicts or negotiation deadlocks can be resolved before the negotiations are enlarged to include selected developed countries or the entire developed world (Rolland, 2007, p. 501). These fora also facilitate 'a pooling of organisational resources, and enable countries with ill-defined interests to avail themselves of the research efforts of allies and a possible country-wise division of research and labour across issue areas' (Narlikar, 2003, p. 14).

Through these fora, the interests of the participating countries would be better and more symmetrically represented (Rolland, 2007, p. 512). The fora would also 'help build capacity for the group's members as they would gain leverage through access to a more central and streamlined channel of information (through the group representation) and, in turn, be able to better formulate their own policy positions' (Rolland, 2007, p. 512). In addition, regional or pro-development fora could help improve the human capital and WTO know-how of less developed countries by 'better coordinat[ing] training of developing country officials and non-governmental representatives' (Shaffer, 2004, p. 478). These capacity-building functions are especially important, considering the fact that some less developed countries have given up their participation in international fora due to a lack of financial resources or political circumstances.

As commentators have pointed out, many less developed countries 'lack the resources ... to send delegates to these fora and thus have resorted to using nongovernmental organizations ... to represent their interests' (McGinnis and Movsesian, 2000, p. 557 n. 256). In one instance, the Foundation for International Environmental Law and Development, a London-based environmental NGO, negotiated a deal to represent Sierra Leone before the WTO Committee on Trade and Environment (Shaffer, 2001, pp. 62–3). Even if countries are willing to send delegates, they may have become formally inactive due to their failure to pay dues for a certain period of time. Within the WTO, for example, their inactive status would prevent them from chairing any bodies (Narlikar, 2003, p. 15). Many delegations are also affected by their limited institutional capacity, delegation size, geopolitical capital, and overall expertise (Rolland, 2007, p. 529).

Coordination at the regional level and among less developed countries becomes even more important in light of the proliferation of bilateral and regional trade agreements initiated by the European Union and the United States. Since these agreements tend to transplant laws based on developed-country models, they are notorious for ignoring local needs, national interests, technological capabilities, institutional capacities, and public health conditions of less developed countries. Even worse, these agreements sometimes call for a higher level of protection than what is currently offered in the developed world (Correa, 2004, p. 93; Yu, 2006c,

p. 41). If the European Union or the United States does not consider it beneficial to have higher protection, one has to wonder why protection needs to be strengthened in countries that have even more limited resources and that do not possess adequate safeguards and correction mechanisms.

If these demands for higher protection are not disturbing enough, less developed countries may be 'induced' into signing conflicting agreements with both the European Union and the United States (Yu, 2006a, p. 407). While these two trading powers are interested in having strong global intellectual property standards, there remain a large number of intellectual property conflicts between the two. In the copyright context, for example, they take different positions on 'the protection of moral rights, fair use, the first sale doctrine, the work-made-for-hire arrangement, and protection against private copying in the digital environment' (Yu, 2002, pp. 625–6). They also approach the patent filing process differently and greatly disagree on how to protect geographical indications (WTO, 2005). Indeed, had the United States refused to include geographical indications in the then-proposed TRIPs Agreement, the European Community's initial ambivalent position toward the creation of the new agreement might not have changed (Watal, 2001, p. 23).

In view of these differences, conflicts may arise when less developed countries sign the trade agreements supplied by both the European Union and the United States without appropriate review and modification. To be certain, it is not the fault of these trading powers that policymakers in less developed countries are unable to review or modify the agreement. Oftentimes, it is the result of a lack of resources, expertise, leadership, negotiation sophistication, bargaining power, or some or all of the above. Many policymakers in less developed countries are also blinded by the benefits that their countries *may* receive in other trade areas under a package deal – or, worse, they are just too eager to appease, or develop 'friendship' with, the trading powers. Nevertheless, it is still highly lamentable that these countries would enter into potentially conflicting agreements that could be avoided with greater caution, coordination, and information. It is bad enough to be forced to sign a bilateral agreement that does not meet local conditions. It is even worse to be put into a position where one may have to juggle two conflicting agreements that do not meet local conditions and are impossible to honour.

Fortunately for less developed countries, regional or pro-development fora may provide the much-needed institutional response to the growing use of bilateral and regional trade agreements to push for stronger intellectual property standards and to further reduce the policy space needed for the development of intellectual property, trade, and public health policies. While the constantly short-staffed Advisory Centre on WTO Law provides legal advice and support in WTO matters and trains government officials in WTO law, they do not provide assistance in coordinating political, judicial and forum-shifting strategies in an increasingly complex international intellectual property law-making environment (Shaffer, 2004, p. 478). They also provide very limited assistance in developing negotiating strategies concerning the bilateral, plurilateral, or regional trade agreements initiated by the European Union and the United States.

By bringing less developed countries together, these fora would allow policymakers in those countries to share their latest experiences and lessons concerning these agreements. In doing so, the participating countries would have more information to evaluate the benefits and drawbacks of the potential treaties. They would also be able to anticipate problems and potential side effects created by these treaties. They might even be able to better design prophylactic or correction measures that would become handy should the treaties prove to be unsuitable for their countries.

Finally, as Sonia Rolland (2007, p. 505) points out, 'the ability or inability of developing countries to form and sustain effective coalitions in the WTO depends not only on the coalitions' inherent characteristics and the political environment ... but also on the institutional and legal framework in which they operate'. Except for supranational entities such as the European Union, special classifications such as least developed countries, or recognized regional trade agreements, the WTO offers very limited support for formal representation by groups in policy deliberation. Thus, if less developed countries can use these regional or pro-development fora to develop strategies to push for greater legal or structural changes within international organizations that will make group representation easier to obtain and the institution more coalition-friendly, they are more likely to be able to increase their bargaining leverage and to develop a stronger voice for the less developed world. After all, 'the ability to sustain developing country coalitions depends in part on the WTO's legal structure ... . [M]embers whose interests might be more effectively served if they are promoted by a group strategy could [also] benefit from a legal framework that better supports developing country coalitions or groupings' (Rolland, 2007, p. 485).

4. CHALLENGES TO BUILDING IPC4D

Although collective action can play an important role in the international intellectual property regime and the use of the coordination strategies described in this chapter can help less developed countries strengthen their collective bargaining position, there are still many challenges. This section highlights some of these challenges.

Historically, less developed countries have had only limited success in using coalition-building efforts to increase their bargaining leverage (Abbott, 2003, p. 42). Their lack of success was perhaps caused by the fact that these coalitions were usually too ambitious. They were set up to include a broad mandate, diverse membership, complex issues, and incompatible interests. As Amrita Narlikar (2003, pp. 122–3) has shown, issue-based coalitions work best for small and very specialized economies with common profiles and interests, such as those 'small island economies with similar geographic/strategic endowments, concentrated interests in tourism exports, and travel imports'. These coalitions, however, do not work well for larger, more diverse, and often internally conflicting economies (Narlikar, 2003, p. 176). They also do not work well for a large bloc of less developed countries that have various strengths, sizes, and interests and that are only linked together in an ad hoc fashion (Rolland, 2007, p. 510).

The lack of success by less developed countries to build or maintain coalitions can be further attributed to their 'high … dependen[ce] on the developed countries as the source of capital, whether it is provided through the IMF [International Monetary Fund] or World Bank, or through investment bankers and securities exchanges' (Abbott, 2003, p. 42). This lack of financial independence is further aggravated by a lack of stability in the economies of less developed countries – for example, in India during the negotiations of the TRIPs Agreement and in South America during the negotiation of the draft International Code of Conduct on the Transfer of Technology (Yu, 2009, pp. 493–505).

Another challenge for less developed countries concerns how to set up a coalition in a way that would prevent the more powerful members from dominating their much weaker and more dependent partners. Since countries with more human capital, technical knowledge, and legal expertise may abuse their leadership roles at the expense of others, it is important to build safeguards into the coalitions to protect the weaker members and to allow them to retain their autonomy and identity. If IPC4D are to be successfully built and maintained, it is also important to develop trust among the participating members so that they can work together closely without worrying about potential exploitation.

These safeguards are particularly important in light of the complex economic interests of the large developing countries, such as Brazil, China, and India, all of which have grown significantly faster than their poorer neighbours. In many areas of international trade, these middle-income countries already 'have gained relatively more than their poorer counterparts from the multilateral trade process [and] have increasingly found themselves adopting positions divergent from those of [their poorer counterparts] on the question of preferential access to rich country markets' (Rolland, 2007, p. 536). If history repeats itself, as in the cases of the United States, Germany, Japan, and South Korea, some of these countries eventually will want stronger intellectual property protection once they become economically developed. They may also benefit from the continued lack of manufacturing capacity in other less developed countries.

To complicate matters, the economic interests of pharmaceutical manufacturers have grown rapidly in large developing countries, and these countries are eager to exploit their comparative advantages by serving as regional research-and-development or supply centres. One may still remember the remark by PhRMA representative Tom Bombelles where he suggested 'South Africa was a pawn used by India and Argentina to undermine TRIPS' (Halbert, 2002, p. 267). Although this remark sought to 'shift the focus [unfairly] away from the enormous health crisis in Africa' (Halbert, 2002, pp. 267–8), it signalled a problem that would arise if the debate became whether the developed or large developing countries would supply medication to other less developed countries.

Moreover, the dynamic development of the pharmaceutical sector has made it difficult for countries to assess their self-interests and for coalitions to be maintained. As Dwijen Rangnekar (2007, pp. 379–80) points out:

> [I]n 1999 [there emerged] a new configuration of pharmaceutical firms, the Indian Pharmaceutical Alliance (the Alliance), consisting of firms like Cipla, Dr Reddy's Laboratories, Lupin Laboratories and Ranbaxy that collectively account for 30% of domestic production and 33% of Indian exports. The Alliance is composed of pharmaceutical firms with mixed interests and areas of expertise: '[the Alliance] … is perhaps a little schizophrenic about where its members' interests lie. On the one hand many of them, such as Ranbaxy, wish to develop as research based companies and see the value of strong patent protection to achieve that. On the other hand, the overwhelming majority of their revenues remain derived from generic production, and accordingly they share many of the concerns of [the Indian Drug Manufacturers' Association, a key domestic group of generic manufacturers].'

As the economy of these countries matures, the structure of the pharmaceutical sector may change even further. In 2007, for example, 'Merck partnered with Advinus Therapeutics, an Indian company, to develop drugs for metabolic disorders, with Merck retaining the right to advance research into late-stage clinical trials. GlaxoSmithKline and Ranbaxy have also teamed up' (Nath, 2008, p. 102). Such partnerships between brand name and generic manufacturers have made it particularly difficult for countries to assess their economic self-interests.

Finally, there are 'IP-irrelevant' factors – factors that are largely unaffected by intellectual property protection (Yu, 2007b, pp. 852–3) – that would make it difficult for countries to co-operate with each other, such as xenophobia, nationalism, racism, mistrust, and resentment. No matter how much more globalized and interdependent the world has become, some countries will always remain reluctant to participate in these coalitions, because of historical conflicts, border disputes, economic rivalries, cultural differences, or spillover issues from other areas.

The existence of all of these challenges, however, does not doom the IPC4D project. Rather, it demonstrates how coalition building is always a work in progress that requires care, vision, and continuous attention between and among the various parties. It also suggests the importance of using regional approaches to alleviate the impact of some of these factors. If the interests of the weaker coalition members are to be protected, a clear and detailed coalition agreement and a carefully designed benefit-sharing arrangement need to be put in place when the coalition is set up. It is also important for the weaker members to obtain a better understanding of how they can take advantage of the coalitions when the interests of the members are still close to each other.

5. CONCLUSION

There are many benefits to building IPC4D. There are some challenges, however. If countries are to work together to develop successful coalitions, they need to clearly articulate their goals, understand each other better, and work out mutually beneficial arrangements. In doing so, the development of IPC4D is not a mere hope but a realistic goal. The resulting coalitions will not only be able to reduce the ongoing push by the European Union and the United States to ratchet up global intellectual property standards, but they will also help enlarge the policy space needed by less developed countries for the development of their intellectual property, trade, and public health policies. With better coordination and greater leverage, these countries may even be able to establish, shape, and enlarge a pro-development negotiating agenda that would restore the balance of the international intellectual property system while promoting access to essential medicines in the less developed world.

Acknowledgements

This chapter has been abridged and adapted from Yu, Peter K. (2008), 'Access to medicines, BRICS alliances, and collective action', *American Journal of Law and Medicine*, **34**(2), 345–94. The author would like to thank Jonathan Soike for excellent research and editorial assistance.

NOTES

1. Although the initial deadline for ratification was 1 December 2007, the deadline has been extended for two years three times until 2013 (WTO, 2010). As of this writing, only more than a third of the 157 WTO member states, including the United States, India, Japan, China, and members of the European Union, have ratified the proposed amendment.
2. The term 'regime complex' originated from Kal Raustiala and David Victor (2004). David Leebron (2002, p. 18) has also advanced the concept of 'conglomerate regime' to describe this new development.

BIBLIOGRAPHY

Abbott, Frederick (2003), 'The future of IPRs in the multilateral trading system', in Christophe Bellmann, Graham Dutfield and Ricardo Melendez-Ortiz (eds), *Trading in Knowledge: Development Perspectives on TRIPS, Trade and Sustainability*, London: Earthscan Publications, pp. 36–44.

Abbott, Frederick M. and Jerome H. Reichman (2003), 'The Doha round's public health legacy: Strategies for the production and diffusion of patented medicines under the amended TRIPS provisions', *Journal of International Economic Law*, **10**(4), 921–87.

Alden, Chris (2007), *China in Africa*, London: Zed Books.

Amoore, Louise, Randall Germain and Rorden Wilkinson (2003), 'Series preface', in Amrita Narlikar (ed.), *International Trade and Developing Countries: Bargaining Coalitions in the GATT and WTO*, London: Routledge, pp. xiii–xiv.

Benvenisti, Eyal and George W. Downs (2007), 'The empire's new clothes: Political economy and the fragmentation of international law', *Stanford Law Review*, **60**(2), 595–631.

Bird, Robert and Daniel R. Cahoy (2008), 'The impact of compulsory licensing on foreign direct investment: A collective bargaining approach', *American Business Law Journal*, **45**(2), 283–330.

Braithwaite, John and Peter Drahos (2000), *Global Business Regulation*, Cambridge: Cambridge University Press.

Cho, Sungjoon (2004), 'A bridge too far: The fall of the fifth WTO ministerial conference in Cancún and the future of trade constitution', *Journal of International Economic Law*, **7**(2), 219–44.

Coleman, William D. and Geoffrey R.D. Underhill (1998), 'Introduction: Domestic politics, regional economic co-operation, and global economic integration', in William D. Coleman and Geoffrey R.D. Underhill (eds), *Regionalism and Global Economic Integration: Europe, Asia and the Americas*, London: Routledge, pp. 1–16.

Correa, Carlos M. (2004), 'Bilateralism in intellectual property: Defeating the WTO system for access to medicines', *Case Western Reserve Journal of International Law*, **36**(1), 79–94.

Davey, William J. (1987), 'Dispute settlement in GATT', *Fordham International Law Journal*, **11**(1), 51–109.

Davey, William J. (2005), 'The WTO dispute settlement system: The first ten years', *Journal of International Economic Law*, **8**(1), 17–50.

Drahos, Peter (2002), 'Developing countries and international intellectual property standard-setting', *Journal of World Intellectual Property*, **5**(5), 765–89.

Drahos, Peter (2008), '"Trust me": Patent offices in developing countries', *American Journal of Law and Medicine*, **34**(2), 151–74.

Halbert, Debora (2002), 'Moralized discourses: South Africa's intellectual property fight for access to AIDS drugs', *Seattle Journal for Social Justice*, **1**(2), 257–88.

Hurrell, Andrew and Amrita Narlikar (2006), 'A new politics of confrontation? Brazil and India in multilateral trade negotiations', *Global Society*, **20**(4), 415–33.

Leebron, David W. (2002), 'Linkages', *American Journal of International Law*, **96**(1), 5–27.

McGinnis, John O. and Mark L. Movsesian (2000), 'The world trade constitution', *Harvard Law Review*, **114**(2), 511–605.

Musungu, Sisule F., Susan Villanueva and Roxana Blasetti (2004), *Utilizing TRIPS Flexibilities for Public Health Protection through South-South Regional Frameworks*, Geneva: South Centre.

Narlikar, Amrita (2003), *International Trade and Developing Countries: Bargaining Coalitions in the GATT and WTO*, London: Routledge.

Nath, Kamal (2008), *India's Century*, New York: McGraw-Hill.

New, William (2007), 'TRIPs Council extends health amendment; targets poor nations' needs', *Intellectual Property Watch*, 23 October, available at http://www.ip-watch.org/weblog/index.php?p=798 (accessed 26 May 2010).

Odell, John S. (2006), 'Introduction', in John S. Odell (ed.), *Negotiating Trade: Developing Countries in the WTO and NAFTA*, Cambridge: Cambridge University Press, pp. 1–38.

Odell, John S. and Susan K. Sell (2006), 'Reframing the issue: The WTO coalition on intellectual property and public health, 2001', in John S. Odell (ed.), *Negotiating Trade: Developing Countries in the WTO and NAFTA*, Cambridge: Cambridge University Press, pp. 85–114.

Rangnekar, Dwijen (2007), 'Context and ambiguity in the making of law: A comment on amending India's patent act', *Journal of World Intellectual Property*, **10**(5), 365–87.

Raustiala, Kal and David G. Victor (2004), 'The regime complex for plant genetic resources', *International Organization*, **58**(2), 277–309.

Rolland, Sonia E. (2007), 'Developing country coalitions at the WTO: In search of legal support', *Harvard International Law Journal*, **48**(2), 483–551.

Rosenberg, Barbara (2006), 'Market concentration of the transnational pharmaceutical industry and the generic industries: Trends on mergers, acquisitions and other transactions', in Pedro Roffe, Geoff Tansey and David Vivas-Eugui (eds), *Negotiating Health: Intellectual Property and Access to Medicines*, London: Earthscan Publications, pp. 65–78.

Shaffer, Gregory C. (2001), 'The World Trade Organization under challenge: Democracy and the law and politics of the WTO's treatment of trade and environment matters', *Harvard Environmental Law Review*, **25**(1), 1–93.

Shaffer, Gregory C. (2004), 'Recognizing public goods in WTO dispute settlement: Who participates? Who decides? The case of TRIPS and pharmaceutical patent protection', *Journal of International Economic Law*, **7**(2), 459–82.

Watal, Jayashree (2001), *Intellectual Property Rights in the WTO and Developing Countries*, The Hague: Kluwer Law International.

World Intellectual Property Organization (WIPO) (2007), *Member States Adopt a Development Agenda for WIPO*, 1 October, available at http://www.wipo.int/pressroom/en/articles/2007/article_0071.html (accessed 26 May 2010).

World Trade Organization [WTO] (1999), *United States – Sections 301–310 of the Trade Act of 1974*, WTO Panel Report, WT/DS152/R.

WTO (2000a), *Canada – Patent Protection of Pharmaceutical Products*, WTO Panel Report, WT/DS114/R.

WTO (2000b), *United States – Section 110(5) of the US Copyright Act*, WTO Panel Report, WT/DS/160/R.

WTO (2002), *United States – Section 211 Omnibus Appropriations Act of 1998*, WTO Appellate Body Report, WT/DS176/AB/R.

WTO (2004), *United States – Measures Affecting the Cross-Border Supply of Gambling and Betting Services*, WTO Panel Report, WT/DS285/R.

WTO (2005), *European Communities – Protection of Trademarks and Geographical Indications for Agricultural Products and Foodstuffs*, WTO Panel Report, WT/DS174/R.

WTO (2010), *Countries Accepting Amendment of the TRIPS Agreement*, available at http://www.wto.org/english/tratop_e/trips_e/amendment_e.htm (accessed 26 May 2010).

Yu, Peter K. (2002), 'Toward a nonzero-sum approach to resolving global intellectual property disputes: What we can learn from mediators, business strategists, and international relations theorists', *University of Cincinnati Law Review*, **70**(2), 569–650.

Yu, Peter K. (2004), 'Currents and crosscurrents in the international intellectual property regime', *Loyola of Los Angeles Law Review*, **38**(1), 323–443.

Yu, Peter K. (2006a), 'TRIPs and its discontents', *Marquette Intellectual Property Law Review*, **10**(2), 369–410.

Yu, Peter K. (2006b), 'From pirates to partners (Episode II): Protecting intellectual property in post-WTO China', *American University Law Review*, **55**(4), 901–1000.

Yu, Peter K. (2006c), 'Anti-circumvention and anti-anticircumvention', *Denver University Law Review*, **84**(1), 13–77.

Yu, Peter K. (2007a), 'Five disharmonizing trends in the international intellectual property regime', in Peter K. Yu (ed.), *Intellectual Property and Information Wealth: Issues and Practices in the Digital Age*, Westport: Praeger Publishers, vol. 4, pp. 73–111.

Yu, Peter K. (2007b), 'The international enclosure movement', *Indiana Law Journal*, **82**(4), 827–907.

Yu, Peter K. (2007c), 'International enclosure, the regime complex, and intellectual property schizophrenia', *Michigan State Law Review*, **2007**(1), 1–33.

Yu, Peter K. (2008), 'Access to medicines, BRICS alliances, and collective action', *American Journal of Law and Medicine*, **34**(2), 345–94.

Yu, Peter K. (2009), 'A tale of two development agendas', *Ohio Northern University Law Review*, **35**(2), 465–573.

Zoellick, Robert B. (2003), 'America will not wait for the won't-do countries', *Financial Times*, 22 September, p. 23.

11. The global governance of HIV/AIDS and the rugged road ahead: An epilogue

Peter K. Yu

> For each day that passes without people accessing treatment we attend funerals. People die. We hear a hundred reasons for not providing people with treatment. For each reason given, lives are lost.
>
> A group of Zambians living with HIV/AIDS in Lusaka (D'Adesky, 2004, p. 324)

> You hear that in my country perhaps one out of nine [is] infected with HIV. Imagine if you represented the South African population, and we counted out, one, two, three, four, five, six, seven, eight, nine – you have AIDS. One, two, three, four, five, six, seven, eight, nine – AIDS. We are in fact speaking about the daughter of, the wife of, the sister of, the husband of, the father of, the brother of someone.
>
> – Archbishop Desmond Mpilo Tutu (Tutu, 2002, p. 253)

Since its discovery more than three decades ago, AIDS has grown from a disease afflicting only a small portion of the world's population to one having major deleterious effects on an ever-growing number of people. To date, over 30 million adults and about 2.5 million children have been infected with the disease (UNAIDS, 2010, p. 180). Another 25 million have died owing to the infection (The Economist, 2011). If we count family members, loved ones and the numerous professionals and volunteers who cared for the infected, HIV/AIDS has disturbed the lives of an incalculable number of individuals and communities from around the world.

Yet, despite the gravity of this public health crisis and the many dedicated responses, we are still nowhere close to finding a solution to containing, if not curing, the disease. As the Joint United Nations Programme on HIV/AIDS (UNAIDS) lamented in its latest report, about two-thirds of the estimated 15 million people living with HIV in less developed countries have no access to affordable life-saving medications (UNAIDS, 2010, p. 7). Such limited access has renewed fears that the disease will continue to plague the globe for decades to come.

In the past two decades, a global governance structure has slowly emerged to address the HIV/AIDS crisis. From programs developed by the World Health Organization (WHO) to the ongoing negotiations in the Doha Development Round of Trade Negotiations (Doha Round) at the World Trade Organization (WTO), governments have worked closely to confront the crisis head-on. Nongovernmental organizations (NGOs) and private foundations have also entered the fold to provide non–state based assistance, especially in areas where national governments alone could not achieve satisfactory outcomes. These organizations include Health Action International, the Health Global Access Project (Health GAP), Knowledge Ecology International (formerly the Consumer Project on Technology), Médecins Sans Frontières, Oxfam, Public Citizen, the Treatment Action Campaign, the Bill and Melinda Gates Foundation and the William J. Clinton Foundation.

Today, HIV/AIDS governance is no longer a simple international initiative building on the Westphalian nation-state model. Rather it reflects a more pluralistic order featuring complex, transnational interactions among state governments, intergovernmental bodies, international donor organizations, sub-state and non-state actors, and the private sector (Dodgson and Lee, 2002; Harman and Lisk, 2009; Hein, Bartsch and Kohlmorgen, 2007). HIV/AIDS governance is global governance in every sense of the word.

In recent years, HIV/AIDS governance has become more complex. Today, it implicates quite a number of disparate international regimes. Although intellectual property issues concerning HIV/AIDS treatments are traditionally governed by conventions developed by the World Intellectual Property Organization (WIPO) and its predecessors, the establishment of the WTO and its Agreement on Trade-Related Aspects of Intellectual Property Rights (TRIPs Agreement) has steered the discussions towards the international trade arena.

In addition, issues lying at the intersection of HIV/AIDS governance and intellectual property protection have been explored in the human rights forum. Since the TRIPs Agreement entered into force, a number of United Nations (UN) human rights bodies – including the Sub-Commission on the Promotion and Protection of Human Rights, the High Commissioner for Human Rights and two Special Rapporteurs on the Right to Health – have issued reports and documents emphasizing the primacy of human rights over the TRIPs Agreement and other international trade, intellectual property and investment instruments (Yu, 2009a, pp. 522–7).

Intellectual property issues concerning HIV/AIDS treatments have also been closely scrutinized in the public health arena. In February 2004, the World Health Assembly established the Commission on Intellectual Property Rights, Innovation and Public Health. The commission's final report reminded us of the many adverse spillover effects of strong protection for pharmaceutical patents and undisclosed clinical trial data (Commission on Intellectual Property Rights, Innovation and Public Health, 2006). That report eventually led to the May 2008 adoption of the Global Strategy and Plan of Action on Public Health, Innovation and Intellectual Property (WHA Resolution 61.21), which seeks to facilitate the development of funding and incentive mechanisms for the creation of new medicines ('t Hoen, 2009, pp. 92–3).

Even in the intellectual property arena, where policymakers and rights holders have traditionally embraced a maximalist, non–evidence based approach to protection, a number of important developments have taken place. The increased assertiveness on the part of the African Group and the rapid rise of emerging economies – the so-called BRICS countries (Brazil, China, India and South Africa) – have altered the political dynamics of the international regulatory system (Deere, 2009, p. 123; Yu, 2008). The ongoing Doha Round, the establishment of the WIPO Development Agenda and the increasing push for greater pro-development efforts at the WHO and in other international fora have also built up the much-needed momentum for promoting access to essential medicines (Yu, 2009a, pp. 511–40).

Moreover, governments in the less developed world and supportive NGOs in both the North and South have fought better and harder to advance policies that are more tailored to local health needs and conditions. For example, during the June 2010 meeting of the WTO Council for Trade-Related Aspects of Intellectual Property Rights, both China and India made important interventions expressing concerns about the inappropriate push for TRIPs-plus enforcement norms through the establishment of the highly controversial Anti-Counterfeiting Trade Agreement and other bilateral, plurilateral and regional trade agreements (Yu, 2011, pp. 518–21). Brazil and India also filed complaints with the WTO Dispute Settlement Body against the European Union and the Netherlands over the seizure of in-transit generic drugs (Chapter 7). Although India and the European Union recently reached an interim settlement, it remains to be seen whether India will eventually withdraw its complaint from the WTO and whether Brazil will follow suit.

As if these developments were not promising enough, new players have emerged from the non-state sector. The substantial resources of the Gates Foundation, for instance, have ushered in exciting initiatives in vaccine development and various types of global health research. Although some commentators have expressed reservation about the Foundation's focus on biomedical science, emphasis on intellectual property rights and limited interest in infrastructural development (Harman, 2010, p. 114; Lee, 2009, p. 32; Rimmer, 2010, pp. 329–32), most are thankful for the many opportunities created by this new player. The foundation's war chest alone exceeds the public health budgets of many less developed countries.

Of equal promise is the growing public awareness of the HIV/AIDS pandemic and the attendant socio-economic problems. When HIV/AIDS was first diagnosed, it was often seen as a stigma of the gay and lesbian communities, prostitutes and intravenous drug users – or, later, as a problem of the global South. Today, it is viewed as a cause for concern for the larger international community. Such growing concern draws attention to not only the disease itself, but also the development of the underlying governance structure and the existence of unanticipated medical complications, notably the shortage of paediatric formulae (Chapter 4). The increased attention given to HIV/AIDS has also raised the public awareness of the disease's many unintended consequences, which range from threats to global security to the needless reduction of human productivity to severe impediments to the progress toward the UN Millennium Development Goals (Lisk, 2010, pp. 59–68; McInnes, 2009; Tansey, 2006, p. 2; Yu, 2007c, pp. 854–5).

Even advocates of strong intellectual property rights have begun to evaluate, or re-evaluate, the expediency of the existing intellectual property system. Some, for example, question whether incentives could be provided through non–property based models, such as grants, subsidies, prizes (including the Health Impact Fund), advance market commitments, reputation gains, open source drug discovery, patent pools, public-private partnerships, or equity-based systems built upon liability rules (Chapter 9; Ho, 2011, pp. 355–72; Pogge, Rimmer and Rubenstein, 2010, pp. 135–283; Van Overwalle, 2009, pp. 3–307). Meanwhile, others explore the need for greater limitations and exceptions in the intellectual property system, including the adoption of compulsory licenses, parallel importation and government use provisions and the introduction of exceptions for development of diagnostics, early working and research ('t Hoen, 2009, pp. 39–59; Commission on Intellectual Property Rights,

2002, pp. 49–51). A minority few go even further to develop or adapt licensing models to facilitate access to HIV/AIDS medications (Chapter 8).

Outside the intellectual property field, commentators have embraced the protection of human rights as part of the needed rhetorical and normative bases for enhancing access to affordable HIV/AIDS treatments (Chapters 2 and 5). Although existing international human rights agreements protect both the right to life and the right to health on the one hand and the human rights interests in intellectual creations on the other (Yu, 2007a; Yu, 2007b), there is no denying that the right to life has now become part of customary international law. The right to health has also been incorporated into strategies for reshaping the HIV/AIDS debate.

Finally, commentators have taken a more holistic view when assessing the need for legal and policy reforms (Poku, Whiteside and Sandkjaer, 2007). After all, the adjustment of the intellectual property system alone is insufficient to address problems created by the HIV/AIDS pandemic. Other contributing factors include inadequate healthcare and drug delivery; lack of medical infrastructure and research capabilities; insufficient sex education and drug control; ill-advised trade, investment and financial policies; political unrests and civil wars; bribery and corruption; abject poverty and colonization-induced underdevelopment. The more comprehensive the analysis is, the better the understanding of the interplay among these factors will be and the more likely policymakers are to adjust their priorities.

The push for a more holistic approach has also opened up the possibility for experts from different disciplines to interact with each other, at both the policy and discursive levels. The workshop that brought together the contributors to this volume represented only one of these cross-disciplinary exchanges. As the discussion of HIV/AIDS governance becomes more inter- and multi-disciplinary, experts have begun to pay greater attention to the multifaceted interfaces between and among the different international regimes (Bartsch, Hein and Kohlmorgen, 2007). These interfaces are not only present in places where the regimes intersect, but they can also be created through legal linkages, technical cooperation, institutional interplay and political alliances (Chapter 10).

Notwithstanding the many promising developments in our efforts to combat HIV/AIDS, at least four challenges remain. These challenges, to date, have hampered access to affordable HIV/AIDS treatments.

First, with the expiry of the transitional periods allowed for developing countries under the TRIPs Agreement, it is unclear whether India, Brazil, China, Thailand and other countries with the capacity to manufacture generic antiretrovirals will still be interested in meeting the demands of countries lacking in such capacity (Chapters 3 and 6). Although the Declaration on the TRIPS Agreement and Public Health (Doha Declaration) delayed the formal introduction of pharmaceutical patents and protection for undisclosed clinical trial data in least developed countries until January 1, 2016, that deadline is fast approaching. It remains to be seen if – or, more likely, how – that deadline will be extended.

Moreover, the TRIPs Agreement remains a major barrier to attaining access to essential medicines in many less developed countries. Although the close to 150 WTO member states adopted a formal proposal to convert the TRIPs waiver into a permanent article 31*bis*, only over a third of these member states have hitherto ratified the proposed amendment (Appendix 6). While the Doha Declaration ensures that a transitional waiver still exists, only one generic manufacturer, Apotex, has ever used the waiver to send drugs from developed to less developed countries – in this case, from Canada to Rwanda. After its pioneering effort, even that firm expressed reluctance to use the arrangement again, citing bureaucratic barriers and the time-consuming process (Apotex, 2009; Intellectual Property Watch, 2009).

Second, the recent global economic and debt crises have raised challenging questions concerning efforts to be undertaken by state governments, NGOs, charities, private foundations and public-private partnerships (such as the Global Fund to Fight AIDS, Tuberculosis and Malaria). As the abilities of these organizations to address the HIV/AIDS crisis decline, additional efforts will have to come from new players or from areas that are unexplored or underexplored. Governments, intergovernmental bodies, international donor organizations and the private sector may also need to better coordinate existing initiatives at both the domestic and international levels. This is particularly important when corporate downsizing has led to a significant reduction in investment in research and development, including the development of new HIV/AIDS treatments (Yu, 2009b, p. 2).

Third, the international regulatory system has become increasingly fragmented. Although fragmentation can create political spaces that help less developed countries strike a better balance between intellectual property protection and public health needs, it will deeply affect the ability of these countries to participate in both the international discourse and global policymaking efforts (Benvenisti and Downs, 2007). The lack of resources not only forces these countries to prioritize but has also made them vulnerable to the ever-increasing forum-manipulating activities undertaken by powerful developed countries. Such vulnerability is particularly troublesome when the latter continue to push for the establishment of bilateral, plurilateral and regional TRIPs-plus trade and investment agreements, which threaten to bypass the multilateral norm-setting process.

Finally, HIV/AIDS is not the only issue concerning access to essential medicines that deserves policy attention (Commission on Intellectual Property Rights, 2002, p. 30; Yu, 2007c, p. 829, n. 6). To be certain, no public health crisis has ever attracted the same amount of political support, resource commitments, public consciousness and civil society participation as the HIV/AIDS pandemic. If we cannot find solutions to combating this pandemic with such support and participation, we most certainly will have a very tough time finding solutions to address other public health challenges.

Nevertheless, it is important not to overstate the importance of the HIV/AIDS crisis to the point that we overshadow the problems created by other important diseases. Our work toward better global health governance and a more appropriate balance between intellectual property protection and public health needs could not stop even if we finally manage to keep the HIV/AIDS pandemic under control. As the damage caused by malaria, tuberculosis and other neglected diseases has shown, and as new communicable diseases such as SARS (Severe Acute Respiratory Syndrome) and H1N1 (swine flu) have emerged to catch policy attention, public health crises that implicate intellectual property laws and policies are plentiful. The tension between the intellectual property system and the public health system, therefore, can only grow, especially when developed countries and intellectual property rights holders continue to actively push for stronger protection and tougher enforcement.

In sum, we still have a rugged road ahead. Although our persistent efforts to combat HIV/AIDS have created new opportunities, many challenges remain. Hopefully this volume will help us advance toward better global health governance and greater access to essential medicines in both the developed and less developed worlds. The human immunodeficiency virus has troubled our world for more than three decades. It is time we come up with effective solutions to address this longstanding public health challenge.

Acknowledgements

The author would like to thank his co-editors for their valuable comments and suggestions; and Linzey Erickson and Lindsey Purdy for excellent research and editorial assistance.

BIBLIOGRAPHY

Apotex (2009), 'CAMR federal law needs to be fixed if life-saving drugs for children are to be developed', http://www.apotex.com/global/about/press/20090514.asp.

Bartsch, Sonja, Wolfgang Hein and Lars Kohlmorgen (2007), 'Interfaces: A concept for the analysis of global health governance', in Hein, Wolfgang, Sonja Bartsch and Lars Kohlmorgen (eds), *Global Health Governance and the Fight Against HIV/AIDS*, Basingstoke and New York: Palgrave Macmillan, pp. 18–37.

Benvenisti, Eyal and George W. Downs (2007), 'The empire's new clothes: Political economy and the fragmentation of international law', *Stanford Law Review*, **60**(2), 595–631.

Commission on Intellectual Property Rights (2002), *Integrating Intellectual Property Rights and Development Policy*, London: Commission on Intellectual Property Rights.

Commission on Intellectual Property Rights, Innovation and Public Health, World Health Organization (2006), *Public Health, Innovation and Intellectual Property Rights*, Geneva: World Health Organization.

D'Adesky, Anne-Christine (2004), *Moving Mountains: The Race to Treat Global AIDS*, London and New York: Verso.

Deere, Carolyn (2009), *The Implementation Game: The TRIPS Agreement and the Global Politics of Intellectual Property Reform in Developing Countries*, Oxford and New York: Oxford University Press.

Dodgson, Richard and Kelley Lee (2002), 'Global health governance: A conceptual review', in Rorden Wilkinson and Steve Hughes (eds), *Global Governance: Critical Perspectives*, London and New York: Routledge, pp. 92–110.

The Economist (2011), 'Thirty Years of a Disease: The End of AIDS', *The Economist*, 2 June, available at http://www.economist.com/node/18774722 (accessed 30 July 2011).

Harman, Sophie (2010), *The World Bank and HIV/AIDS: Setting a Global Agenda*, London and New York: Routledge.

Harman, Sophie and Franklyn Lisk (eds) (2009), *Governance of HIV/AIDS: Making Participation and Accountability Count*, London and New York: Routledge.

Hein, Wolfgang, Sonja Bartsch and Lars Kohlmorgen (eds) (2007), *Global Health Governance and the Fight Against HIV/AIDS*, Basingstoke and New York: Palgrave Macmillan.

Ho, Cynthia M. (2011), *Access to Medicine in the Global Economy: International Agreements on Patents and Related Rights*, Oxford and New York: Oxford University Press.

Intellectual Property Watch (2009), 'Last cheaper AIDS medicines for Rwanda under WTO', *Intellectual Property Watch*, 17 September, available at http://www.ip-watch.org/weblog/2009/09/17/last-cheaper-aids-medicines-for-rwanda-under-wto/ (accessed 30 July 2011).

Lee, Kelley (2009), 'Understandings of global health governance: The contested landscape', in Adrian Kay and Owain David Williams (eds), *Global Health*

Governance: Crisis, Institutions and Political Economy, Basingstoke and New York: Palgrave Macmillan, pp. 27–41.

Lisk, Franklyn (2010), *Global Institutions and the HIV/AIDS Epidemic: Responding to an International Crisis*, London and New York: Routledge.

McInnes, Colin (2009), 'National security and global health governance', in Adrian Kay and Owain David Williams (eds), *Global Health Governance: Crisis, Institutions and Political Economy*, Basingstoke and New York: Palgrave Macmillan, pp. 42–59.

Pogge, Thomas, Matthew Rimmer and Kim Rubenstein (eds) (2010), *Incentives for Global Public Health: Patent Law and Access to Essential Medicines*, Cambridge and New York: Cambridge University Press.

Poku, Nana K., Alan Whiteside and Bjorg Sandkjaer (eds) (2007), *AIDS and Governance*, Aldershot and Burlington: Ashgate.

Rimmer, Matthew (2010), 'The Lazarus Effect: The (RED) Campaign and Creative Capitalism', in Thomas Pogge, Matthew Rimmer and Kim Rubenstein (eds), *Incentives for Global Public Health: Patent Law and Access to Essential Medicines*, Cambridge and New York: Cambridge University Press, pp. 313–40.

Tansey, Geoff (2006), 'Introduction: Legal fictions and public health', in Pedro Roffe, Geoff Tansey and David Vivas-Eugui (eds), *Negotiating Health: Intellectual Property and Access to Medicines*, London: Earthscan Publications, pp. 1–5.

't Hoen, Ellen F.M. (2009), *The Global Politics of Pharmaceutical Monopoly Power: Drug Patents, Access, Innovation and the Application of the WTO Doha Declaration on TRIPS and Public Health*, Diemen: AMB Publishers.

Tutu, Desmond Mpilo (2002), 'We can be human only together', *Seattle Journal for Social Justice*, **1**(2), 253–6.

UNAIDS (2010), *Global Report: UNAIDS Report on the Global AIDS Epidemic 2010,* Geneva: UNAIDS.

Van Overwalle, Geertrui (ed.) (2009), *Gene Patents and Collaborative Licensing Models: Patent Pools, Clearinghouses, Open Source Models and Liability Regimes*, Cambridge and New York: Cambridge University Press.

Yu, Peter K. (2007a), 'Ten common questions about intellectual property and human rights', *Georgia State University Law Review*, **23**(4), 709–53.

Yu, Peter K. (2007b), 'Reconceptualizing intellectual property interests in a human rights framework', *U.C. Davis Law Review*, **40**(3), 1039–149.

Yu, Peter K. (2007c), 'The international enclosure movement', *Indiana Law Journal*, **82**(4), 827–907.

Yu, Peter K. (2008), 'Access to medicines, BRICS alliances, and collective action', *American Journal of Law and Medicine*, **34**(2), 345–94.

Yu, Peter K. (2009a), 'A tale of two development agendas', *Ohio Northern University Law Review*, **35**(2), 465–573.

Yu, Peter K. (2009b), 'The global intellectual property order and its undetermined future', *The WIPO Journal*, **1**(1), 1–15.

Yu, Peter K. (2011), 'TRIPS and Its Achilles' Heel', *Journal of Intellectual Property Law*, **18**(2), 479–531 (2011).

Appendices

APPENDIX 1 AGREEMENT ON TRADE-RELATED ASPECTS OF INTELLECTUAL PROPERTY RIGHTS, 15 APRIL 1994 (SELECTED PROVISIONS)

Members,

Desiring to reduce distortions and impediments to international trade, and taking into account the need to promote effective and adequate protection of intellectual property rights, and to ensure that measures and procedures to enforce intellectual property rights do not themselves become barriers to legitimate trade;

Recognizing, to this end, the need for new rules and disciplines concerning:

(a) the applicability of the basic principles of GATT 1994 and of relevant international intellectual property agreements or conventions;
(b) the provision of adequate standards and principles concerning the availability, scope and use of trade-related intellectual property rights;
(c) the provision of effective and appropriate means for the enforcement of trade-related intellectual property rights, taking into account differences in national legal systems;
(d) the provision of effective and expeditious procedures for the multilateral prevention and settlement of disputes between governments; and
(e) transitional arrangements aiming at the fullest participation in the results of the negotiations;

Recognizing the need for a multilateral framework of principles, rules and disciplines dealing with international trade in counterfeit goods;

Recognizing that intellectual property rights are private rights;

Recognizing the underlying public policy objectives of national systems for the protection of intellectual property, including developmental and technological objectives;

Recognizing also the special needs of the least-developed country Members in respect of maximum flexibility in the domestic implementation of laws and regulations in order to enable them to create a sound and viable technological base;

Emphasizing the importance of reducing tensions by reaching strengthened commitments to resolve disputes on trade-related intellectual property issues through multilateral procedures;

Desiring to establish a mutually supportive relationship between the WTO and the World Intellectual Property Organization (referred to in this Agreement as "WIPO") as well as other relevant international organizations;

Hereby agree as follows:

Article 1
Nature and Scope of Obligations

1. Members shall give effect to the provisions of this Agreement. Members may, but shall not be obliged to, implement in their law more extensive protection than is required by this Agreement, provided that such protection does not contravene the provisions of this Agreement. Members shall be free to determine the appropriate method of implementing the provisions of this Agreement within their own legal system and practice.
2. For the purposes of this Agreement, the term "intellectual property" refers to all categories of intellectual property that are the subject of Sections 1 through 7 of Part II.
3. Members shall accord the treatment provided for in this Agreement to the nationals of other Members. In respect of the relevant intellectual property right, the nationals of other Members shall be understood as those natural or legal persons that would meet the criteria for eligibility for protection provided for in the Paris Convention (1967), the Berne Convention (1971), the Rome Convention and the Treaty on Intellectual Property in Respect of Integrated Circuits, were all Members of the WTO members of those conventions. Any Member availing itself of the possibilities provided in paragraph 3 of Article 5 or paragraph 2 of Article 6 of the Rome Convention shall make a notification as foreseen in those provisions to the Council for Trade-Related Aspects of Intellectual Property Rights (the "Council for TRIPS").

Article 2
Intellectual Property Conventions

1. In respect of Parts II, III and IV of this Agreement, Members shall comply with Articles 1 through 12, and Article 19, of the Paris Convention (1967).
2. Nothing in Parts I to IV of this Agreement shall derogate from existing obligations that Members may have to each other under the Paris Convention, the Berne Convention, the Rome Convention and the Treaty on Intellectual Property in Respect of Integrated Circuits.

Article 6
Exhaustion

For the purposes of dispute settlement under this Agreement, subject to the provisions of Articles 3 and 4 nothing in this Agreement shall be used to address the issue of the exhaustion of intellectual property rights.

Article 7
Objectives

The protection and enforcement of intellectual property rights should contribute to the promotion of technological innovation and to the transfer and dissemination of technology, to the mutual advantage of producers and users of technological knowledge and in a manner conducive to social and economic welfare, and to a balance of rights and obligations.

Article 8
Principles

1. Members may, in formulating or amending their laws and regulations, adopt measures necessary to protect public health and nutrition, and to promote the public interest in sectors of vital importance to their socio-economic and technological development, provided that such measures are consistent with the provisions of this Agreement.
2. Appropriate measures, provided that they are consistent with the provisions of this Agreement, may be needed to prevent the abuse of intellectual property rights by right holders or the resort to practices which unreasonably restrain trade or adversely affect the international transfer of technology.

Article 27
Patentable Subject Matter

1. Subject to the provisions of paragraphs 2 and 3, patents shall be available for any inventions, whether products or processes, in all fields of technology, provided that they are new, involve an inventive step and are capable of industrial application. Subject to paragraph 4 of Article 65, paragraph 8 of Article 70 and paragraph 3 of this Article, patents shall be available and patent rights enjoyable without discrimination as to the place of invention, the field of technology and whether products are imported or locally produced.
2. Members may exclude from patentability inventions, the prevention within their territory of the commercial exploitation of which is necessary to protect *ordre public* or morality, including to protect human, animal or plant life or health or to avoid serious prejudice to the environment, provided that such exclusion is not made merely because the exploitation is prohibited by their law.
3. Members may also exclude from patentability:
   (a) diagnostic, therapeutic and surgical methods for the treatment of humans or animals;
   (b) plants and animals other than micro-organisms, and essentially biological processes for the production of plants or animals other than non-biological and microbiological processes. However, Members shall provide for the protection of plant varieties either by patents or by an effective *sui generis* system or by any combination thereof. The provisions of this subparagraph shall be reviewed four years after the date of entry into force of the WTO Agreement.

Article 30
Exceptions to Rights Conferred

Members may provide limited exceptions to the exclusive rights conferred by a patent, provided that such exceptions do not unreasonably conflict with a normal exploitation of the patent and do not unreasonably prejudice the legitimate interests of the patent owner, taking account of the legitimate interests of third parties.

Article 31
Other Use Without Authorization of the Right Holder

Where the law of a Member allows for other use of the subject matter of a patent without the authorization of the right holder, including use by the government or third parties authorized by the government, the following provisions shall be respected:

(a) authorization of such use shall be considered on its individual merits;
(b) such use may only be permitted if, prior to such use, the proposed user has made efforts to obtain authorization from the right holder on reasonable commercial terms and conditions and that such efforts have not been successful within a reasonable period of time. This requirement may be waived by a Member in the case of a national emergency or other circumstances of extreme urgency or in cases of public non-commercial use. In situations of national emergency or other circumstances of extreme urgency, the right holder shall, nevertheless, be notified as soon as reasonably practicable. In the case of public non-commercial use, where the government or contractor, without making a patent search, knows or has demonstrable grounds to know that a valid patent is or will be used by or for the government, the right holder shall be informed promptly;
(c) the scope and duration of such use shall be limited to the purpose for which it was authorized, and in the case of semi-conductor technology shall only be for public non-commercial use or to remedy a practice determined after judicial or administrative process to be anti-competitive;
(d) such use shall be non-exclusive;
(e) such use shall be non-assignable, except with that part of the enterprise or goodwill which enjoys such use;
(f) any such use shall be authorized predominantly for the supply of the domestic market of the Member authorizing such use;
(g) authorization for such use shall be liable, subject to adequate protection of the legitimate interests of the persons so authorized, to be terminated if and when the circumstances which led to it cease to exist and are unlikely to recur. The competent authority shall have the authority to review, upon motivated request, the continued existence of these circumstances;

(h) the right holder shall be paid adequate remuneration in the circumstances of each case, taking into account the economic value of the authorization;

(i) the legal validity of any decision relating to the authorization of such use shall be subject to judicial review or other independent review by a distinct higher authority in that Member;

(j) any decision relating to the remuneration provided in respect of such use shall be subject to judicial review or other independent review by a distinct higher authority in that Member;

(k) Members are not obliged to apply the conditions set forth in subparagraphs (b) and (f) where such use is permitted to remedy a practice determined after judicial or administrative process to be anti-competitive. The need to correct anti-competitive practices may be taken into account in determining the amount of remuneration in such cases. Competent authorities shall have the authority to refuse termination of authorization if and when the conditions which led to such authorization are likely to recur;

(l) where such use is authorized to permit the exploitation of a patent ("the second patent") which cannot be exploited without infringing another patent ("the first patent"), the following additional conditions shall apply:

    (i) the invention claimed in the second patent shall involve an important technical advance of considerable economic significance in relation to the invention claimed in the first patent;

    (ii) the owner of the first patent shall be entitled to a cross-licence on reasonable terms to use the invention claimed in the second patent; and

    (iii) the use authorized in respect of the first patent shall be non-assignable except with the assignment of the second patent.

Article 40
[Control of Anti-Competitive Practices in Contractual Licences]

1. Members agree that some licensing practices or conditions pertaining to intellectual property rights which restrain competition may have adverse effects on trade and may impede the transfer and dissemination of technology.
2. Nothing in this Agreement shall prevent Members from specifying in their legislation licensing practices or conditions that may in particular cases constitute an abuse of intellectual property rights having an adverse effect on competition in the relevant market. As

provided above, a Member may adopt, consistently with the other provisions of this Agreement, appropriate measures to prevent or control such practices, which may include for example exclusive grantback conditions, conditions preventing challenges to validity and coercive package licensing, in the light of the relevant laws and regulations of that Member.

3. Each Member shall enter, upon request, into consultations with any other Member which has cause to believe that an intellectual property right owner that is a national or domiciliary of the Member to which the request for consultations has been addressed is undertaking practices in violation of the requesting Member's laws and regulations on the subject matter of this Section, and which wishes to secure compliance with such legislation, without prejudice to any action under the law and to the full freedom of an ultimate decision of either Member. The Member addressed shall accord full and sympathetic consideration to, and shall afford adequate opportunity for, consultations with the requesting Member, and shall cooperate through supply of publicly available non-confidential information of relevance to the matter in question and of other information available to the Member, subject to domestic law and to the conclusion of mutually satisfactory agreements concerning the safeguarding of its confidentiality by the requesting Member.
4. A Member whose nationals or domiciliaries are subject to proceedings in another Member concerning alleged violation of that other Member's laws and regulations on the subject matter of this Section shall, upon request, be granted an opportunity for consultations by the other Member under the same conditions as those foreseen in paragraph 3.

Article 44
Injunctions

1. The judicial authorities shall have the authority to order a party to desist from an infringement, inter alia to prevent the entry into the channels of commerce in their jurisdiction of imported goods that involve the infringement of an intellectual property right, immediately after customs clearance of such goods. Members are not obliged to accord such authority in respect of protected subject matter acquired or ordered by a person prior to knowing or having reasonable grounds to know that dealing in such subject matter would entail the infringement of an intellectual property right.

2. Notwithstanding the other provisions of this Part and provided that the provisions of Part II specifically addressing use by governments, or by third parties authorized by a government, without the authorization of the right holder are complied with, Members may limit the remedies available against such use to payment of remuneration in accordance with subparagraph (h) of Article 31. In other cases, the remedies under this Part shall apply or, where these remedies are inconsistent with a Member's law, declaratory judgments and adequate compensation shall be available.

Article 65
Transitional Arrangements

1. Subject to the provisions of paragraphs 2, 3 and 4, no Member shall be obliged to apply the provisions of this Agreement before the expiry of a general period of one year following the date of entry into force of the WTO Agreement.
2. A developing country Member is entitled to delay for a further period of four years the date of application, as defined in paragraph 1, of the provisions of this Agreement other than Articles 3, 4 and 5.
3. Any other Member which is in the process of transformation from a centrally-planned into a market, free-enterprise economy and which is undertaking structural reform of its intellectual property system and facing special problems in the preparation and implementation of intellectual property laws and regulations, may also benefit from a period of delay as foreseen in paragraph 2.
4. To the extent that a developing country Member is obliged by this Agreement to extend product patent protection to areas of technology not so protectable in its territory on the general date of application of this Agreement for that Member, as defined in paragraph 2, it may delay the application of the provisions on product patents of Section 5 of Part II to such areas of technology for an additional period of five years.
5. A Member availing itself of a transitional period under paragraphs 1, 2, 3 or 4 shall ensure that any changes in its laws, regulations and practice made during that period do not result in a lesser degree of consistency with the provisions of this Agreement.

Article 66
Least-Developed Country Members

1. In view of the special needs and requirements of least-developed country Members, their economic, financial and administrative constraints, and their need for flexibility to create a viable technological base, such Members shall not be required to apply the provisions of this Agreement, other than Articles 3, 4 and 5, for a period of 10 years from the date of application as defined under paragraph 1 of Article 65. The Council for TRIPS shall, upon duly motivated request by a least-developed country Member, accord extensions of this period.
2. Developed country Members shall provide incentives to enterprises and institutions in their territories for the purpose of promoting and encouraging technology transfer to least-developed country Members in order to enable them to create a sound and viable technological base.

APPENDIX 2 DOHA DECLARATION ON THE TRIPS AGREEMENT AND PUBLIC HEALTH OF 14 NOVEMBER 2001, WT/MIN(01)/DEC/2

1. We recognize the gravity of the public health problems afflicting many developing and least-developed countries, especially those resulting from HIV/AIDS, tuberculosis, malaria and other epidemics.
2. We stress the need for the WTO Agreement on Trade-Related Aspects of Intellectual Property Rights (TRIPS Agreement) to be part of the wider national and international action to address these problems.
3. We recognize that intellectual property protection is important for the development of new medicines. We also recognize the concerns about its effects on prices.
4. We agree that the TRIPS Agreement does not and should not prevent Members from taking measures to protect public health. Accordingly, while reiterating our commitment to the TRIPS Agreement, we affirm that the Agreement can and should be interpreted and implemented in a manner supportive of WTO Members' right to protect public health and, in particular, to promote access to medicines for all.

   In this connection, we reaffirm the right of WTO Members to use, to the full, the provisions in the TRIPS Agreement, which provide flexibility for this purpose.
5. Accordingly and in the light of paragraph 4 above, while maintaining our commitments in the TRIPS Agreement, we recognize that these flexibilities include:
   a. In applying the customary rules of interpretation of public international law, each provision of the TRIPS Agreement shall be read in the light of the object and purpose of the Agreement as expressed, in particular, in its objectives and principles.
   b. Each Member has the right to grant compulsory licences and the freedom to determine the grounds upon which such licences are granted.
   c. Each Member has the right to determine what constitutes a national emergency or other circumstances of extreme urgency, it being understood that public health crises, including those relating to HIV/AIDS, tuberculosis, malaria and other epidemics, can represent a national emergency or other circumstances of extreme urgency.

d. The effect of the provisions in the TRIPS Agreement that are relevant to the exhaustion of intellectual property rights is to leave each Member free to establish its own regime for such exhaustion without challenge, subject to the MFN and national treatment provisions of Articles 3 and 4.

6. We recognize that WTO Members with insufficient or no manufacturing capacities in the pharmaceutical sector could face difficulties in making effective use of compulsory licensing under the TRIPS Agreement. We instruct the Council for TRIPS to find an expeditious solution to this problem and to report to the General Council before the end of 2002.

7. We reaffirm the commitment of developed-country Members to provide incentives to their enterprises and institutions to promote and encourage technology transfer to least-developed country Members pursuant to Article 66.2. We also agree that the least-developed country Members will not be obliged, with respect to pharmaceutical products, to implement or apply Sections 5 and 7 of Part II of the TRIPS Agreement or to enforce rights provided for under these Sections until 1 January 2016, without prejudice to the right of least-developed country Members to seek other extensions of the transition periods as provided for in Article 66.1 of the TRIPS Agreement. We instruct the Council for TRIPS to take the necessary action to give effect to this pursuant to Article 66.1 of the TRIPS Agreement.

APPENDIX 3 DECISION OF THE GENERAL COUNCIL ON THE IMPLEMENTATION OF PARAGRAPH 6 OF THE DOHA DECLARATION ON THE TRIPS AGREEMENT AND PUBLIC HEALTH, 30 AUGUST 2003, WT/L/540

The General Council,

Having regard to paragraphs 1, 3 and 4 of Article IX of the Marrakesh Agreement Establishing the World Trade Organization ("the WTO Agreement");

Conducting the functions of the Ministerial Conference in the interval between meetings pursuant to paragraph 2 of Article IV of the WTO Agreement;

Noting the Declaration on the TRIPS Agreement and Public Health (WT/MIN(01)/DEC/2) (the "Declaration") and, in particular, the instruction of the Ministerial Conference to the Council for TRIPS contained in paragraph 6 of the Declaration to find an expeditious solution to the problem of the difficulties that WTO Members with insufficient or no manufacturing capacities in the pharmaceutical sector could face in making effective use of compulsory licensing under the TRIPS Agreement and to report to the General Council before the end of 2002;

Recognizing, where eligible importing Members seek to obtain supplies under the system set out in this Decision, the importance of a rapid response to those needs consistent with the provisions of this Decision;

Noting that, in the light of the foregoing, exceptional circumstances exist justifying waivers from the obligations set out in paragraphs (f) and (h) of Article 31 of the TRIPS Agreement with respect to pharmaceutical products;

Decides as follows:

1. For the purposes of this Decision:
   (a) "pharmaceutical product" means any patented product, or product manufactured through a patented process, of the pharmaceutical sector needed to address the public health problems as recognized in paragraph 1 of the Declaration. It is understood that active ingredients necessary for its manufacture and diagnostic kits needed for its use would be included;
   (b) "eligible importing Member" means any least-developed country Member, and any other Member that has made a notification to the Council for TRIPS of its intention to use the system as an

importer, it being understood that a Member may notify at any time that it will use the system in whole or in a limited way, for example only in the case of a national emergency or other circumstances of extreme urgency or in cases of public non-commercial use. It is noted that some Members will not use the system set out in this Decision as importing Members and that some other Members have stated that, if they use the system, it would be in no more than situations of national emergency or other circumstances of extreme urgency;

(c) "exporting Member" means a Member using the system set out in this Decision to produce pharmaceutical products for, and export them to, an eligible importing Member.

2. The obligations of an exporting Member under Article 31(f) of the TRIPS Agreement shall be waived with respect to the grant by it of a compulsory licence to the extent necessary for the purposes of production of a pharmaceutical product(s) and its export to an eligible importing Member(s) in accordance with the terms set out below in this paragraph:

(a) the eligible importing Member(s) has made a notification to the Council for TRIPS, that:

(i) specifies the names and expected quantities of the product(s) needed;

(ii) confirms that the eligible importing Member in question, other than a least developed country Member, has established that it has insufficient or no manufacturing capacities in the pharmaceutical sector for the product(s) in question in one of the ways set out in the Annex to this Decision; and

(iii) confirms that, where a pharmaceutical product is patented in its territory, it has granted or intends to grant a compulsory licence in accordance with Article 31 of the TRIPS Agreement and the provisions of this Decision;

(b) the compulsory licence issued by the exporting Member under this Decision shall contain the following conditions:

(i) only the amount necessary to meet the needs of the eligible importing Member(s) may be manufactured under the licence and the entirety of this production shall be exported to the Member(s) which has notified its needs to the Council for TRIPS;

(ii) products produced under the licence shall be clearly identified as being produced under the system set out in this Decision through specific labelling or marking. Suppliers should distinguish such products through special packaging and/or special colouring/shaping of the products themselves, provided that such distinction is feasible and does not have a significant impact on price; and

(iii) before shipment begins, the licensee shall post on a website the following information:
- the quantities being supplied to each destination as referred to in indent (i) above; and
- the distinguishing features of the product(s) referred to in indent (ii) above;

(c) the exporting Member shall notify the Council for TRIPS of the grant of the licence, including the conditions attached to it. The information provided shall include the name and address of the licensee, the product(s) for which the licence has been granted, the quantity(ies) for which it has been granted, the country(ies) to which the product(s) is (are) to be supplied and the duration of the licence. The notification shall also indicate the address of the website referred to in subparagraph (b)(iii) above.

3. Where a compulsory licence is granted by an exporting Member under the system set out in this Decision, adequate remuneration pursuant to Article 31(h) of the TRIPS Agreement shall be paid in that Member taking into account the economic value to the importing Member of the use that has been authorized in the exporting Member. Where a compulsory licence is granted for the same products in the eligible importing Member, the obligation of that Member under Article 31(h) shall be waived in respect of those products for which remuneration in accordance with the first sentence of this paragraph is paid in the exporting Member.

4. In order to ensure that the products imported under the system set out in this Decision are used for the public health purposes underlying their importation, eligible importing Members shall take reasonable measures within their means, proportionate to their administrative capacities and to the risk of trade diversion to prevent re-exportation of the products that have actually been imported into their territories under the system. In the event that an eligible importing Member that is a developing country Member or a least-developed country Member experiences difficulty in implementing this provision, developed country Members shall provide, on request and on mutually agreed terms and conditions, technical and financial cooperation in order to facilitate its implementation.

5. Members shall ensure the availability of effective legal means to prevent the importation into, and sale in, their territories of products

produced under the system set out in this Decision and diverted to their markets inconsistently with its provisions, using the means already required to be available under the TRIPS Agreement. If any Member considers that such measures are proving insufficient for this purpose, the matter may be reviewed in the Council for TRIPS at the request of that Member.

6. With a view to harnessing economies of scale for the purposes of enhancing purchasing power for, and facilitating the local production of, pharmaceutical products:
   (i) where a developing or least-developed country WTO Member is a party to a regional trade agreement within the meaning of Article XXIV of the GATT 1994 and the Decision of 28 November 1979 on Differential and More Favourable Treatment Reciprocity and Fuller Participation of Developing Countries (L/4903), at least half of the current membership of which is made up of countries presently on the United Nations list of least developed countries, the obligation of that Member under Article 31(f) of the TRIPS Agreement shall be waived to the extent necessary to enable a pharmaceutical product produced or imported under a compulsory licence in that Member to be exported to the markets of those other developing or least developed country parties to the regional trade agreement that share the health problem in question. It is understood that this will not prejudice the territorial nature of the patent rights in question;
   (ii) it is recognized that the development of systems providing for the grant of regional patents to be applicable in the above Members should be promoted. To this end, developed country Members undertake to provide technical cooperation in accordance with Article 67 of the TRIPS Agreement, including in conjunction with other relevant intergovernmental organizations.

7. Members recognize the desirability of promoting the transfer of technology and capacity building in the pharmaceutical sector in order to overcome the problem identified in paragraph 6 of the Declaration. To this end, eligible importing Members and exporting Members are encouraged to use the system set out in this Decision in a way which would promote this objective. Members undertake to cooperate in paying special attention to the transfer of technology and capacity building in the pharmaceutical sector in the work to be undertaken pursuant to Article 66.2 of the TRIPS

Agreement, paragraph 7 of the Declaration and any other relevant work of the Council for TRIPS.

8. The Council for TRIPS shall review annually the functioning of the system set out in this Decision with a view to ensuring its effective operation and shall annually report on its operation to the General Council. This review shall be deemed to fulfil the review requirements of Article IX:4 of the WTO Agreement.
9. This Decision is without prejudice to the rights, obligations and flexibilities that Members have under the provisions of the TRIPS Agreement other than paragraphs (f) and (h) of Article 31, including those reaffirmed by the Declaration, and to their interpretation. It is also without prejudice to the extent to which pharmaceutical products produced under a compulsory licence can be exported under the present provisions of Article 31(f) of the TRIPS Agreement.
10. Members shall not challenge any measures taken in conformity with the provisions of the waivers contained in this Decision under subparagraphs 1(b) and 1(c) of Article XXIII of GATT 1994.
11. This Decision, including the waivers granted in it, shall terminate for each Member on the date on which an amendment to the TRIPS Agreement replacing its provisions takes effect for that Member. The TRIPS Council shall initiate by the end of 2003 work on the preparation of such an amendment with a view to its adoption within six months, on the understanding that the amendment will be based, where appropriate, on this Decision and on the further understanding that it will not be part of the negotiations referred to in paragraph 45 of the Doha Ministerial Declaration (WT/MIN(01)/DEC/1).

Annex

Assessment of Manufacturing Capacities in the Pharmaceutical Sector

Least-developed country Members are deemed to have insufficient or no manufacturing capacities in the pharmaceutical sector.

For other eligible importing Members insufficient or no manufacturing capacities for the product(s) in question may be established in either of the following ways:

(i) the Member in question has established that it has no manufacturing capacity in the pharmaceutical sector;

OR

(ii) where the Member has some manufacturing capacity in this sector, it has examined this capacity and found that, excluding any capacity owned or controlled by the patent owner, it is currently insufficient for the purposes of meeting its needs. When it is established that such capacity has become sufficient to meet the Member's needs, the system shall no longer apply.

APPENDIX 4 GENERAL COUNCIL CHAIRPERSON'S STATEMENT ON DECISION OF 30 AUGUST 2003, WT/GC/M/82, PARA. 29

On 30 August 2003, the General Council approved a decision to make it easier for countries in need to import cheaper generic medicines made under compulsory licensing if they are unable to manufacture the medicines themselves. A separate statement by General Council chairperson Carlos Pérez del Castillo, Uruguay's ambassador, was designed to provide comfort to those who feared that the decision might be abused and undermine patent protection. Below is the statement:

The General Council has been presented with a draft Decision contained in document IP/C/W/405 to implement paragraph 6 of the Doha Declaration on the TRIPS Agreement and Public Health. This Decision is part of the wider national and international action to address problems as recognized in paragraph 1 of the Declaration. Before adopting this Decision, I would like to place on the record this Statement which represents several key shared understandings of Members regarding the Decision to be taken and the way in which it will be interpreted and implemented. I would like to emphasize that this Statement is limited in its implications to paragraph 6 of the Doha Declaration on the TRIPS Agreement and Public Health.

First, Members recognize that the system that will be established by the Decision should be used in good faith to protect public health and, without prejudice to paragraph 6 of the Decision, not be an instrument to pursue industrial or commercial policy objectives.

Second, Members recognize that the purpose of the Decision would be defeated if products supplied under this Decision are diverted from the markets for which they are intended. Therefore, all reasonable measures should be taken to prevent such diversion in accordance with the relevant paragraphs of the Decision. In this regard, the provisions of paragraph 2(b)(ii) apply not only to formulated pharmaceuticals produced and supplied under the system but also to active ingredients produced and supplied under the system and to finished products produced using such active ingredients. It is the understanding of Members that in general special packaging and/or special colouring or shaping should not have a significant impact on the price of pharmaceuticals.

In the past, companies have developed procedures to prevent diversion of products that are, for example, provided through donor programmes. "Best practices" guidelines that draw upon the experiences of companies are attached to this statement for illustrative purposes. Members and producers are encouraged to draw from and use these practices, and to share information on their experiences in preventing diversion.

Third, it is important that Members seek to resolve any issues arising from the use and implementation of the Decision expeditiously and amicably:

- To promote transparency and avoid controversy, notifications under paragraph 2(a)(ii) of the Decision would include information on how the Member in question had established, in accordance with the Annex, that it has insufficient or no manufacturing capacities in the pharmaceutical sector.
- In accordance with the normal practice of the TRIPS Council, notifications made under the system shall be brought to the attention of its next meeting.
- Any Member may bring any matter related to the interpretation or implementation of the Decision, including issues related to diversion, to the TRIPS Council for expeditious review, with a view to taking appropriate action.
- If any Member has concerns that the terms of the Decision have not been fully complied with, the Member may also utilise the good offices of the Director General or Chair of the TRIPS Council, with a view to finding a mutually acceptable solution.

Fourth, all information gathered on the implementation of the Decision shall be brought to the attention of the TRIPS Council in its annual review as set out in paragraph 8 of the Decision.

In addition, as stated in footnote 3 to paragraph 1(b) of the Decision, the following Members have agreed to opt out of using the system as importers: Australia, Austria, Belgium, Canada, Denmark, Finland, France, Germany, Greece, Iceland, Ireland, Italy, Japan, Luxembourg, Netherlands, New Zealand, Norway, Portugal, Spain, Sweden, Switzerland, United Kingdom and United States of America.

Until their accession to the European Union, Czech Republic, Cyprus, Estonia, Hungary, Latvia, Lithuania, Malta, Poland, Slovak Republic and Slovenia agree that they would only use the system as importers in situations of national emergency or other circumstances of extreme urgency. These countries further agree that upon their accession to the European Union, they will opt out of using the system as importers.

As we have heard today, and as the Secretariat has been informed in certain communications, some other Members have agreed that they would only use the system as importers in situations of national emergency or other circumstances of extreme urgency: Hong Kong

China, Israel, Korea, Kuwait, Macao China, Mexico, Qatar, Singapore, Chinese Taipei, Turkey, United Arab Emirates.

Attachment
"Best practices" guidelines

Companies have often used special labelling, colouring, shaping, sizing, etc. to differentiate products supplied through donor or discounted pricing programmes from products supplied to other markets. Examples of such measures include the following:

- Bristol Myers Squibb used different markings/imprints on capsules supplied to sub Saharan Africa.
- Novartis has used different trademark names, one (Riamet®) for an anti-malarial drug provided to developed countries, the other (Coartem®) for the same products supplied to developing countries. Novartis further differentiated the products through distinctive packaging.
- GlaxoSmithKline (GSK) used different outer packaging for its HIV/AIDS medications Combivir, Epivir and Trizivir supplied to developing countries. GSK further differentiated the products by embossing the tablets with a different number than tablets supplied to developed countries, and plans to further differentiate the products by using different colours.
- Merck differentiated its HIV/AIDS antiretroviral medicine CRIXIVAN through special packaging and labelling, i.e., gold-ink printing on the capsule, dark green bottle cap and a bottle label with a light-green background.
- Pfizer used different colouring and shaping for Diflucan pills supplied to South Africa.

Producers have further minimized diversion by entering into contractual arrangements with importers/distributors to ensure delivery of products to the intended markets.

To help ensure use of the most effective anti-diversion measures, Members may share their experiences and practices in preventing diversion either informally or through the TRIPS Council. It would be beneficial for Members and industry to work together to further refine anti-diversion practices and enhance the sharing of information related to identifying, remedying or preventing specific occurrences of diversion.

APPENDIX 5 PROTOCOL TO AMEND THE TRIPS AGREEMENT ALLOWING INCLUSION OF ARTICLE 31BIS – GENERAL COUNCIL DECISION OF 6 DECEMBER 2005, WT/L/641

The General Council;

Having regard to paragraph 1 of Article X of the Marrakesh Agreement Establishing the World Trade Organization ("the WTO Agreement");

Conducting the functions of the Ministerial Conference in the interval between meetings pursuant to paragraph 2 of Article IV of the WTO Agreement;

Noting the Declaration on the TRIPS Agreement and Public Health (WT/MIN(01)/DEC/2) and, in particular, the instruction of the Ministerial Conference to the Council for TRIPS contained in paragraph 6 of the Declaration to find an expeditious solution to the problem of the difficulties that WTO Members with insufficient or no manufacturing capacities in the pharmaceutical sector could face in making effective use of compulsory licensing under the TRIPS Agreement;

Recognizing, where eligible importing Members seek to obtain supplies under the system set out in the proposed amendment of the TRIPS Agreement, the importance of a rapid response to those needs consistent with the provisions of the proposed amendment of the TRIPS Agreement;

Recalling paragraph 11 of the General Council Decision of 30 August 2003 on the Implementation of Paragraph 6 of the Doha Declaration on the TRIPS Agreement and Public Health;

Having considered the proposal to amend the TRIPS Agreement submitted by the Council for TRIPS (IP/C/41);

Noting the consensus to submit this proposed amendment to the Members for acceptance;

Decides as follows:

1. The Protocol amending the TRIPS Agreement attached to this Decision is hereby adopted and submitted to the Members for acceptance.
2. The Protocol shall be open for acceptance by Members until 1 December 2007 or such later date as may be decided by the Ministerial Conference.
3. The Protocol shall take effect in accordance with the provisions of paragraph 3 of Article X of the WTO Agreement.

Attachment
Protocol Amending the TRIPS Agreement

Members of the World Trade Organization;

Having regard to the Decision of the General Council in document WT/L/641, adopted pursuant to paragraph 1 of Article X of the Marrakesh Agreement Establishing the World Trade Organization ("the WTO Agreement");

Hereby agree as follows:

1. The Agreement on Trade-Related Aspects of Intellectual Property Rights (the "TRIPS Agreement") shall, upon the entry into force of the Protocol pursuant to paragraph 4, be amended as set out in the Annex to this Protocol, by inserting Article 31*bis* after Article 31 and by inserting the Annex to the TRIPS Agreement after Article 73.
2. Reservations may not be entered in respect of any of the provisions of this Protocol without the consent of the other Members.
3. This Protocol shall be open for acceptance by Members until 1 December 2007 or such later date as may be decided by the Ministerial Conference.
4. This Protocol shall enter into force in accordance with paragraph 3 of Article X of the WTO Agreement.
5. This Protocol shall be deposited with the Director-General of the World Trade Organization who shall promptly furnish to each Member a certified copy thereof and a notification of each acceptance thereof pursuant to paragraph 3.
6. This Protocol shall be registered in accordance with the provisions of Article 102 of the Charter of the United Nations.

Done at Geneva this sixth day of December two thousand and five, in a single copy in the English, French and Spanish languages, each text being authentic.

Annex to the Protocol Amending the TRIPS Agreement
Article 31*bis*

1. The obligations of an exporting Member under Article 31(f) shall not apply with respect to the grant by it of a compulsory licence to

the extent necessary for the purposes of production of a pharmaceutical product(s) and its export to an eligible importing Member(s) in accordance with the terms set out in paragraph 2 of the Annex to this Agreement.

2. Where a compulsory licence is granted by an exporting Member under the system set out in this Article and the Annex to this Agreement, adequate remuneration pursuant to Article 31(h) shall be paid in that Member taking into account the economic value to the importing Member of the use that has been authorized in the exporting Member. Where a compulsory licence is granted for the same products in the eligible importing Member, the obligation of that Member under Article 31(h) shall not apply in respect of those products for which remuneration in accordance with the first sentence of this paragraph is paid in the exporting Member.
3. With a view to harnessing economies of scale for the purposes of enhancing purchasing power for, and facilitating the local production of, pharmaceutical products: where a developing or least developed country WTO Member is a party to a regional trade agreement within the meaning of Article XXIV of the GATT 1994 and the Decision of 28 November 1979 on Differential and More Favourable Treatment Reciprocity and Fuller Participation of Developing Countries (L/4903), at least half of the current membership of which is made up of countries presently on the United Nations list of least developed countries, the obligation of that Member under Article 31(f) shall not apply to the extent necessary to enable a pharmaceutical product produced or imported under a compulsory licence in that Member to be exported to the markets of those other developing or least developed country parties to the regional trade agreement that share the health problem in question. It is understood that this will not prejudice the territorial nature of the patent rights in question.
4. Members shall not challenge any measures taken in conformity with the provisions of this Article and the Annex to this Agreement under subparagraphs 1(b) and 1(c) of Article XXIII of GATT 1994.
5. This Article and the Annex to this Agreement are without prejudice to the rights, obligations and flexibilities that Members have under the provisions of this Agreement other than paragraphs (f) and (h) of Article 31, including those reaffirmed by the Declaration on the TRIPS Agreement and Public Health (WT/MIN(01)/DEC/2), and to their interpretation. They are also without prejudice to the extent to which pharmaceutical products produced under a compulsory licence can be exported under the provisions of Article 31(f).

Annex to the TRIPS Agreement

1. For the purposes of Article 31*bis* and this Annex:
   (a) "pharmaceutical product" means any patented product, or product manufactured through a patented process, of the pharmaceutical sector needed to address the public health problems as recognized in paragraph 1 of the Declaration on the TRIPS Agreement and Public Health (WT/MIN(01)/DEC/2). It is understood that active ingredients necessary for its manufacture and diagnostic kits needed for its use would be included;
   (b) "eligible importing Member" means any least-developed country Member, and any other Member that has made a notification to the Council for TRIPS of its intention to use the system set out in Article 31*bis* and this Annex ("system") as an importer, it being understood that a Member may notify at any time that it will use the system in whole or in a limited way, for example only in the case of a national emergency or other circumstances of extreme urgency or in cases of public non-commercial use. It is noted that some Members will not use the system as importing Members and that some other Members have stated that, if they use the system, it would be in no more than situations of national emergency or other circumstances of extreme urgency;
   (c) "exporting Member" means a Member using the system to produce pharmaceutical products for, and export them to, an eligible importing Member.
2. The terms referred to in paragraph 1 of Article 31*bis* are that:
   (a) the eligible importing Member(s) has made a notification to the Council for TRIPS, that:
      (i) specifies the names and expected quantities of the product(s) needed;
      (ii) confirms that the eligible importing Member in question, other than a least developed country Member, has established that it has insufficient or no manufacturing capacities in the pharmaceutical sector for the product(s) in question in one of the ways set out in the Appendix to this Annex; and
      (iii) confirms that, where a pharmaceutical product is patented in its territory, it has granted or intends to grant a compulsory licence in accordance with Articles 31 and 31*bis* of this Agreement and the provisions of this Annex;

(b) the compulsory licence issued by the exporting Member under the system shall contain the following conditions:
   (i) only the amount necessary to meet the needs of the eligible importing Member(s) may be manufactured under the licence and the entirety of this production shall be exported to the Member(s) which has notified its needs to the Council for TRIPS;
   (ii) products produced under the licence shall be clearly identified as being produced under the system through specific labelling or marking. Suppliers should distinguish such products through special packaging and/or special colouring/shaping of the products themselves, provided that such distinction is feasible and does not have a significant impact on price; and
   (iii) before shipment begins, the licensee shall post on a website the following information:
      – the quantities being supplied to each destination as referred to in indent (i) above; and
      – the distinguishing features of the product(s) referred to in indent (ii) above;

(c) the exporting Member shall notify the Council for TRIPS of the grant of the licence, including the conditions attached to it. The information provided shall include the name and address of the licensee, the product(s) for which the licence has been granted, the quantity(ies) for which it has been granted, the country(ies) to which the product(s) is (are) to be supplied and the duration of the licence. The notification shall also indicate the address of the website referred to in subparagraph (b)(iii) above.

3. In order to ensure that the products imported under the system are used for the public health purposes underlying their importation, eligible importing Members shall take reasonable measures within their means, proportionate to their administrative capacities and to the risk of trade diversion to prevent re-exportation of the products that have actually been imported into their territories under the system. In the event that an eligible importing Member that is a developing country Member or a least-developed country Member experiences difficulty in implementing this provision, developed country Members shall provide, on request and on mutually agreed terms and conditions, technical and financial cooperation in order to facilitate its implementation.

4. Members shall ensure the availability of effective legal means to prevent the importation into, and sale in, their territories of products

produced under the system and diverted to their markets inconsistently with its provisions, using the means already required to be available under this Agreement. If any Member considers that such measures are proving insufficient for this purpose, the matter may be reviewed in the Council for TRIPS at the request of that Member.

5. With a view to harnessing economies of scale for the purposes of enhancing purchasing power for, and facilitating the local production of, pharmaceutical products, it is recognized that the development of systems providing for the grant of regional patents to be applicable in the Members described in paragraph 3 of Article 31*bis* should be promoted. To this end, developed country Members undertake to provide technical cooperation in accordance with Article 67 of this Agreement, including in conjunction with other relevant intergovernmental organizations.
6. Members recognize the desirability of promoting the transfer of technology and capacity building in the pharmaceutical sector in order to overcome the problem faced by Members with insufficient or no manufacturing capacities in the pharmaceutical sector. To this end, eligible importing Members and exporting Members are encouraged to use the system in a way which would promote this objective. Members undertake to cooperate in paying special attention to the transfer of technology and capacity building in the pharmaceutical sector in the work to be undertaken pursuant to Article 66.2 of this Agreement, paragraph 7 of the Declaration on the TRIPS Agreement and Public Health and any other relevant work of the Council for TRIPS.
7. The Council for TRIPS shall review annually the functioning of the system with a view to ensuring its effective operation and shall annually report on its operation to the General Council.

Appendix to the Annex to the TRIPS Agreement
Assessment of Manufacturing Capacities in the Pharmaceutical Sector

Least-developed country Members are deemed to have insufficient or no manufacturing capacities in the pharmaceutical sector.

For other eligible importing Members insufficient or no manufacturing capacities for the product(s) in question may be established in either of the following ways:

(i) the Member in question has established that it has no manufacturing capacity in the pharmaceutical sector;

or

(ii) where the Member has some manufacturing capacity in this sector, it has examined this capacity and found that, excluding any capacity owned or controlled by the patent owner, it is currently insufficient for the purposes of meeting its needs. When it is established that such capacity has become sufficient to meet the Member's needs, the system shall no longer apply.

APPENDIX 6 LIST OF MEMBERS ACCEPTING AMENDMENT OF THE TRIPS AGREEMENT PROPOSED IN GENERAL COUNCIL DECISION OF 6 DECEMBER 2005 (AS OF 1 JANUARY 2013)

WTO members on 6 December 2005 approved changes to the WTO's intellectual property (TRIPS) agreement making permanent a decision on patents and public health originally adopted in 2003. This will now be formally built into the TRIPS Agreement when two thirds of the WTO's members have accepted the change. They originally set themselves until 1 December 2007 to do this. The General Council extended the deadline to 31 December 2009 and then to 31 December 2011 by decisions on 18 December 2007 and 17 December 2009.

Once two thirds of members have formally accepted it, the amendment will take effect in those members and will replace the 2003 waiver for them. For each of the remaining members: the waiver will continue to apply until that member accepts the amendment and it takes effect.

Members and dates of acceptance

United States (17 December 2005)
Switzerland (13 September 2006)
El Salvador (19 September 2006)
Rep. of Korea (24 January 2007)
Norway (5 February 2007)
India (26 March 2007)
Philippines (30 March 2007)
Israel (10 August 2007)
Japan (31 August 2007)
Australia (12 September 2007)
Singapore (28 September 2007)
Hong Kong, China (27 November 2007)
China (28 November 2007)
European Union (30 November 2007)
Mauritius (16 April 2008)
Egypt (18 April 2008)
Mexico (23 May 2008)
Jordan (6 August 2008)
Brazil (13 November 2008)
Morocco (2 December 2008)
Albania (28 January 2009)

Macau, China (16 June 2009)
Canada (16 June 2009)
Bahrain (4 August 2009)
Colombia (7 August 2009)
Zambia (10 August 2009)
Nicaragua (25 January 2010)
Pakistan (8 February 2010)
Former Yugoslav Republic of Macedonia (16 March 2010)
Uganda (12 July 2010)
Mongolia (17 September 2010)
Croatia (6 December 2010)
Senegal (18 January 2011)
Bangladesh (15 March 2011)
Argentina (20 October 2011)
Indonesia (20 October 2011)
New Zealand (21 October 2011)
Cambodia (1 November 2011)
Panama (24 November 2011)
Costa Rica (8 December 2011)
Rwanda (12 December 2011)
Honduras (16 December 2011)
Togo (13 March 2012)
Saudi Arabia (29 May 2012)
Chinese Taipei (31 July 2012)

Source: World Trade Organization (2013), *Countries Accepting Amendment of the TRIPS Agreement*, available at http://www.wto.org/english/tratop_e/trips_e/amendment_e.htm (accessed 21 January 2013).

APPENDIX 7 NOTIFICATION BY RWANDA OF INTENTION TO IMPORT UNDER PARAGRAPH 2(A) OF THE DECISION OF 30 AUGUST 2003 ON THE IMPLEMENTATION OF PARAGRAPH 6 OF THE DOHA DECLARATION ON THE TRIPS AGREEMENT AND PUBLIC HEALTH, 19 JULY 2007, IP/N/9/RWA/1

The following notification from Rwanda's Government Centre for the Treatment & Research on AIDS (TRAC) has been received from the Delegation of Rwanda on 17 July 2007 for circulation to the Council for TRIPS.

Based on Rwanda's present evaluation of its public health needs, we expect to import during the next two years 260,000 packs of TriAvir, a fixed-dose combination product of Zidovudine, Lamivudine and Nevirapine (hereinafter referred to as the "Product") manufactured in Canada by Apotex, Inc. However, because it is not possible to predict with certainty the extent of the country's public health needs, we reserve the right to modify the foregoing estimate as necessary or appropriate.

Pursuant to Paragraph 7 of the Doha Declaration and implementation thereof by the TRIPS Council (Decision of the Council for TRIPS of 27 June 2002), we have decided that we will not enforce rights provided under Part II Section 5 of the TRIPS Agreement that may have been granted within Rwanda's territory with respect to the Product.

APPENDIX 8 NOTIFICATION BY CANADA OF INTENTION TO IMPORT UNDER PARAGRAPH 2(C) OF THE DECISION OF 30 AUGUST 2003 ON THE IMPLEMENTATION OF PARAGRAPH 6 OF THE DOHA DECLARATION ON THE TRIPS AGREEMENT AND PUBLIC HEALTH, 8 OCTOBER 2007, IP/N/10/CAN/1

The following notification has been received from the delegation of Canada on 4 October 2007 for circulation to the Council for TRIPS.

In accordance with paragraph 2(c) of the WTO General Council Decision of 30 August 2003 on the Implementation of Paragraph 6 of the Doha Declaration on the TRIPS Agreement and Public Health, attached is the authorization granted on 19 September 2007 by Canada's Commissioner of Patents to Apotex, Inc, pursuant to section 21.04 of the Patent Act. Rwanda had previously filed a related notification, dated 17 July 2007, pursuant to paragraph 2(a) of the same Decision of the WTO General Council (IP/N/9/RWA/1).

Pursuant to paragraph 2(c) and 2(b)(iii) of the Decision of 30 August 2003 on the Implementation of paragraph 6 of the Doha Declaration on the TRIPS Agreement and Public Health, the information on the shipment (quantities and distinguishing features) will be posted on the licensee's website at: www.apotex.com/apotriavir/abouttriavir.asp.

Annex
Authorization under Section 21.04 of the Patent Act

In the matter of application for authorization number CAMR–1 by Apotex, Inc. for export to Rwanda of the following pharmaceutical product:

(a) if the pharmaceutical product is a drug as set out in section 2 of the Food and Drugs Act: A fixed dose combination tablet of lamivudine (150mg) + nevirapine (200mg) + zidovudine (300mg), as provided in Schedule 1 to the Patent Act

(b) if the pharmaceutical product is a medical device:

1. I hereby authorize Apotex, Inc. whose postal address is
150 Signet Drive
Toronto, Ontario
M9L 1T9

to make, construct and use, the patented inventions identified in patent numbers 2,311,988; 2,070,230; 2,068,790; 2,286,126; 2,216,634; 2,105,487; 2,059,263; 2,009,637 and 2,030,056 solely for purposes directly related to the manufacture of the above-mentioned pharmaceutical product, and to sell it for export to the above-mentioned country or WTO Member.

2. The quantity of the pharmaceutical product authorized to be manufactured by this authorization is 15,600,000 tablets.
3. In accordance with section 21.09 of the Act, this authorization is valid for a period of two years, beginning on the date shown below.

Granted at Gatineau, Quebec, the 19th day of September, 2007

Mary Carman
Commissioner of Patents

Index